Civil Procedure

BLACK LETTER OUTLINES

Civil Procedure

by Kevin M. Clermont
Flanagan Professor of Law,
Cornell University

EIGHTH EDITION

THOMSON

WEST

Mat #40709272

 PRINTED ON 10% POST CONSUMER RECYCLED PAPER

Summary of Contents

■ PART ONE: GENERAL CONSIDERATIONS

■ PART TWO: LITIGATING STEP–BY–STEP

■ PART THREE: AUTHORITY TO ADJUDICATE

■ PART FOUR: COMPLEX LITIGATION

■ PART FIVE: GOVERNING LAW

■ PART SIX: FORMER ADJUDICATION

APPENDICES

Table of Contents

■ PART TWO: LITIGATING STEP–BY–STEP

■ PART THREE: AUTHORITY TO ADJUDICATE

■ PART FOUR: COMPLEX LITIGATION

■ PART FIVE: GOVERNING LAW

■ PART SIX: FORMER ADJUDICATION

APPENDICES

App.

Capsule Summary of Civil Procedure

■ PART ONE: GENERAL CONSIDERATIONS

I. CIVIL PROCEDURE ANALYZED

Most courses, and this outline, approach the seamless web of civil procedure by (1) presenting in survey fashion the whole subject of the conduct of litigation and then (2) studying a series of fundamental problems inherent therein.

II. CIVIL PROCEDURE SYNTHESIZED

A. Nature of Civil Procedure

Civil procedure concerns the society's noncriminal process for submitting and resolving factual and legal disputes over the rights and duties recognized by substantive law, which rights and duties concern primary conduct in the private and public life that transpires essentially outside the courthouse or other forum. In shaping this law of civil procedure, the shapers—constitutions, legislatures, courts, and litigants—observe both outcome and process values.

B. Content of Civil Procedure

Turbulent policies and misleadingly concrete rules constitute the law of civil procedure. One underlying theme is that our society has generally opted to dispense justice by *adjudication* involving an *adversary system* wherein the parties are represented by *advocates*.

C. History of Civil Procedure

1. English Roots

The old English system had two distinct sets of courts, procedure, remedies, and substantive law.

a. Common Law

b. Equity

2. State Developments

The American states basically followed the English model until the code reforms of the 19th century, beginning with the Field Code in 1848.

3. Federal Developments

The federal legal system followed traditional ways from 1789 until well into the 20th century, which saw the Rules Enabling Act of 1934 and the Federal Rules of Civil Procedure in 1938.

■ PART TWO: LITIGATING STEP–BY–STEP

III. PRELIMINARY CONSIDERATIONS

A. Federal Focus

This capsule summary of Part Two focuses on federal practice.

B. Selecting a Court with Authority to Adjudicate

First, plaintiff must select a court with *subject-matter jurisdiction* and *territorial authority to adjudicate*. He commences a federal lawsuit by filing a complaint with the selected federal district court. Rule 3. Second, the persons whose interests are to be affected must receive adequate *notice*. This usually is achieved by service of process. Rule 4.

IV. PRETRIAL

A. Pleading Stage

This stage is usually short in duration and seldom determinative in effect.

1. General Rules

a. Purposes of Pleadings

Federal pleading is primarily notice pleading.

b. Form of Pleadings

The formal requirements—from caption to signing—are quite lenient.

c. Contents of Pleadings

Pleadings should be simple, direct, and brief. The pleader should carry his burden of allegation, without pleading irrelevancies or detail.

d. Flexibility of Pleadings

Alternative and inconsistent pleading is permissible, and there is liberal joinder of claims and parties.

e. Governing Law

In any federal action, federal law governs the mechanics of pleadings, as well as most of the other mechanics of civil procedure.

2. Steps in Pleading Stage

a. Complaint

Rule 8(a) requires (1) a jurisdictional allegation, (2) "a short and plain statement of the claim," and (3) a demand for judgment.

b. Motion and/or Answer

To avoid default, defendant must under Rule 12(a) make a timely response, such as (1) pre-answer objections by motion for a more definite statement and by motion to strike, (2) disfavored defenses under Rule 12(b)(2)–(5) by pre-answer motion or answer, (3) defenses on the merits by including denials and affirmative defenses in the answer, (4) favored defenses under Rule 12(b)(6) and (7) by motion and answer, and (5) the subject-matter jurisdiction defense under Rule 12(b)(1) by raising it in any fashion. This scheme leaves considerable room for tactics; but Rule 12(g) and (h) imposes complicated consolidation and waiver prescriptions.

c. Motion, Reply, and/or Answer

Usually plaintiff does not respond to an answer. However, there is the significant requirement that plaintiff make a timely response to any counterclaim denominated as such in the defendant's answer.

3. Amendments

There are liberal provisions for amending the pleadings, either by amendment as a matter of course within certain time limits or by amendment later with written consent of the adversary or with leave of court. Rule 15(a). The court freely gives leave "when justice so requires," and amendments are possible at or after trial. Rule 15(c) provides that the effective date of a nondrastic amendment is the date of the original pleading.

B. Disclosure

In 1993, amid much controversy, the rulemakers introduced a new stage called disclosure.

1. Purposes

Disclosure aims at achieving some savings in time and expense by automatically getting certain core information on the table, and also at moderating litigants' adversary behavior in the pretrial phase.

2. Scope

Parties must disclose (1) at the outset, favorable occurrence witnesses and documents, as well as insurance coverage, (2) at a specified time, identity of any expert who may be called at trial, along with a detailed expert report, and (3) shortly before trial, trial witness lists and the like regarding nonimpeachment evidence.

3. Mechanics

Disclosure is meant to proceed in an atmosphere of cooperation. A key feature is the requirement in Rule 26(f) that the litigants confer early, before discovery proceeds, to consider the case, the disclosures, and a discovery plan.

4. Problems

The swirling controversy arises from doubts that the benefits of overlaying a system of disclosure can match its costs.

C. Discovery

The pivotal feature of the federal procedural system is the availability of a significant discovery stage.

1. General Rules

a. Purposes of Discovery

Discovery allows a party to expand on the notice given by the pleadings and any disclosures and to prepare for disposition of the case.

b. Scope of Discovery

The scope is very wide, extending to any matter that is "relevant" and that is "nonprivileged." Rule 26(b)(1). Additional provisions restrict discovery of work product, treat discovery of expert information and electronically stored information, and permit control of discovery on a case-by-case basis.

c. Mechanics of Discovery

Discovery is meant to work almost wholly by action of the parties, without intervention by the court. Nevertheless, to remedy abuse, the respondent or any party may seek a protective order. Rule 26(c). Alternatively, to remedy recalcitrance, the discovering party may go to court to obtain an order compelling discovery and then a sanction. Rule 37.

d. Problems of Discovery

Serious questions persist on whether the benefits of discovery outweigh its costs, and on how to control those costs.

2. Specific Devices

There are six major types of discovery devices:

(1) oral depositions;

(2) written depositions;

(3) interrogatories;

(4) production of documents and such;

(5) physical and mental examination; and

(6) requests for admission.

D. Pretrial Conference

Judicially supervised conferences (1) help move the case through the pretrial process and toward trial and (2) focus the case after the skeletal pleading stage and the dispersive effects of disclosure and discovery. The pretrial procedure of Rule 16 was traditionally rather loose, but recent amendments have embraced the notion of judicial case management.

1. Purposes

A pretrial conference allows the court and the litigants to confer generally about the case, so moving it along to disposition and molding it for trial.

2. Procedural Incidents

The court may direct the attorneys and unrepresented parties to appear before it for one or more pretrial conferences. There is no uniform practice, but pretrial conferences should usually be voluntary in tone and relatively simple, flexible, and informal in format.

3. Order

After a pretrial conference, the court must enter a binding but amendable order reciting the action taken.

E. Other Steps

Other procedural steps can be taken in the pretrial period, and not necessarily in any fixed order.

1. Provisional Remedies

The claimant may seek temporary relief to protect himself from loss or injury while his action is pending.

a. Seizure of Property

Rule 64 incorporates state law on seizure of property, which law typically provides such remedies as *attachment* and *garnishment* to ensure that assets will still be there to satisfy any eventual judgment.

b. **Injunctive Relief**
Rule 65 governs the stopgap *temporary restraining order*, which can be granted without a hearing and sometimes even without notice, and the *preliminary injunction*, which can be granted only after notice and hearing.

2. **Summary Judgment and Other Steps That Avoid Trial**
Most often trial is ultimately avoided, either by a motion attacking the pleadings or more likely by one of the following steps.

a. **Summary Judgment**
Rule 56 is an important and broadly available device by which any party may without trial obtain a summary judgment on all or part of any claim, if he is "entitled to judgment as a matter of law" and if "there is no genuine issue as to any material fact." The party may move on the pleadings alone, or use other factual materials to pierce the pleadings. In determining whether there is a genuine issue as to any fact, the court construes all factual matters in the light reasonably most favorable to the party opposing the motion and then asks whether reasonable minds could differ.

b. **Other Steps That Avoid Trial**
There are four other steps that may avoid trial:

(1) voluntary dismissal;

(2) involuntary dismissal;

(3) default; and

(4) settlement.

3. **Masters and Magistrate Judges**
Another possible step involves referring the case to one of these "parajudges."

V. TRIAL

A. **Scenario**
Trial follows a relatively settled order, although trial practice is largely confided to the trial judge's discretion. Assume for the following that there is a federal jury trial, although a nonjury trial has a basically similar scenario.

1. **Plaintiff's Case**

   Ordinarily, plaintiff and then defendant make *opening statements*. Plaintiff then presents his evidence on all elements with respect to which he bears the initial burden of production.

2. **Motions**

   When plaintiff rests, defendant may move for *judgment as a matter of law* under Rule 50(a).

3. **Defendant's Case**

   If the trial has not been short-circuited by the granting of judgment as a matter of law, defendant may present her evidence.

4. **Motions**

   When defendant rests, plaintiff may move for judgment as a matter of law. There can be further stages of rebuttal, rejoinder, and so on. When both sides finally rest at the close of all the evidence, either side may move for judgment as a matter of law. As usual, this can be granted if, looking only at all the evidence that is favorable to the opponent of the motion but not incredible and also the unquestionable evidence that is favorable to the movant, the judge believes that a reasonable jury could not find for the opponent.

5. **Submission of Case**

   If the trial still has not been short-circuited by judgment as a matter of law, the parties usually make *closing arguments*, with plaintiff ordinarily speaking first and last. After and/or before closing arguments, the judge gives oral *instructions* to the jury. Then, the jury retires to reach a *verdict*.

6. **Motions**

   Two motions are available to change the outcome of the trial, but these motions must be filed no later than 10 days after entry of judgment. First, a *renewed motion for judgment as a matter of law* under Rule 50(b) asks to have the adverse verdict and any judgment thereon set aside and to have judgment entered in the movant's favor. The movant must have earlier moved for judgment as a matter of law under Rule 50(a). The standard for the renewed motion is the same as that for the original motion. Second, a *motion for a new trial* under Rule 59(a) asks to have the adverse verdict and any judgment thereon set aside and to hold a new trial to prevent injustice. This can be granted if, looking at all the evidence, the judge is clearly convinced that the jury was in error. It can also be granted on such grounds as error by the judge or misconduct by the participants in the course of the trial or on the ground of newly discovered evidence.

B. Jury and Judge

Many of the complications of trial practice result from the presence of a jury and its interaction with the judge.

1. Trial by Jury

a. Formal Characteristics of a Jury

A federal civil jury normally has 6 to 12 members acting unanimously.

b. Selection of a Jury

By an elaborate process including the judge's voir dire examination and the parties' challenges, an impartial and qualified trial jury is selected.

c. Right to Trial by Jury

Upon timely written demand of any party, there will be trial by jury on those contested factual issues:

(1) that are triable of right by a jury under the *Seventh Amendment* to the Federal Constitution, which is read expansively and includes at least any issue arising in a case such that the issue would have been triable of right to a common-law jury in 1791; or

(2) that are triable of right by a jury under some federal *statute*.

Also, the court, in its discretion with the *consent* of both parties, can order a trial by jury under Rule 39(c)(2).

d. State Practice

State jury practice is widely similar to federal. However, the Seventh Amendment and its expansive reading do not apply to the states.

2. Judicial Controls

Federal practice, unlike that of some states, leans toward maximizing judicial control of the jury.

VI. JUDGMENT

A. Entry of Judgment
Rule 58 requires prompt entry of a judgment as the formal expression of the outcome of federal litigation.

B. Kinds of Relief

1. Coercive Relief
Courts in their judgments generally can give active relief that the government will enforce.

a. Legal Relief
There can be an award to the prevailing party of damages, restoration of property, and costs.

b. Equitable Relief
There can be an order to defendant to do or not to do something, as by an injunction or an order of specific performance.

2. Declaratory Relief
Courts generally can give passive relief that declares legal relationships, as in an action for declaratory judgment.

C. Enforcement of Judgment

1. Legal Coercive Relief
The usual tool for enforcing a legal-type judgment is a *writ of execution.*

2. Equitable Coercive Relief
The usual tool for enforcing an equitable-type judgment is the court's *contempt* power.

D. Relief from Judgment
Relief from judgment, other than in the ordinary course of review in the trial and appellate courts, is available in narrow circumstances of extraordinary harm.

VII. APPEAL

A. Appealability

1. Routes to Court of Appeals
The basic jurisdictional rule is that only *final* decisions of a district court are appealable to the appropriate court of appeals, but the courts and Congress have created a series of exceptions.

a. **Final Decisions**

This final decision rule appears in 28 U.S.C.A. § 1291. However, there are masked exceptions in (1) such judge-made doctrines as the collateral order doctrine of the *Cohen* case, (2) the ad hoc approach of the *Gillespie* case, and (3) the treatment of complex litigation in Rule 54(b).

b. **Interlocutory Decisions**

There are also explicit exceptions that directly allow immediate review of avowedly interlocutory decisions in (1) 28 U.S.C.A. § 1292(a), which allows appeal of decisions concerning preliminary injunctions and of other specified decisions, (2) 28 U.S.C.A. § 1651(a), which allows review by mandamus, (3) 28 U.S.C.A. § 1292(b), which allows appeal if the district court and the court of appeals so agree, and (4) 28 U.S.C.A. § 1292(e), which authorizes Federal Rule 23(f) on appeal from class-action certification orders.

2. **Routes to Supreme Court**

Under 28 U.S.C.A. § 1254, there are two routes from the court of appeals to the Supreme Court. The usual route is by certiorari, which is a matter of the Court's discretion and not of right; but there is also the slim possibility of certification.

B. **Reviewability**

1. **Standards of Review**

The appellate court applies one of three degrees of scrutiny to reviewable issues.

a. **Nondeferential Review**

The appellate court makes a virtually fresh determination of questions of law.

b. **Middle–Tier Review**

The appellate court shows deference to fact-findings by a judge in a nonjury trial and to discretionary rulings, affirming unless it is clearly convinced there was error.

c. **Highly Restricted Review**

The appellate court will overturn only in the most extreme situations a decision denying a new trial motion based on the weight of the evidence.

2. Appellate Procedure

Appeal does not entail a retrial of the case, but a rather academic reconsideration of the reviewable issues in search of prejudicial error.

■ PART THREE: AUTHORITY TO ADJUDICATE

VIII. SUBJECT–MATTER JURISDICTION

A. Introduction to Subject–Matter Jurisdiction

For a court properly to undertake a civil adjudication, the court must have, under applicable constitutional and statutory provisions, *authority to adjudicate the type of controversy before the court*—that is, it must have jurisdiction over the subject matter.

B. State Courts

A state may organize its judicial branch as it wishes. A state has considerable freedom in allocating jurisdiction to its courts of *original* and *appellate* jurisdiction, subject to occasional federal statutes excluding state courts from certain subject areas.

1. General Versus Limited Jurisdiction

Typically, a state's courts of original jurisdiction include one set of courts of *general* jurisdiction, which can hear any type of action not specifically prohibited to them, and several sets of courts of *limited* jurisdiction, which can hear only those types of actions specifically consigned to them.

2. Exclusive Versus Concurrent Jurisdiction

A great number of cases can be heard only in state courts. For some other cases, the federal and state courts have *concurrent* jurisdiction. A few types of cases are restricted by federal statute to the *exclusive* jurisdiction of the federal courts.

C. Federal Courts

Article III of the Federal Constitution establishes the Supreme Court, and Articles I and III give Congress the power to establish lower federal courts as it sees fit. The result is a number of federal courts, including the basic pyramid of 91 district courts, 13 courts of appeals, and the Supreme Court. These federal courts are courts of limited jurisdiction. Accordingly, for a case to come within the jurisdiction of a federal court, the case normally must fall (1) within a federal statute bestowing jurisdiction on the court and (2) within the outer bounds of federal jurisdiction marked by Article III and the Eleventh Amendment.

1. Federal Questions

As the most important example of federal subject-matter jurisdiction, the district courts have original jurisdiction over cases arising under the Constitution, federal statutory or common law, or treaties.

a. Constitutional Provision

Article III extends the federal judicial power to such "arising under" cases, and it has been broadly read to embrace all cases that include a federal "ingredient."

b. Statutory Provisions

Congress has acted under the constitutional provision to vest federal question jurisdiction in the district courts:

(1) the general provision in 28 U.S.C.A. § 1331 uses the key constitutional words, but it has been narrowly read to require an *adequate federal element* that would appear on the face of a *well-pleaded complaint* stating a federal claim that is *not insubstantial*; and

(2) there is a string of special federal question statutes, applicable to special subject areas, that might avoid some of the restrictions read into § 1331, might impose other restrictions, or might make the jurisdiction exclusive.

2. Diversity of Citizenship

For another example, the district courts have original jurisdiction over cases that are between parties of diverse citizenship, usually provided that they satisfy a jurisdictional amount requirement.

a. Constitutional Provision

Article III extends the federal judicial power to such diversity cases, and it has been broadly read to require only "partial diversity."

b. Statutory Provisions

Congress has acted under the constitutional provision to vest diversity jurisdiction in the district courts:

(1) the general provision in 28 U.S.C.A. § 1332(a) bestows jurisdiction only in certain cases of "complete diversity" where the matter in controversy exceeds $75,000; and

(2) there are a few special statutes such as 28 U.S.C.A. § 1335 bestowing jurisdiction for interpleader actions involving partial diversity where the amount in controversy equals or exceeds $500.

c. Jurisdictional Amount

Jurisdictional amount requirements, intended to keep petty controversies out of the federal courts but very complicated to apply, are of statutory origin.

3. Removal

Congress has provided for removal of specified cases within the federal judicial power from a state trial court to the local federal district court. The basic statute is 28 U.S.C.A. § 1441, which most importantly allows all defendants together promptly to remove any civil action against them that is within the district courts' original jurisdiction—subject to certain exceptions, such as the prohibition of removal of a case not founded on a federal question if any served defendant is a citizen of the forum state.

4. Supplemental Jurisdiction

The courts generally read the Constitution and the jurisdictional statutes to permit the district courts when desirable to hear state claims that were related to pending federal claims. Now Congress has codified this doctrine in 28 U.S.C.A. § 1367.

IX. TERRITORIAL AUTHORITY TO ADJUDICATE

A. Introduction to Territorial Authority to Adjudicate

For a court properly to undertake a civil adjudication, the court must have *authority to hear the case despite any nonlocal elements in the case*—that is, it must have territorial authority to adjudicate.

1. Territorial Jurisdiction and Venue

These two types of restrictions on the place of litigation together constitute the concept of territorial authority to adjudicate.

2. **Current Due Process Doctrine**

The principal limitation on territorial authority to adjudicate is the federal due process provision, which under the *World-Wide Volkswagen* case now requires the categorization of the action and then the application of both the power and the unreasonableness tests.

a. **Categorization**

First the action must be categorized in terms of the target of the action, be it a person or some kind of thing.

b. **Jurisdictional Tests**

Then it must be determined whether (1) the forum has *power* over the target ("minimum contacts") *and* (2) litigating the action there would be *unreasonable* in light of all interests ("fair play and substantial justice").

3. **Future Due Process Doctrine**

Several commentators argue that the due process doctrine should evolve toward directly applying only a reasonableness test, as was done in the *Mullane* case.

B. **Application of Current Due Process Doctrine**

First categorize the action.

1. **In Personam**

For personal jurisdiction, there must be power over the individual or corporate defendant, and the exercise of jurisdiction must not be unreasonable. There are several recognized bases of power:

(1) *General Jurisdiction.* Both *presence* and *domicile* of defendant give power to adjudicate any personal claim.

(2) *Specific Jurisdiction.* The lesser contacts of *consent* and certain *forum-directed acts* (such as sufficiently substantial tortious acts, business activity, acts related to property, and litigating acts) by defendant give power to adjudicate only those personal claims related to the contacts.

2. **In Rem**

a. **Pure In Rem**

Jurisdiction in rem can result in a judgment affecting the interests of *all* persons in a designated thing. To satisfy the power test, such an action normally must be brought where the thing is. Unreasonableness will then be the key test.

b. Jurisdiction over Status

This subtype of jurisdiction can result in a judgment establishing or terminating a status. To satisfy the power test, such an action must be brought in a place to which one party in the relationship has a significant connection. The exercise of jurisdiction must not be unreasonable.

3. Quasi In Rem

a. Subtype One

This variety of jurisdiction quasi in rem can result in a judgment affecting only the interests of *particular* persons in a designated thing, and may be invoked by a plaintiff seeking to establish a *pre-existing interest* in the thing as against the defendant's interest. To satisfy the power test, such an action normally must be brought where the thing is. Unreasonableness will then be the key test.

b. Subtype Two

This variety of jurisdiction quasi in rem can result in a judgment affecting only the interests of *particular* persons in a designated thing, and may be invoked by a plaintiff seeking to apply the defendant's property to the satisfaction of a claim against defendant that is *unrelated* to the property. To satisfy the power test, such an action normally must be brought where the thing is. Unreasonableness will then be the key test, but is here so difficult to satisfy that such jurisdiction is available only in rather special situations.

C. Other Limitations on Territorial Authority to Adjudicate

1. Limits on State Trial Courts

a. Federal Law

The principal federal limitation on state-court territorial authority to adjudicate is the already described Due Process Clause of the Fourteenth Amendment.

b. International Law

International law imposes no significant additional restrictions on state-court territorial authority to adjudicate.

c. State Law

First, state constitution, statute, or decision may further limit state-court territorial jurisdiction, such as by a restricted long-arm statute or the doctrine of forum non conveniens. *Second*, related to these limits are state venue restrictions, which most often are defined as those requirements of territorial authority to adjudicate that specify as proper fora only certain courts within a state having territorial jurisdiction, but which would be better defined as those requirements of territorial authority to adjudicate that are not founded on the Federal Constitution.

d. Agreements Among Parties

The parties generally may, by agreement, restrict any potential litigation to one or more courts.

2. Limits on Federal District Courts

a. Federal Law

First, the principal constitutional limitation on a federal court's territorial jurisdiction is the Due Process Clause of the Fifth Amendment. The variety of federal statutes and Rules treating service of process further limits federal-court territorial jurisdiction. The federal courts have also developed a number of limiting doctrines, such as immunity from service of process. *Second*, related to all these limits are federal venue restrictions, which most often are defined as those requirements of territorial authority to adjudicate that are not linked to service provisions, but which would be better defined as those requirements of territorial authority to adjudicate that are not founded on the Federal Constitution.

b. International Law

International law imposes no significant additional restrictions on federal-court territorial authority to adjudicate.

c. State Law

State jurisdictional limits frequently apply in federal court through the federal service provisions, most often because the applicable federal provision incorporates that state law.

d. Agreements Among Parties

The parties generally may, by agreement, restrict any potential litigation to one or more courts.

X. NOTICE

A. Introduction to Notice
For a court properly to undertake a civil adjudication, the persons whose property or liberty interests are to be significantly affected must receive *adequate notice*.

B. Constitutional Requirement

1. General Rule
For any adjudication, due process requires fair notice of the pendency of the action to the affected person or her representative. Most importantly, fair notice must be either (1) actual notice or (2) notice that is reasonably calculated to result in actual notice.

2. Notice Before Seizing Property
Due process also requires certain procedural protections before governmental action may unduly impair a person's property interest.

C. Nonconstitutional Requirements
The provisions for service of process further specify the manner of giving notice. Local law may strictly enforce some of these nonconstitutional requirements for giving notice, but today the trend is toward ignoring irregularities (1) where there was actual notice received or (2) where the form of the notice and the manner of transmitting it substantially complied with the prescribed procedure.

D. Contractual Waiver of Protections
By voluntary, intelligent, and knowing act, a person may waive in advance all these procedural protections.

XI. PROCEDURAL INCIDENTS OF FORUM–AUTHORITY DOCTRINES

A. Procedure for Raising

1. Subject–Matter Jurisdiction
Satisfaction of this requirement is open to challenge throughout the ordinary course of the initial action.

2. Territorial Authority to Adjudicate and Notice
In the initial action the key for defendant is to raise these personal defenses in a way that avoids waiving them.

a. **Special Appearance**

This is the procedural technique by which defendant can effectively raise these defenses. Defendant must be very careful to follow precisely the required procedural steps of a special appearance. In federal court, a "special appearance" comes in the form of a Rule 12(b)(2)–(5) defense.

b. **Limited Appearance**

To be sharply distinguished from a special appearance is this procedural technique by which defendant restricts her appearance to defending a nonpersonal action on the merits, without submitting to personal jurisdiction.

B. **Consequences of Raising**

1. **Subject–Matter Jurisdiction**

A finding in the ordinary course of the initial action of the existence of subject-matter jurisdiction is *res judicata*, precluding the parties from attacking the resultant judgment on that ground in subsequent litigation—except in special circumstances.

2. **Territorial Authority to Adjudicate and Notice**

A finding in the ordinary course of the initial action of the existence of territorial authority to adjudicate or adequate notice is *res judicata*, precluding the appearing parties from attacking the resultant judgment on either ground in subsequent litigation.

C. **Consequences of Not Raising**

1. **Litigated Action**

a. **Subject–Matter Jurisdiction**

Unraised subject-matter jurisdiction in a litigated action is later treated as *res judicata*.

b. **Territorial Authority to Adjudicate and Notice**

By failing properly to raise any such threshold defense, an appearing defendant *waives* it.

2. **Complete Default**

a. **Subject–Matter Jurisdiction**

In case of complete default, a party usually may later obtain *relief from judgment* on the ground of lack of subject-matter jurisdiction.

b. **Territorial Authority to Adjudicate and Notice**
A defaulting party usually may later obtain *relief from judgment* on the ground of an important defect in territorial authority to adjudicate or notice.

■ PART FOUR: COMPLEX LITIGATION

XII. PRELIMINARY CONSIDERATIONS

A. Historical Note
Historically, there has been a general movement in our legal systems toward more broadly requiring joinder of multiple claims and parties and toward permitting even more extensive joinder.

B. Federal Focus
This capsule summary of Part Four focuses on federal practice.

1. Governing Law
In any federal action, federal law governs joinder.

2. Federal Joinder Rules
The critical provisions are Rules 13–14, 17–24, and 42.

3. Jurisdiction and Venue
Each claim against a particular party must satisfy the federal requirements of subject-matter jurisdiction, territorial jurisdiction, and venue. Especially relevant here, however, are the ameliorating doctrines of supplemental jurisdiction and ancillary venue.

C. Abuses
Efficiency and fairness demand that there be techniques to compel joinder, as well as means to simplify the structure of a case.

1. Defenses of Nonjoinder and Misjoinder
A party can raise by the defense of *nonjoinder* the opposing pleader's violation of the minimal rules of compulsory joinder, and can raise by the defense of *misjoinder* the opposing pleader's violation of the very liberal bounds on permissive joinder.

2. **Judicial Power to Combine and Divide**

Even where the pleaders have initially formulated a proper case in that wide area between the limits of compulsory and permissive joinder, the court may reshape the litigation for efficient and fair disposition. The court may expand the case by ordering either *a joint trial* or *consolidation* of separate actions pending before it and involving a common question of law or fact, or may contract the case by ordering either *a separate trial* or *severance* of individual claims against particular parties.

XIII. MULTICLAIM LITIGATION

A. Compulsory Joinder

Requirements are quite limited concerning what additional claims *must* be joined in the parties' pleadings.

1. **Claim Preclusion**

Res judicata does not require a party to join separate claims against his opponent, but it generally does in effect require him to put any asserted claim entirely before the court. This requirement follows from the rule that the eventual judgment will preclude later suit on any part of that whole claim, which is defined in transactional terms.

2. **Compulsory Counterclaims**

Analogously, Rule 13(a) generally requires a defending party to put forward any claim that she has against any opposing party, if it "arises out of the transaction or occurrence that is the subject matter of the opposing party's claim." Failure to assert such a counterclaim will preclude subsequently suing thereon.

B. Permissive Joinder

Permissiveness is almost unbounded concerning what additional claims *may* be joined in the parties' pleadings.

1. **Parallel Claims**

Rule 18(a) says that any party "asserting a claim, counterclaim, crossclaim, or third-party claim may join, as independent or alternative claims, as many claims as it has against an opposing party."

2. **Permissive Counterclaims**

Analogously, Rule 13(b) permits a defending party to assert any claim that she has against an opposing party.

3. Crossclaims

Rule 13(g) permits, but does not compel, a party to assert a transactionally related claim against another party who is not yet in an opposing posture.

XIV. MULTIPARTY LITIGATION

A. General Joinder Provisions

1. Compulsory Joinder

Rule 19 governs what persons *must* be joined when any party pleads a claim other than a class action.

a. Necessary Parties

Rule 19(a) specifies those persons who are so closely connected to an action that they must be joined, unless joinder is not feasible under the requirements of jurisdiction and venue.

b. Indispensable Parties

Rule 19(b) guides the court in deciding whether to dismiss an action on the ground of the absence of a necessary party who cannot be joined because of the restrictions of jurisdiction and venue.

c. Procedure

All persons joined pursuant to Rule 19 are normally brought in as defendants.

2. Permissive Joinder

The subject of "proper parties" controls what persons *may* be joined when any party pleads a claim, and that subject entails three relevant limitations.

a. Rule 20

This Rule permits certain related plaintiffs to join together to sue, and also permits plaintiff to join certain related defendants.

b. Real Party in Interest

Rule 17(a) requires every claim to be prosecuted only in the name of "real parties in interest," who are the persons entitled under applicable substantive law to enforce the right sued upon.

c. **Capacity**
Rule 17(b) and (c) imposes the further and separate limitation of "capacity" to sue or be sued, which comprises the personal qualifications legally needed by a person to litigate.

B. **Special Joinder Devices**
Five major devices expand the scope of permissive joinder beyond Rule 20.

1. **Impleader**
Impleader allows a *defending party* (as third-party plaintiff) to assert a claim against a *nonparty* (as third-party defendant) who is or may contingently be liable to that party for all or part of a claim already made against that party. Rule 14.

2. **Interpleader**
Interpleader allows a person (as stakeholder) to avoid the risk of *multiple liability* by requiring two or more persons with actual or prospective claims against him to assert their respective *adverse* claims in a single action.

   a. **Procedure**
   The stakeholder can invoke interpleader by an original action or by counterclaim, whether or not the stakeholder claims part or all of the stake.

   b. **Kinds of Interpleader**
   There are two kinds:

      (1) *Rule Interpleader*. Rule 22(a) governs this kind, subject to the normal restrictions of jurisdiction and venue.

      (2) *Statutory Interpleader*. An alternative lies in 28 U.S.C.A. §§ 1335, 2361, and 1397, which provide specially permissive limits on jurisdiction and venue.

3. **Class Action**
A class action allows one or more members of a class of similarly situated persons to sue, or be sued, as representative parties litigating on behalf of the other class members without actually bringing them into court. Rule 23. However, to justify such efficiency and substantive goals, the essential due process requirement of adequate representation must be met.

a. **Requirements**

The proposed class action must (1) meet the four initial requirements that Rule 23(a) imposes, (2) fall into one of the three situations specified in Rule 23(b), and (3) satisfy the requirements of jurisdiction and venue.

b. **Mechanics**

Class actions pose major management problems for the courts, accounting for the special management provisions in Rule 23(c)–(h).

c. **Termination**

Class actions also pose major settlement problems, accounting for the special notice and court approval provisions in Rule 23(e).

d. **State Practice**

States have their own class-action provisions, of lesser or greater scope and detail.

4. **Shareholders' Derivative Action**

A derivative action allows one or more persons to sue for the benefit of similarly situated persons on a claim that their common fiduciary refuses to assert. Rule 23.1 deals specifically with derivative actions by shareholders of a corporation *or* by members of an unincorporated association.

5. **Intervention**

Intervention allows a person not named as a party to enter an existing lawsuit, coming in on the appropriate side of the litigation. Rule 24(a) governs *intervention of right* by closely connected persons, and Rule 24(b) governs *permissive intervention* by other persons.

■ PART FIVE: GOVERNING LAW

XV. CHOICE OF LAW

A pervasive problem in litigation that involves nonlocal elements is choosing which sovereign's law to apply.

A. Techniques

Generally, it is the forum court's task to choose the governing law for each issue by using some technique for choice of law, such as interest analysis.

B. Constitutional Limits

Constitutionally, courts have a very free hand in choosing the governing law.

XVI. CHOICE BETWEEN STATE AND FEDERAL LAW

A special choice-of-law problem frequently encountered in our federal system is the choice between state and federal law.

A. State Law in Federal Court: *Erie*

1. Constitutional Limits

The Federal Constitution can dictate a choice in favor of federal law applicable in federal court, as it has done in the Seventh Amendment's guarantee of trial by jury. Conversely, the Constitution requires the application of state law in areas of extremely high state interest, such as title to real estate. However, these relatively rare and easy cases of constitutionally mandated choice of law are of limited practical significance. Usually, the Constitution does not directly enter into solving a state-federal choice-of-law problem.

2. Legislative Limits

Within constitutional limits, Congress can make the choice between state and federal law, and its choice will bind the federal courts. Indeed, the Rules of Decision Act of 1789 looks as if Congress has broadly made a choice in favor of state law, but that statute is generally read to preserve judicial choice-of-law power.

3. Choice–of–Law Technique

In the absence of constitutional and congressional directive, how then should a federal court choose between state and federal law for application to a particular issue in a case before it?

a. Competing Methodologies

Since 1938 the Supreme Court has progressed through a sequence of choice-of-law techniques for the federal courts to use in handling that problem:

(1) Erie *Decision*. The fountainhead vaguely offered a discussion of relevant policies.

(2) *Substance/Procedure Test*. Next came this crude and mechanical technique.

(3) *Outcome-determinative Test*. The *Guaranty Trust* case eventually led to this other crude and mechanical technique.

(4) *Interest Analysis*. The *Byrd* case developed this sensitive and flexible, but obviously uncertain, approach.

(5) Hanna *Formulas*. This case both requires the application of valid Federal Rules in all federal actions and also establishes a refined outcome-determinative test for use outside the realm of the Federal Rules.

Thus, the Court has not yet arrived at any truly clear or optimal solution. In its latest attempt in *Gasperini*, it seems to have rejected certainty in favor of ad hoc balancing of state and federal interests.

b. ***Erie* Precepts**
Regardless of the choice-of-law technique adopted, the federal courts observe three precepts:

(1) the choice-of-law technique applies issue-by-issue in each case, so the type of subject-matter jurisdiction does not fix state or federal law as applicable to all issues in the case;

(2) the *Klaxon* rule says that for matters governed by state law under *Erie*, the forum state's conflicts law tells which state's law governs; and

(3) to determine the content of state law where it is unclear, the federal court should fabricate state law as if it were then sitting as the forum state's highest court.

c. **Federal Law in Federal Court**
Under this whole scheme, federal law frequently applies in federal court. When it is left to the federal courts to formulate the content of that federal law, the result is called federal

common law. Often the federal courts perform this task by adopting state law as the federal common law.

B. Federal Law in State Court: Reverse–*Erie*

   1. Constitutional Limits
   As in the *Erie* setting, the Federal Constitution can dictate a choice in favor of federal law applicable in state court. Conversely, the Constitution requires the application of state law in areas of high state interest.

   2. Legislative Limits
   Within constitutional limits, Congress can make the choice between state and federal law, and its choice will bind the courts.

   3. Choice–of–Law Technique
   In the absence of constitutional and congressional directive, the state courts and ultimately the Supreme Court must decide whether state or federal law applies in state court by employing a federally mandated choice-of-law technique similar to the *Erie* technique.

C. Summary
In areas of clear state "substantive" concern, state law governs in both state and federal courts. As one moves into "procedural" areas, state law *tends* to govern in state court and federal law *tends* to govern in federal court. Finally, as one moves into areas of clear federal "substantive" concern, federal law governs in both state and federal courts.

■ PART SIX: FORMER ADJUDICATION

XVII. PRELIMINARY CONSIDERATIONS

A. Introduction to Former Adjudication
The subject here is the impact of a previously rendered judgment in subsequent civil litigation.

   1. Modern Focus
   This capsule summary of Part Six focuses on the modern approach to res judicata.

2. **Rules**

The centrally important doctrine of res judicata has two main branches:

(1) *Claim Preclusion.* Outside the context of the initial action, a party generally may not relitigate a claim decided therein by a valid and final judgment. If that judgment was for plaintiff, *merger* applies. If instead that judgment was for defendant, *bar* applies.

(2) *Issue Preclusion.* Outside the context of the initial action, a party generally may not relitigate any issue actually litigated and determined therein if the determination was essential to a valid and final judgment. If the two actions were on the same claim, *direct estoppel* applies. If the two actions were on different claims, *collateral estoppel* applies.

3. **Comparisons and Contrasts**

Res judicata should be distinguished from:

(1) stare decisis;

(2) law of the case;

(3) former recovery;

(4) estoppel; and

(5) election of remedies.

B. **Rationale of Res Judicata**

Efficiency and fairness demand that there be an end to litigation.

C. **Application of Res Judicata**

1. **Raising the Doctrine**

The person wishing to rely on res judicata must affirmatively raise it. It can be so raised only after the prior judgment was rendered, and outside the context of the initial action (and any appeal).

2. **Conditions for Application: Validity and Finality**

For a judgment to have res judicata effects, it must be "valid" and "final."

a. **Validity**

To be treated as valid, the judgment must withstand any attack in the form of a request for relief from judgment.

b. **Finality**

An adjudication can be treated as a final judgment for issue preclusion at an earlier stage than for claim preclusion.

XVIII. CLAIM PRECLUSION

A. Requirements of Claim Preclusion

Claim preclusion prohibits repetitive litigation of the same claim. The modern view is that a "claim" includes all rights of plaintiff to remedies against defendant with respect to the transaction from which the action arose.

B. Exceptions to Claim Preclusion

Predictably, this broad conception of claim preclusion has generated several significant exceptions, such as where there was:

(1) a jurisdictional or procedural impediment to presenting the entire claim;

(2) a party agreement to claim-splitting;

(3) judicial permission to split a claim; or

(4) an adjudication on one of those grounds labeled "not on the merits."

C. Counterclaims

1. **Interposition of Counterclaim**

A defendant who asserts a counterclaim is generally treated, with respect to that claim, as a plaintiff under the normal rules of claim preclusion.

2. **Failure to Interpose Counterclaim**

A defendant who does not assert a counterclaim is unaffected by claim preclusion with respect to that claim, unless that claim (1) falls within a compulsory counterclaim statute or rule or (2) constitutes a common-law compulsory counterclaim.

XIX. ISSUE PRECLUSION

A. Requirements of Issue Preclusion

Where claim preclusion does not apply, issue preclusion acts to prevent relitigation of essential issues. There are three requirements.

      1. Same Issue

      2. Actually Litigated and Determined

      3. Essential to Judgment

B. Exceptions to Issue Preclusion
Courts apply issue preclusion quite flexibly by invoking many exceptions, such as where, *in certain circumstances*:

(1) an issue of law is involved;

(2) the initial court was an inferior court;

(3) there is a change in the burden of persuasion;

(4) there was an inability to appeal in the initial action; or

(5) the application of issue preclusion was unforeseeable.

C. Multiple Issues

      1. Cumulative Determinations
      If several issues in a case were litigated and determined, each is precluded provided that its determination was essential to judgment.

      2. Ambiguous Determinations
      If one cannot tell which of several possible issues was determined in a case, then none is precluded.

      3. Alternative Determinations
      If the adjudicator determined several issues in a case and each of those determinations without the others sufficed to support the judgment, then some authorities say that none by itself is precluded unless it was affirmed on appeal.

XX. NONORDINARY JUDGMENTS

Special attention must be given to the res judicata effects of special kinds of judgment when used in subsequent civil litigation.

A. **Nonpersonal Judgments**

    1. **Pure In Rem**

    2. **Jurisdiction over Status**

    3. **Quasi In Rem—Subtype One**

    4. **Quasi In Rem—Subtype Two**

B. **Noncoercive Judgments**
The subject here is declaratory judgment, which has limited claim-preclusion effects but normal issue-preclusion effects.

C. **Nonjudicial or Noncivil Proceedings**

    1. **Administrative Adjudication**

    2. **Arbitration Award**

    3. **Criminal Judgment**

XXI. NONPARTY EFFECTS

A. **Privies**
Certain nonparties to an action are in certain circumstances subjected to generally the same rules of res judicata as are the former parties, the basis for this treatment being some sort of representational relationship between former party and nonparty. These nonparties are then labeled "privies."

B. **Strangers**
A person who had nothing to do with a judgment *might benefit* from its res judicata effects, but good policy dictates that the judgment *cannot bind* such a person who is neither party nor privy. The most important example of the possible benefits is that, mutuality of estoppel having been rejected, the stranger may sometimes use the prior judgment for collateral estoppel against a former party.

XXII. NONDOMESTIC JUDGMENTS

A. **General Rules**
Special attention must be given to the treatment a judgment should receive in subsequent civil litigation in another judicial system.

1. **Recognition**

   A court will "recognize," or give effect under the doctrine of res judicata to, a nondomestic judgment that is valid and final. The applicable law on recognition generally is the law of the judgment-rendering sovereign.

2. **Enforcement**

   The second court will enforce a judgment entitled to recognition. The applicable law on method of enforcement generally is the law of the enforcing court's sovereign, which might provide for an action upon the judgment or registration of the judgment.

B. **Judgments of American Courts**

   The Federal Constitution and federal legislation make these rules for handling a nondomestic judgment in large part obligatory on American courts when that judgment comes from another American court.

C. **Judgments of Foreign Nations**

   American courts treat judgments of foreign nations pretty much like American judgments, although their approach to such foreign judgments is more flexible because their respect generally flows from comity rather than from legal obligation.

Perspective

■ APPROACH TO THE SUBJECT

The course in civil procedure usually turns out to be the most pleasant surprise of the first year of law school. (Those of you studying for the bar examination know this already, and so I direct these comments primarily to first-year law students.) Civil procedure provides a series of revelations: it is not a how-to-do-it course, but is instead a course centered on a number of engrossing problems; it does not limit itself to the tactical mechanics of litigation, but extends to fundamental issues lurking at the fringes and in the interstices of those mechanics; it involves more than mere rules, as it plunges to the profundities of policies, values, and needs lying below; and it conveys much information, but it addresses the unanswerable as well. The subject matter is quite foreign to the lay person and is not simple, but that provides challenge. In short, the study of civil procedure should turn out to be interesting, new, challenging, and fun.

The topic of civil procedure concerns the societal process for handling disputes of a noncriminal sort. Your course will probably focus on the current law governing American court procedure in ordinary civil actions. In Part One of my outline I have tried to analyze, or break down, this subject into comprehensible components; and still in Part One I have tried to synthesize, or reassemble, the parts into a more meaningful whole. I shall here spare you repetition of all that and pass quickly to more specific suggestions on approaching civil procedure. But permit me first to stress the importance of the subject: civil procedure is important in its own right as an integral part of a system of justice; moreover, as the machinery of the legal system, civil procedure implements substantive law and, in so doing, inevitably affects substantive law in profound ways; and, finally, every lawyer can profit from a sophisticated knowledge of civil procedure, just as any law student can make much more sense of his or her other courses through an attentive study of civil procedure. See generally Judith Resnik, Civil Procedure, in Looking at Law School 177 (Stephen Gillers ed., 4th ed. 1997).

Now, let me turn to those specific suggestions, of which I offer four.

(1) *Day-to-Day Study.* In civil procedure as in your other courses, day-to-day preparation for and intentness in class and daily review after class are utterly essential. More specifically, you should approach your reading carefully (analyzing with excruciating word-by-word attention), critically (questioning the soundness of everything written in cases), and actively (constantly asking yourself questions and answering your own and the casebook's questions, thinking beyond the confines of the case in front of you, and continually summarizing and synthesizing the materials). Briefing cases and taking class notes are special law-school skills to be perfected, and reviewing your briefs and notes after each class is a practice to be followed religiously. See generally Kenney F. Hegland, Introduction to the Study and Practice of Law in a Nutshell (4th ed. 2003).

Buried in all this usual advice is the single most important determinant of law-school success: the idea that the only way to get anything out of your study is careful, critical, and active reading and rereading. True, your ultimate goal is perceiving the big picture, but you will not get there by a passive and uncritical skimming. Such skimming may have worked to give you the gist as an undergraduate. But a casebook is no ordinary textbook, and so skimming a casebook will yield nothing more than a collection of meaningless fact patterns from unrelated cases and perhaps a few rules that by themselves are of little or no importance. Instead, under the case method, only a long series of painstaking microscopic views will reveal the big picture. In brief, reading should be a struggle.

From this idea flow at least four corollaries. First, do not read any case for the "rule of the case." As just explained, the rule of the case by itself is likely to be of little or no importance. The case is important as a learning process. It matters less where the case ends up than how the case got there. Naturally, then, a detailed reading of and thinking about the whole case are necessary. Second, you should be constantly asking yourself questions about the materials. Indeed, the frequency of such questions is a measure of your progress in mastering this new reading skill. Third, as you read word-by-word, lots of those words will be unfamiliar, especially at first. For a full understanding of the materials, you should look up all these words. So you should be aware of the existence of Black's Law Dictionary (Bryan A. Garner ed., 8th ed. 2004), as well as the glossary that I offer in Appendix C below. Fourth, a special technique in civil procedure is reading every court rule and statute referred to in your materials.

Do not delude yourself—law is of necessity essentially self-taught. Truly learning law is not a process of receiving information, but rather one of recreating in your own mind the understanding of others and then creating your own understanding. The case method is brilliantly suited to this difficult process, but it places great demands on you.

(2) *Final Synthesis.* The pointillist case method also necessitates a review and overview at the end of the semester. Without diligent day-to-day study, this synthesis will be beyond your reach. Without this synthesis, your daily diligence will have been largely wasted effort.

Your final synthesis should not involve memorization of law or acquisition of detail. You should instead be reflectively looking for the big picture, by fitting the parts together. Law school must leave this task to you. Take it seriously, and the returns will be immense.

(3) *Outside Reading.* Marvelously useful readings on civil procedure exist out in the world beyond your casebook and rules pamphlet. They fall into three groups.

First, there are introductory books, which can do much at the outset to orient you in civil procedure. Reading a book like John A. Humbach, Whose Monet? An Introduction to the American Legal System (2007), which relates the full story of an actual case, will do wonders in calming you down and getting you started in the right direction. Or you might read on your own some other "case" study such as (1) Joyce Bichler, DES Daughter: The Joyce Bichler Story (1981), (2) David Crump & Jeffrey B. Berman, The Story of a Civil Case (3d ed. 2001), (3) Marc A. Franklin, The Biography of a Legal Dispute (1968), (4) Sandra M. Gilbert, Wrongful Death: A Medical Tragedy (1995), (5) Brandt Goldstein, Storming the Court (2005), now elaborated in Brandt Goldstein & Rodger Citron, A Documentary Companion to *Storming the Court* (2008), (6) Jonathan Harr, A Civil Action (1995), now elaborated in Lewis A. Grossman & Robert G. Vaughn, A Documentary Companion to *A Civil Action* (4th ed. 2008), (7) Nan D. Hunter, The Power of Procedure: The Litigation of *Jones v. Clinton* (2002), (8) Jonathan Mahler, The Challenge: *Hamdan v. Rumsfeld* and the Fight over Presidential Power (2008), (9) Samuel Mermin, Law and the Legal System (2d ed. 1982), (10) Peter N. Simon, The Anatomy of a Lawsuit (rev. ed. 1996), (11) Jeffrey W. Stempel, Litigation Road: The

Story of *State Farm v. Campbell* (2008), (12) Gerald M. Stern, The Buffalo Creek Disaster (1976), (13) Barry Werth, Damages: One Family's Legal Struggles in the World of Medicine (1998), or (14) William Zelermyer, The Legal System in Operation (1977).

Second, there are hornbooks and other texts on civil procedure. Here more caution is required. Avoid over-reliance on them. They will not prove very helpful because they focus on summarizing the law, which is only one of your lesser concerns in law school. Moreover, these books can do actual damage by derailing the learning process. They do this by discouraging in-depth reading of particular cases; also, for series of cases, they tend to abort incipient confusion, often by glossing over problems. Bear in mind that a degree of confusion is an essential part of the learning process, as confusion instigates thought and eventually leads to true understanding. In short, such texts should not become a crutch or even a part of your regular study pattern.

However, for shedding light on specific problems to which your study leads you and for some review purposes, texts on civil procedure can be useful. Thus, a few words on these books are in order. The most useful books are (1) Federal Practice and Procedure, written by Professors Wright and Miller and others, and (2) Moore's Federal Practice, written by James Wm. Moore and recently revised by others; these two multi-volume works are very easy to use, generally being arranged by Federal Rule number, and they are complete and superb. Among single-volume works, the most helpful, in my opinion, are Charles Alan Wright & Mary Kay Kane, Law of Federal Courts (6th ed. 2002), and the more general Fleming James, Jr., Geoffrey C. Hazard, Jr. & John Leubsdorf, Civil Procedure (5th ed. 2001). But very good and quite helpful are (1) Michael Allen & Michael Finch, An Illustrated Guide to Civil Procedure (2006), (2) Steven Baicker–McKee, William M. Janssen & John B. Corr, A Student's Guide to the Federal Rules of Civil Procedure (11th ed. 2008), (3) James R. Devine, Problems in Civil Procedure (2007), (4) David A. Dittfurth, Learning Civil Procedure (2007), (5) Jack H. Friedenthal, Mary Kay Kane & Arthur R. Miller, Civil Procedure (4th ed. 2005), (6) Howard Erichson, Inside Civil Procedure (2008), (7) Richard D. Freer, Introduction to Civil Procedure (2006), (8) Joseph W. Glannon, Civil Procedure: Examples and Explanations (6th ed. 2008), (9) Geoffrey C. Hazard, Jr. & Michele Taruffo, American Civil Procedure (1993), (10) David Charles Hricik, Mastering Civil Procedure (2008), (11) Samuel Issacharoff, Civil Procedure (2005), (12) Mary Kay Kane, Civil Procedure in a Nutshell (6th ed. 2007), and also the books on related subjects in the Nutshell Series, (13) Carolyn J. Nygren, Starting Off Right in Civil Procedure (1999), (14) Suzanna Sherry & Jay Tidmarsh, Essentials: Civil Procedure (2007), (15) Gene R. Shreve & Peter Raven–Hansen, Understanding Civil Procedure (3d ed. 2002), (16) A. Benjamin Spencer, Acing Civil Procedure (2d ed. 2008), (17) A.J. Stephani & Glen Weissenberger, Weissenberger's Federal Civil Procedure 2005 Litigation Manual (2005), (18) Stephen N. Subrin & Margaret Y.K. Woo, Litigating in America (2006), (19) Larry L. Teply & Ralph U. Whitten, Civil Procedure (3d ed. 2004), and (20) Ann E. Woodley, Litigating in Federal Court: A Guide to the Rules (1999). Alternatively, I flesh out this outline in Kevin M. Clermont, Principles of Civil Procedure (2d ed. 2009).

Third, you should eventually consider reading in the depths of civil procedure and somewhat beyond the confines of that subject. Law review articles and books cited in your casebook mark the route to the depths, and a fine collection of such readings lies in Geoffrey C. Hazard, Jr. & Jan Vetter, Perspectives on Civil Procedure (1987), and David I. Levine, Donald L. Doernberg & Melissa L. Nelken, Civil Procedure Anthology (1998). A good but aging way to find your way beyond civil procedure is Robert M. Cover & Owen M. Fiss, The Structure of Procedure (1979), an excellent collection of readings that can take you from civil procedure to procedure in general, to jurisprudence, and to interdisciplinary studies. A more integrated consideration of procedure as a generalized subject is Judith Resnik, Processes of the Law (2004).

(4) *Other Study Techniques.* Outlines, yours and mine, can help. So can preparation for the examination. I shall discuss these in the next two sections of this perspective.

■ APPROACH TO THIS BOOK

The world might be better off without commercial outlines. But they exist, and so I have tried to give you a careful outline. In it I have expressed my current conception of civil procedure—the relationships among the ideas and the law that constitute the subject. I have tried to use the strengths of the outline format to convey relationships, while avoiding staccato senselessness; I have tried not to sacrifice substance altogether, while avoiding uninterrupted prose. To put it somewhat pompously, the resulting "structured thoughtfulness" should orient you and provide a framework, answer some of your questions and inform you, and verify and expand your own understanding. It might even stimulate you to think about the important.

However, this outline has significant limits. It is not a treatise, bristling with footnotes. Indeed, a great deal of effort has gone into condensing the subject.

Brevity pays dividends, but the outline consequently leaves to you the task of elaborating it with detailed knowledge. Also, the outline's emphasis will surely not coincide perfectly with the emphasis of your course, so you must adapt and supplement it.

More significantly, a law-school course in civil procedure has many goals, both more profound and more practical, beyond those of this outline. A casebook too has aims very different from an outline's. Do not to any extent permit any study aid to supplant your casebook in *day-to-day study*. You would be cheating yourself and endangering success.

Moreover, the task of *final synthesis* is still yours. Do your own outline, as a tangible record of systematic final review and overview. On the one hand, very important is the actual thought process of fitting your course together. If you fall for the illusion of someone else doing it for you, you have gained nothing of value. On the other hand, some students become so enmeshed in the mechanics of outlining that they miss the big picture. Some indeed use going through the motions of outlining as a mental excuse for not doing hard thinking in those final pressurized days of the semester. So use my outline to give you the courage to keep your own outline very brief. My concrete suggestion to you is to compose your own short outline by marking up the capsule summary of civil procedure that I offer at the outset of this book or, better yet, by marking up the table of contents of your casebook.

Thus, recognize the limits of my outline. But how should you exploit what uses it has? The best way to explain is to run through this book division-by-division.

In the front of this book are a *summary of contents* and a detailed *table of contents*. You can use these to locate easily the pages of immediate interest.

Then there is a *capsule summary of civil procedure*. It should serve to orient you generally and quickly, both before and after final studying. To facilitate entry into the main outline, the capsule summary uses the same headings as the outline itself. Indeed, you may treat the capsule summary as an annotated table of contents. However, it is obviously not a substitute for the main outline or for diligent and reflective study.

Here this *perspective* makes suggestions on how to approach civil procedure, this book, and your examination.

Next comes the main *outline* itself. At the outset of Part One thereof, I have explained the organization of the outline and shall not repeat it here. As to style,

I have used various devices in trying to help you. For example, I have included an analysis at the beginning of each part and chapter to orient you, I have used italic type for emphasis of important rules and ideas, and I have liberally given examples to render rules and ideas more concrete. But these and other devices should be self-explanatory. All I wish to add here is a warning on my citation convention in this book: the multi-volume Federal Practice and Procedure, written by Professors Wright and Miller and others, I have referred to only by the number of the particular volume and the last names of that volume's authors; similarly, I have used "Wright's Hornbook" to refer to Charles Alan Wright & Mary Kay Kane, Law of Federal Courts (6th ed. 2002); and, finally, I have cited Restatement (Second) of Judgments (1982) and Restatement (Second) of Conflict of Laws (1971) (amended 1988) as "Judgments Second" and "Conflict of Laws Second," respectively. In this book, I have referred to these, and by full citation to other texts and cases, in order to facilitate your in-depth study.

After each major part of the main outline, I have provided sample *review questions*, in the belief that practicing on examination questions is an important study technique. I offer true-false, multiple-choice, and traditional law-school hypothetical questions. Incidentally, because Part One of the outline gives a general orientation in the whole subject of civil procedure, thus serving as both introduction and summation, the questions for Part One are geared to both specific and comprehensive review.

The appendices follow the main outline. Appendix A provides, for the sample review questions just described, sample *answers to review questions*. I explain my answers, because even for an objective question it is critical to understand the reasoning behind the answer. Appendix B sets out a sample comprehensive *practice examination*. This should give you an idea of how a three-hour examination in civil procedure might look.

Appendix C is a *glossary*. It lists and defines those words of art that are important to civil procedure, words that you should be familiar with and that you should use correctly.

In the back of this book are a few more tools to guide you through it. Appendix D is a rather specific *text correlation chart*. This enables you to find quickly the relevant chapters of the main outline that correlate to certain pages in your casebook, and vice versa. Incidentally, my outline is not geared to any particular casebook. Appendices E and F contain a *table of cases* and a *table of statutes and court rules*. You can use either of these to locate quickly the pages in this book of immediate interest. Finally, Appendix G gives you an *index*.

■ APPROACH TO THE EXAMINATION

Assuming that you have diligently studied day-to-day and that you have finally synthesized the subject, you are then prepared to face the examination. It is well to realize that there are all sorts of examination questions—such as objective, short answer, policy essay, and traditional law-school hypothetical questions. With these the professor may be testing any or all of a variety of attributes and skills—for example, your diligence, knowledge, or comprehension of policy or your logic, creativity, and ability to analyze, organize, and express your arguments. A key to success on the examination is to be responsive to the kind of question asked, giving what it is looking for. That follows from common sense.

Here I shall focus primarily on the traditional law-school hypothetical question, because it is least familiar to the new law student, because it is the most common kind in law schools, and because it tests the widest range of attributes and skills. There are five steps in answering such a question, some of which steps involve more than common sense.

(1) *Getting Started.* Bring a watch! It is absolutely essential to establish a schedule at the outset and then to stick to it. A brutal fact is that you will always do better with equally hurried answers to all questions than with some answers you think are pretty good and some total blanks in your answer booklet. Time will fly in the examination room. Only a schedule will save you. (Incidentally, do not write "Time" at the end of any of your answers. At best, it indicates that you cannot plan your time. At worst, it proves that you spent more time on the other questions, and thus received more credit for your other answers, than you should have.)

Begin by reading the general instructions carefully, by glancing over the whole examination, and by finalizing your schedule. A good lawyer follows instructions. Moreover, those instructions presumably appear on the examination for good reason. Therefore, professors often take departures from instructions into account when grading.

Next, read through quickly the question that you plan to answer first. Give special attention to the last part of the question, which usually asks precise and narrow subquestions. These often greatly affect your answer by giving you a special role in a special setting, such as a judge hearing an appeal or a lawyer giving office advice. Also, these subquestions often specify some particular issues or put bounds on your answer.

With these subquestions in mind, now reread the whole question very carefully. Jot down notes to yourself as you go.

(2) *Analysis.* Now think long and hard about the question. Try to uncover every issue the question presents. Some are hidden. This task of inclusion is called issue spotting. Also, try to eliminate every issue the question does not fairly raise. Some are red herrings. This task of exclusion is called issue rejecting. Quite simply, this is work. But so is lawyering. It is difficult to be comprehensive while avoiding irrelevancies.

How should you accomplish this task? The trick is to think. Thus, in an open-book examination, do not research. Such an examination still aims at testing something more important than the ability to do high-speed research. Indeed, there is usually little reason to consult your notes or books, other than checklists you have prepared and the rules pamphlet you have brought. Those professors who permit bringing materials into the examination room do so primarily to give you psychological comfort. (Incidentally, there is no need to name cases in your answers, unless one is blatantly in point or unless referring to a case like *Klaxon* is a useful shorthand. In other words, refer to cases only where it feels natural or where it makes life easier for you. On the other hand, especially in a code-type course like civil procedure, you should cite court rules and statutes wherever relevant.)

One helpful technique of analysis is to go through the question fact-by-fact, asking yourself why each fact appears. Also, reconsider the question by thinking through your whole course part-by-part. For example, if your course was organized like my outline, you might pose to yourself a series of six queries. First, does this examination question raise any policy-based issues concerning the big picture of civil procedure? Second, does the question present issues involving the mechanics of litigation? Third, does the court have authority to adjudicate, with the requirements of subject-matter jurisdiction, territorial jurisdiction, venue, and notice being satisfied? Fourth, are there problems of multiclaim or multiparty litigation? Fifth, which sovereign's law governs? Sixth, are the effects of former adjudication in issue?

Almost always there will be analytic difficulties in the form of ambiguity in the question or missing facts or, more likely, indeterminate issues. The only possible advice is to treat these difficulties intelligently. Usually that means to treat them in the alternative.

(3) *Organization.* Now outline your answer in detail on scrap paper. This is the single most important step. It helps you to think clearly and rigorously, and thus to tighten the preceding analysis step. It helps you to write clearly and orderly, and thus lays the foundation for the subsequent writing step.

You should begin your outline, and eventually your answer, with a very brief introductory conclusion or summary. This will allow the reader to follow your answer more easily. Do everything you can to demonstrate clearly that you understand the question and its solution. Anything that will help the reader will help you. (Incidentally, you should close with a final conclusion as well.)

You should choose an organizational structure that both resolves the precise subquestions posed by the examiner and also covers all the relevant issues revealed by your analysis. This organization should be responsive to the nature of the question. Similarly, your approach to and depth of discussion on each issue must be responsive to the nature of the question. On each particular issue, is the question looking for a categorical response with brief reasons or for a balanced and extended discussion of the two sides or, most likely, for something in-between?

All these preliminary steps should have consumed almost half the time that you allotted to the question. In all seriousness, you are in deep trouble if you have more quickly rushed through them in order to seek the false security of starting to write. Take your time. If the person next to you starts writing immediately, do not feel nervous—feel sympathetic.

(4) *Writing.* When you are ready to start, writing is a simple process. Just flesh out your outline of the answer. Indeed, carry over the higher-order headings and even the related numbers and letters from your outline. Do everything conceivable to help the reader see your thought pattern. Do not forget that you are trying to communicate.

You should avoid adding stuff now that did not fit naturally into your outline. That is, do not repeat the question, but instead answer it. Do not recite the facts, but instead work them into your answer where relevant. Do not launch into abstract discussions of the law or of interesting-cases-I-have-read, but instead apply the relevant law to the facts. Do not otherwise pad your answer, as by quoting from your casebook or rules pamphlet or by writing little essays on things you know but unhappily were not asked. Instead, on each particular issue, stick to that difficult middle ground by only finding the relevant facts, mentioning the relevant legal considerations, and applying law to fact in order to reach a conclusion. (Incidentally, you may briefly record the more significant fruits of your issue rejecting, so demonstrating that you saw the red herrings but saw through them. However, do so with few words and much restraint.)

You should accomplish all this with a decent respect for the language. Spelling and grammar matter. Avoid abbreviations and slang. Write complete sentences.

Use to your advantage that crucial element of communication, the paragraph. The examiner may and should be testing your ability to express your thoughts.

Finally, do all this neatly, a luxury permitted by careful planning of your time. Write legibly with a decent blue pen. Or, better yet, keyboard.

(5) *Finishing Up*. Take the last one or two minutes of your allotted time for the question to read your answer. You will be amazed by some of the things— inadvertent mistakes of substance—that spilled from you in the heat of the moment. The returns from such review will surely exceed the returns from the extra minutes of scribbling or pounding. (Incidentally, now you should write that final conclusion at the end of your answer that will tie it all together.)

In order to avoid being too depressed by what you read when reviewing your answer, you really should practice in advance. Answering examinations is difficult work, involving the challenges of analysis, organization, and writing. Happily, these are the skills that mark a good lawyer. These skills are worth practicing.

So practice by doing any old examinations that are available. Establishing a study group that only does old examinations from all your courses, whereby once each week during the last half of the semester a member selects and reproduces three or four appropriate questions for all the members to answer under examination conditions and then to discuss together, requires extraordinary dedication but virtually guarantees success.

For practice on your own, I would suggest William V. Dorsaneo, III & Elizabeth G. Thornburg, Questions & Answers: Civil Procedure (LexisNexis, 2d ed. 2007) or Linda S. Mullenix, Civil Procedure (West's Exam Pro Series, 2d ed. 2007) (objective questions only). Additional sources of civil procedure questions, with answers, are Roy L. Brooks, Questions and Answers: Civil Procedure (Spectra's Winning in Law School Series 1987), Joseph W. Glannon, The Glannon Guide to Civil Procedure: Learning Civil Procedure Through Multiple–Choice Questions and Analysis (Aspen 2003), and Lazor Emanuel, Siegel's Civil Procedure: Essay and Multiple–Choice Questions and Answers (Siegel's Series, 5th ed. 2005). In that spirit, I also offer a selection of questions and answers in this book.

*

PART ONE

General Considerations

■ ANALYSIS

*

I

Civil Procedure Analyzed

■ ANALYSIS

A. **Approaches to Civil Procedure**
B. **Approach of Outline**
    1.   General Considerations
    2.   Litigating Step-by-Step
    3.   Authority to Adjudicate
    4.   Complex Litigation
    5.   Governing Law
    6.   Former Adjudication

A. APPROACHES TO CIVIL PROCEDURE

The chief difficulty in breaking down civil procedure for study is that interdependencies so dominate and characterize the subject. To understand anything the student must understand everything. The difficulty of access has prompted teachers to blaze many different approaches into this seamless web. The usual approach, however, is first to present the whole subject in survey fashion and then to study a series of fundamental problems of procedure: the opening orientation facilitates the subsequent in-depth study, while this later study ultimately will illuminate that initial overview. Additionally, within this or any other approach, teachers have found room for a nearly infinite variety of emphasis and perspective.

B. APPROACH OF OUTLINE

This outline tries to break down the subject of civil procedure along the usual lines: an orientation and overview followed by a closer inspection of four major procedural problems. Study of these four problems appropriately aims at informing students about the legal system under which they live: one in which allocation of power among the states is key, one in which the federal and state power relation is key, and one in which the separation of powers between the judiciary and other branches is key. Study of all these problems is all the more appropriate because today they continue to arise in an increasingly complex and globalized setting.

1. GENERAL CONSIDERATIONS

This Part One of the outline provides a general orientation in the whole subject of civil procedure, serving as both introduction and summation. Initial focus should be on the whole. Final review should seek the big picture by reconsidering the whole.

2. LITIGATING STEP–BY–STEP

Part Two provides an overview, at a somewhat more detailed level, by tracing the steps from commencing a lawsuit in some trial court to completing the final appeal in the highest available appellate court: pretrial, trial, judgment, and appeal. These mechanics of litigation appear to the untutored as the totality of procedure, but in fact many proceduralists and many procedure courses are devoted instead to the major problems lurking at the fringes and in the interstices of these mechanics. Nevertheless, exploring these mechanics at the outset serves to give a structure to the subject of civil procedure.

3. AUTHORITY TO ADJUDICATE

Part Three treats the first major problem of civil procedure. In the overview, it was assumed that plaintiff had properly selected a court with authority to adjudicate. In fact, that preliminary step can be a most difficult and significant one. It involves satisfying three basic threshold requirements: *subject-matter jurisdiction, territorial authority to adjudicate,* and *notice.* Moreover, these requirements entail consideration of such subsumed matters as state and federal court systems, territorial jurisdiction, service of process, and venue.

4. COMPLEX LITIGATION

Part Four investigates the restrictions on which claims and parties the litigants must or may join in their lawsuit. In the overview, it was generally assumed that a single plaintiff was properly suing a single defendant on a single claim. In practice, much more complex *multiclaim* and *multiparty* lawsuits enjoy ever-increasing frequency and importance.

5. GOVERNING LAW

Part Five examines a question that pervades the overview and deserves systematic treatment: When should a court choose to apply the law of some sovereign other than its own? This poses problems of interstate and international *choice of law* and also problems involving the *Erie* doctrine.

6. FORMER ADJUDICATION

Part Six studies a question that arises at the end of the overview: What impact does a judgment have in subsequent civil litigation? This primarily entails problems of *res judicata,* or the effects of the judicial branch's end-product.

*

II

Civil Procedure Synthesized

■ ANALYSIS

A. NATURE OF CIVIL PROCEDURE

This outline begins with the desired end-product of study: a suggestion of the nature of the subject.

1. DEFINITION

The subject concerns the societal process for handling disputes of a noncriminal sort. Consider separately the two words "civil procedure."

a. "Civil"

This sweeping word distinguishes the subject from the criminal process. "Civil" thus encompasses the particular processes of administrative adjudication, arbitration, and other alternative dispute-resolution formats, as well as today's court procedure in typical civil actions.

b. "Procedure"

This word distinguishes the subject from substance. That distinction is an especially fuzzy one, and the line is drawn in different spots for different purposes. Speaking roughly, then, "procedure" means the societal process for submitting and resolving factual and legal disputes over the rights and duties recognized by substantive law, which rights and duties concern primary conduct in the private and public life that transpires essentially outside the courthouse or other forum. As the machinery of a legal system, procedure implements substantive law and, in doing so, inevitably affects substantive law in profound ways. But procedure is important in its own right as an integral part of a system of justice.

c. Narrow Focus

After the limiting effect of definition, civil procedure is still a broad subject. But in this outline the primary focus will be a narrower one, being on the *current* law governing *American court* procedure in *ordinary* civil actions. For good reasons, most law-school courses in civil procedure are to a considerable extent limited to these same three italicized concerns. Using the three as distinctional dimensions of civil procedure (time, forum, form of action), the following diagram illuminates the rest of this Chapter II by depicting that focus as the diagram's solid portion near the center.

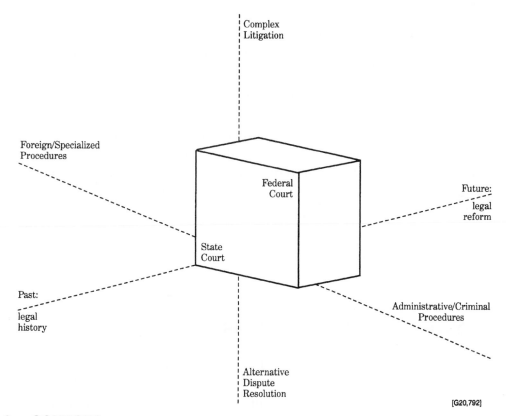

Complex
Litigation

Foreign/Specialized
Procedures

Federal
Court

Future:
legal
reform

State
Court

Past:
legal
history

Administrative/Criminal
Procedures

Alternative
Dispute
Resolution

[G20,792]

2. SOURCES

Who generates the law of civil procedure that applies in American courts? The state and/or federal *constitution* provides some basics (e.g., Federal Constitution's Seventh Amendment guarantee of trial by jury) and also establishes the structure for filling in the rest. The pattern of most states and of the federal system is as follows: Within constitutional limits the *legislature* has very broad power to regulate the courts' civil procedure (e.g., Federal Rules of Evidence). Within constitutional limits the *courts* themselves have power to regulate their own civil procedure, whether pursuant to proper delegation of legislative power (e.g., Federal Rules of Civil Procedure), or at the sufferance of and subject to the ultimate control of the legislature (e.g., res judicata), or by exercise of a narrow inherent judicial power to conduct the courts' own business (e.g., discipline of individual attorneys for misconduct before the courts). Finally, *the parties and their attorneys* bear much of the responsibility for running the resultant procedural machinery and hence for giving final content to the law of civil procedure (e.g., litigants' approach to discovery provisions).

3. MOTIVATION

Ultimately, why have the constitutions, legislatures, and courts created this complicated law of civil procedure? These are the basic reasons: the inevitability of unsettled disputes over substantive law and the attendant facts, the social necessity of resolving those disputes, and the unavoidability of limits on the resources available for such resolution. Together these mean that there must be, to some degree, an established way to submit and resolve with finality those disputes. However, more than such basic needs motivates the lawmakers. Preferably, the resolution should be accurate; in this important sense, civil procedure serves substantive law. Moreover, civil procedure embodies independent values as well; the means to the end should, for example, be efficient but fair. In sum, a *just* law of civil procedure goes beyond (1) responding to felt needs by (2) trying to yield an outcome that serves substantive values and by (3) embodying independent values concerning process.

B. CONTENT OF CIVIL PROCEDURE

The basic societal needs and values regarding outcome and process shape the law of civil procedure for American courts, inducing the lawmakers to generate certain procedural policies and rules. But there are conflicts among these needs and values and also tensions within each. The elusive goal for everyone involved in shaping the law of civil procedure is to strike a sound balance amid these conflicts and tensions.

1. POLICIES

Policies include the general principles that underlie the rules of civil procedure.

a. Adversary System

With regard to fundamentals, our society has generally opted to dispense justice by third-party *adjudication* involving an *adversary system* wherein the parties are represented by partisan *advocates*. Archetypically, then, acting through their attorneys active parties combatively formulate a case and also propel it to decision by a passive judge acting merely as an umpire and representing impartially an appropriately disinterested society. The adversary system, implying active and unhindered combatants *formulating* and *propelling* the case with equal but waivable procedural opportunities, is at the heart of this scheme. It reflects a human attempt to maximize the sum total of a number of turbulent justice values: truth or accuracy, procedural efficiency and fairness, systemic legitimacy, party-satisfaction, and others. Being but a good compromise in an imperfect world, the adversary system has been subject to frequent and sometimes justifiable criticism. Consequently, the adversary system today exists nowhere in pure form and, indeed, is everywhere to some degree a policy in flux. Further reforms are possible that would not endanger the beneficial essence of the adversary system, but that would slightly alter the roles of the participants—with the net effect of ameliorating such shortcomings as excessive combativeness or inequalities between opponents in trying their cases. More radical restructuring might also be desirable for certain cases in these changing times—as perhaps along the lines of the alternative model of public law litigation that gives the judge a greatly more active role in unearthing and solving society's ills.

b. Other Policies

The basic societal needs and values propagate other policies, some almost as fundamental and general as those already suggested but some more arbitrary and associated with a particular place and time. The intelligent study of civil procedure will reveal many policies, such as those in favor of deciding the case on its merits, resolving all disputes concerning the whole transaction in one shot, and forging a cooperative federalism. An individual policy sometimes is in the process of evolution, and one policy often collides with others. Such turmoil is a very important source of the surprisingly considerable *uncertainty* in the law of civil procedure, and also a very certain indicator of the surprisingly considerable *importance* of that law.

2. RULES

The policies are often partially reduced to concrete rules, appearing in the form of statutes, court rules, or doctrines. Indeed, the untutored usually picture civil procedure as comprising nothing but such rules. It is surely true that technical mastery of the use of these rules is critical. But the focus cannot be only on these rules, because some are very untrustworthy guides to the highly practical profundities of policy lurking below.

C. HISTORY OF CIVIL PROCEDURE

Perhaps no single perspective reveals the subject of civil procedure better than the historical one. For a very basic introduction, see Frederick G. Kempin, Jr., Historical Introduction to Anglo–American Law in a Nutshell (3d ed. 1990).

1. ENGLISH ROOTS

Our legal system can be fairly clearly traced back to roots in the English system of a millennium ago. Over the ensuing centuries, England's system fundamentally divided into "common law" and "equity," which were two distinct sets of courts, procedure, remedies, and substantive law. See generally J.H. Baker, An Introduction to English Legal History (4th ed. 2002).

a. Common Law

The system of common law was the older of the two. Its courts offered trial by jury, but gave relief only in the form of money damages or recovery of possession pursuant to a rigid regime of substantive law.

1) Origins

Local communal bodies wielded most of the judicial power under the Anglo–Saxons. The Norman Conquest in 1066 resulted in a strengthened set of feudal courts. However, in the 12th century the English kings started to expand their judicial influence by drawing on their traditional prerogative powers, especially the power to keep the peace. Royal attention at first focused on criminal and land cases, but later expanded to other types of disputes. A principal technique in this expansion of powers was the issuance of "writs," which were royal orders that eventually had the effect of bringing cases before the king and his councillors ("Curia Regis"). Significantly, royal justice was a vast improvement over its competitors. Ultimately, the central royal system of common law came to dominate the judicial scene.

2) Courts

Originally the king and his councillors heard and decided judicial cases, in addition to governing the country. But eventually administrative convenience prompted division of labor, as when in the 12th century the royal treasury became the special concern of the barons of the "Exchequer." The growing judicial business shifted to some of these special bodies, and beginning in the 13th century they began slowly to look more like modern courts. The *Court of Common Pleas* emerged to provide a royal forum stationary at Westminster Hall to hear ordinary cases between the king's subjects. The *Court of King's Bench*, which continued for some time to travel with the king, handled his judicial business. Finally, from the Exchequer evolved the *Court of Exchequer*. Certainly well before the 16th century, these three bodies had developed into true courts sitting at Westminster. But by then, the jurisdictions of the three superior courts of common law had begun to overlap so extensively as to make their continued coexistence fairly senseless as well as very confusing.

3) Procedure
The writ system shaped the law of procedure.

a) Writ System
Most actions were commenced by obtaining an original writ from the king, or more precisely by purchasing an original writ from the king's chief secretarial officer ("chancellor"). At first, these writs were flexibly framed and granted. But in the 13th century, in reaction to the expanding royal power that had by then conquered all of criminal law and much of civil law, the feudal barons succeeded in imposing limits on the development of new writs. This produced a fixed set of "writs of course," such as covenant, debt, detinue, and trespass, each covering a specific grievance of an ordinary sort. Although by the 14th century the common law had begun growing again, it did so by stretching and fictionalizing the established writs to reach such matters as trespass on the case, trover, special assumpsit, and general assumpsit.

b) Forms of Action
Each writ generated its own form of action, with a distinctive procedural, remedial, and substantive law. Generally, the plaintiff established jurisdiction by obtaining a writ, and he had to pick the correct writ for his grievance. The particular writ dictated the bounds on the pleadings (declaration, demurrer or plea, replication, rejoinder, etc.), which were oral and informal in early times but later written and technical. These pleadings were supposed to produce on each count a single issue of law or fact. If that issue was legal, the whole court of four or five judges decided it in banc. If factual, the court sent it out to be heard at *nisi prius*, i.e., before one of the judges on circuit sitting with a local jury; testimony was oral, but this efficiency was offset by the limitation that kept the parties themselves from testifying because they were interested witnesses; a jury decided the factual dispute, in early times acting somewhat as a body of witnesses but later finding facts solely on the evidence

presented in the hearing. Appeal in the modern sense was unknown; but there was a complicated, illogical, limited, and changing scheme for review of decisions on law in some court of error, characteristically only after final judgment. See generally Benjamin J. Shipman, Handbook of Common–Law Pleading (3d ed. 1923).

4) Remedies

If plaintiff succeeded, the court gave relief as an order that plaintiff recover money damages, or sometimes that he recover possession of land (ejectment) or a chattel (replevin), which order the sheriff executed.

5) Substantive Law

Each form of action generated its own substantive law—for example, a law of trespass. Outside the particular form invoked, there was in effect no law. Thus, pigeonholed procedure shaped substance. Moreover, a limit on the number of procedural pigeonholes limited the range of substantive law.

6) Problems

Early on, the common law sank into rigidity and narrowness. To mitigate this, fictionalized thinking became rampant. The consequently uncertain boundaries on the forms of action caused all sorts of difficulties. The whole system inevitably came to exalt hideous technicality. In sum, the inadequacies of wooden procedure, limited remedies, and bounded substantive law were all too evident.

b. Equity

The system of equity arose to overcome the evolving inadequacies of the common law. Its courts did not conduct jury trials, but did give relief in the form of ordering defendant to do or not to do something pursuant to a rather dynamic substantive law.

1) Origins

All along the king and his councillors continued to act on direct petition to remedy injustice. But in the 14th century litigants came to use this route more heavily to circumvent the inadequacies of the common law, in effect creating the separate system of equity.

2) Courts

Soon the king and his councillors (by then called King's Council) began referring most of these petitions regularly to the chancellor, an important official who had legal experience and a large staff ("Chancery"). Shortly thereafter, litigants began addressing their petitions directly to the chancellor. Certainly by the 16th century, a recognizable *Court of Chancery* had arisen around the chancellor and his staff. It was to be the most notable of the various courts of equity.

3) Procedure

Equitable procedure vastly differed from legal procedure. At first, it was quite informal. But soon pleadings (bill, answer, etc.) became long and detailed documents. All testimony was written, but equity had the advantage of being able to compel a party's testimony and thus to examine his "conscience." The judge decided the case himself, although he could refer disputed facts on an advisory basis to a common-law jury. There was a fairly complicated scheme for review of both interlocutory and final decisions.

4) Remedies

Relief was typically a direct personal order to do or not to do something, which order might be conditional and was enforceable by contempt. The most distinctive remedies were injunctions and orders of specific performance. But equity offered other remedies such as discovery, accounting, administration of estates, receivership, reformation, and rescission.

5) Substantive Law

Equity interceded, in the judge's discretion, when the common law was inadequate. Early on, equity served primarily to overcome the procedural inadequacies of the common law. Jealous of its turf, the common law successfully strove through Parliament to prevent such intrusions by equity. But equity had begun to create its own distinctive remedies and substantive law in order to overcome omissions and defects in the scope of the common law—for example, the equitable doctrines concerning uses and trusts, accident, mistake, and fraud. This intensified the conflict between equity and law. In the 17th century equity prevailed, becoming entitled to the last word in case of conflict. Equity went on to evolve a highly developed, regularized, and distinctive body of doctrine within its restricted jurisdiction, acting when the common-law system was inadequate. This law/equity bifurcation profoundly affected the development of our law. See generally Henry L. McClintock, Handbook of the Principles of Equity (2d ed. 1948).

6) **Problems**

By the 19th century, equitable procedure bogged down, becoming incredibly cumbersome and expensive. Equity and the common law overlapped to an uncertain degree, adding confusion to the inefficiency of having two imperfectly meshed systems of justice.

a) **Joinder**

Plaintiff could not join equitable and legal causes, but normally had to bring them separately in the different courts. However, in equity, at the plaintiff's request, the equity court had discretion to retain jurisdiction in order to pass on additional or sometimes even alternative legal relief ("clean-up doctrine").

b) **Equitable Counterclaims and Defenses**

If plaintiff sued at law, as in the example of a contract action, defendant might have a defense cognizable only in equity, such as mutual mistake. In that situation, the law-defendant would immediately sue in equity, say, for reformation. The equity court would as a matter of course temporarily enjoin the law-plaintiff from pursuing his law action, and then would try the equitable issues. If the law-defendant prevailed on those issues, the law action would be permanently enjoined. If not, the law action would be allowed to proceed. This complicated scenario followed from the law/equity bifurcation. Later some of the equitable doctrines, such as fraud, became cognizable as defenses at law as well.

2. STATE DEVELOPMENTS

The American states basically followed the English model until the code reforms of the 19th century. See generally Lawrence M. Friedman, A History of American Law 3–23, 79–104, 111–12, 279–308 (3d ed. 2005); Robert Wyness Millar, Civil Procedure of the Trial Court in Historical Perspective 39–42, 52–57 (1952).

a. Early Period

The colonies combined local innovations with rudimentary English imports to create a legal system suitable for simple American life. Sensibly, the multiple common-law trial courts were united. Equity almost missed being transplanted, only slowly developing to different degrees in the various colonies; then some young states rejected equity altogether (e.g., Massachusetts), some had a single court system with separate law and equity jurisdictions (e.g., Connecticut), and some created separate law and equity courts (e.g., New York). English procedure came to enjoy an increasing influence, bringing along its forms of action and infamous technicality. In short, America eventually shared most of the problems of the English system.

b. Code Reform

In 1848 the first code revolutionized civil procedure.

1) Field Code

The greatest procedural reform in American history has been the comprehensive code of civil procedure. The preeminent one was the New York Code of Procedure of 1848, which was primarily the work of David Dudley Field. The Field Code *merged* law and equity and *abolished* the forms of action, resulting in "but one form of action" offering the full range of legal and equitable remedies and substantive law. For that unitary civil action, the Field Code simplified and reformed procedure, taking the best of law, equity, and more modern thinking. See generally Charles E. Clark, Handbook of the Law of Code Pleading (2d ed. 1947).

2) Subsequent Developments

The Field Code swept through most of the states—including California, which produced in 1850 a code version that served in turn as a basis of codes in several western states. Finally, the Field Code served as one of the models for the Federal Rules of Civil Procedure, which most states have since used as a model for renewed procedural reform. All this leaves a very few states in a sort of pre-code status subject to piecemeal reforms, some states with the Field Code or one of its variants, and most states substantially in the Federal Rules camp.

3. FEDERAL DEVELOPMENTS

The federal legal system followed traditional ways well into the 20th century. See generally Richard H. Fallon, Jr., Daniel J. Meltzer & David L. Shapiro, Hart and Wechsler's The Federal Courts and the Federal System chs. I, VI–1 (5th ed. 2003); Erwin C. Surrency, History of the Federal Courts (2d ed. 2001); Wright's Hornbook §§ 1, 61–63.

a. Pre–Reform Period

The federal courts were established in 1789. Consider the trial level: There were no separate law and equity courts; instead, the same federal judges administered the two jurisdictions in quite separate law and equity "sides" of the court. Congress required the procedure in *actions at law* to conform to the procedure for like causes in the state where the particular federal court sat; at first federal courts had to conform to the state procedure prevailing at some fixed date ("static conformity"), but under the Conformity Act of 1872 federal courts were to conform to the currently prevailing state procedure ("dynamic conformity"). Because equity was so stunted in such divergent degrees in the new states, Congress instructed the federal courts hearing *suits in equity* to follow generally the procedure of English equity, but Congress also gave the Supreme Court rulemaking power for such suits; from time to time, the Court promulgated comprehensive sets of uniform rules on equitable procedure—including the progressive Equity Rules of 1912, which was to serve as another model for the Federal Rules of Civil Procedure. Many statutory and judge-made exceptions further complicated this extraordinarily complex scheme, which exceptions were usually adopted in an effort to mitigate the above-discussed problems that haunted all traditional systems.

b.　Rules Reform

In 1938 the Federal Rules of Civil Procedure became effective, making federal procedure the prime model of modern civil procedure.

1)　Rules Enabling Act

Decades of pressure for reform produced the Rules Enabling Act of 1934, with some changes now 28 U.S.C.A. §§ 2072–2074 [hereinafter REA], which authorized uniting law and equity "so as to secure one form of civil action and procedure for both" and which in its present form reads in part:

§ 2072.

(a) The Supreme Court shall have the power to prescribe general rules of practice and procedure and rules of evidence for cases in the United States district courts (including proceedings before magistrates thereof) and courts of appeals.

(b) Such rules shall not abridge, enlarge or modify any substantive right. All laws in conflict with such rules shall be of no further force or effect after such rules have taken effect.

. . . .

§ 2074.

(a)   The Supreme Court shall transmit to the Congress not later than May 1 of the year in which a rule prescribed under section 2072 is to become effective a copy of the proposed rule. Such rule shall take effect no earlier than December 1 of the year in which such rule is so transmitted unless otherwise provided by law. . . .

2)   **Federal Rules of Civil Procedure**

Four years later, a distinguished Advisory Committee had drafted and the Supreme Court had approved a set of Federal Rules of Civil Procedure, effective September 16, 1938. Those Rules merged law and equity and abandoned the idea of conformity to state procedure; Rule 2 thus provides: "There is one form of action—the civil action." For that civil action, the Rules further simplified and reformed procedure, creating a highly successful and influential scheme marked by very simple pleading, broad joinder, and extensive discovery. Of course, perfection was not achieved, leading to significant sets of amendments from time to time, and also prompting fundamental questions such as whether reform has gone too far toward producing a single form of action for functionally or substantively different kinds of cases. See Rule 1.

3)   *Sibbach*

Early on, the validity of the Rules was challenged unsuccessfully in *Sibbach v. Wilson & Co.*, 312 U.S. 1, 61 S.Ct. 422 (1941) (Rule 35). The Supreme Court broadly interpreted the REA as authorizing rulemaking throughout the whole realm of civil "procedure"—"the judicial process for enforcing rights and duties recognized by substantive law and for justly administering remedy and redress for disregard or infraction of them." Thus, the first sentence of the REA restricted civil rulemaking to matters of procedure. Although some scholarly dispute persists on the point, the *Sibbach* Court apparently read the REA's second sentence concerning "substantive" rights as imposing no additional restriction on rulemaking. Consequently, the Supreme Court has never invalidated a Federal Rule of Civil Procedure.

REVIEW QUESTIONS

1. **T or F**   The law of civil procedure in American courts is largely the product of the discretion of trial judges.

2. **T or F**   A common-law court could enforce a contract by granting an order of specific performance.

3. **T or F**   At common law, most actions were commenced by obtaining an original writ.

4. **T or F**   At common law, plaintiff could testify as to the defendant's acts.

5. **T or F**   Courts of equity did not conduct jury trials.

6. **T or F**   The great defect of the Field Code was its failure to merge law and equity.

7. **T or F**   Under the Rules Enabling Act, federal procedural rules become effective upon their approval by the Chief Justice of the United States.

8. **T or F**   A federal procedural rule is invalid if it abridges, enlarges, or modifies any important right.

9. By failing to deliver a horse upon payment, D breached a sales contract with P in the 18th century. P thereby lost out on a very favorable deal. Which of the following best represents P's situation?

    a.   P must sue in the Court of Exchequer, because money is at stake.

    b.   P cannot sue in the Court of Exchequer.

    c.   P can choose to seek an injunction against breach of contract.

    d.   P must select a form of action.

    e.   P must waive trial by jury in order to seek damages.

10. P objects to undergoing a physical examination in a personal-injury case in federal district court, on the ground that Federal Rule 35 does not validly authorize any such examination. What result on P's objection?

a. P prevails because personal-injury cases cannot be brought in federal court.

b. P loses because state law governs this issue.

c. P prevails because Rule 35 is invalid to the extent that it infringes on the substantive right of personal privacy.

d. P prevails because Rule 35 cannot validly, and does not, authorize physical examinations of plaintiffs.

e. P loses because Rule 35 validly applies.

11. Prepare an essay in response to this comprehensive question for final review:

Driver One ("D.O."), a citizen of New Jersey, sued Master ("M"), a citizen of New York, for injuries sustained in a Manhattan traffic accident involving D.O. and Servant ("S"), M's employee who was and is a citizen of New Jersey living in Hackensack. Suit was brought in the United States District Court for the Southern District of New York, and D.O. sought $100,000 in damages.

M immediately impleaded S, and she had him personally served with process at his home. Then D.O. added a claim directly against S, seeking $100,000 for his injuries in that same accident. After answering, S litigated the merits fully, although S did not challenge subject-matter jurisdiction. Ultimately, D.O. lost both his claims on the merits.

Now S sues D.O. in New Jersey state court, seeking damages for personal injury in that same accident. Immediately, D.O. moves to dismiss on the ground of res judicata. In response, S argues that res judicata does not bar his action and also attacks the subject-matter jurisdiction in the first action. What result?

Incidentally, New York is a code state with no compulsory counterclaims, and New Jersey is a Federal Rules state in all relevant respects.

*

PART TWO

Litigating Step–by–Step

■ **ANALYSIS**

*

III

Preliminary Considerations

■ **ANALYSIS**

A. **Federal Focus**
B. **Selecting a Court with Authority to Adjudicate**
    1.   General Requirements
    2.   Specific Assumptions

A. FEDERAL FOCUS

In this Part Two on the mechanics of procedure, the primary focus will be on federal practice. A number of reasons make this choice the natural one:

(1) *Need for a Procedural Model.* In order to achieve economically an understanding of the subject of civil procedure, the student needs first to look at a single, complete, concise procedural system. That model can later serve as a basis for comparison when dealing with other systems.

(2) *Importance of the Federal Model.* The federal judicial system is the single most important set of courts in the country, handling a considerable number of important cases and being a concern of every lawyer in the nation.

(3) *Success of the Federal Model.* The concise and effective procedural law followed in the federal courts is representative of the modern approach to procedure, being far from perfect but representing a vast improvement over more traditional models.

(4) *Influence of the Federal Model.* Most states substantially adhere to the federal model, making study thereof widely practical.

There will be occasional references to contrasting state practice, where appropriate.

B. SELECTING A COURT WITH AUTHORITY TO ADJUDICATE

The preliminary step for plaintiff in commencing a lawsuit is to select a court with authority to hear and decide the case.

1. GENERAL REQUIREMENTS

First, commencing a lawsuit involves determining whether to sue in the state or the federal court system and, within that system, selecting a trial court with *subject-matter jurisdiction.* That is, the court must have authority to adjudicate the type of controversy put before the court. Second, plaintiff must further select a court having *territorial authority to adjudicate.* That is, there are limits on the court's authority to entertain litigation with nonlocal elements, and so plaintiff must select a place of litigation that satisfies those restrictions of territorial jurisdiction and venue. Third, the persons whose interests are to be affected must receive adequate *notice.* That is, for example, defendant must be notified of the commencement of the lawsuit. These three basic threshold requirements are given detailed treatment in Part Three below, along with how to satisfy them and how to challenge whether they are indeed satisfied.

2. SPECIFIC ASSUMPTIONS

For most purposes of this Part Two, assume that plaintiff has sued in a United States District Court, which court has subject-matter jurisdiction because the case is within the federal question or diversity of citizenship provisions. Also assume that plaintiff has selected a court with territorial authority to adjudicate—envisage perhaps a single plaintiff having brought a typical in personam and transitory action on a single claim against a single individual defendant in the district where defendant is domiciled. Finally, assume that defendant has received adequate notice of the lawsuit in accordance with the Federal Rules of Civil Procedure.

a. Rule 3

Plaintiff registers his selection of court by filing a complaint with the selected federal court. According to Rule 3, this *commences* the civil action. Assume that plaintiff has done so. Note that under the practice of some states, service of process is instead the act that is deemed to commence an action.

b. Rule 4

Service of process pursuant to Rule 4 formally asserts power over defendant and notifies her that plaintiff has commenced an action. Assume that a process server has served defendant by handing her a copy of the summons and complaint. Note that service and filing of subsequent papers in the action normally follow the simpler procedure of Rule 5. See also Rule 6(d) (additional time to act after service by mail, by delivery to court clerk, or by consented means).

*

IV

Pretrial

■ ANALYSIS

A. PLEADING STAGE

In federal practice, the pleading stage is usually short in duration and seldom determinative in effect. In brief, the pleading stage is relatively unimportant, in contrast to the situation prevailing in more traditional procedural systems.

See generally R. Lawrence Dessem, Pretrial Litigation in a Nutshell (4th ed. 2008); Wright's Hornbook §§ 66–69A.

1. GENERAL RULES

A number of policies and rules apply throughout the pleading stage in federal court.

a. Purposes of Pleadings

The primary purpose of federal pleadings has long been to give fair notice of the pleader's contentions to the adversary, the court, and the public. See *Conley v. Gibson*, 355 U.S. 41, 78 S.Ct. 99 (1957). This purpose implies that there is little need for detail in the pleadings. This simple mission of pleadings also implies that there is little sense in spending time and money skirmishing over them. Contrast this so-called *notice pleading* with:

(1) *Fact Pleading.* The code approach requires more detail; for example, a complaint must state the facts constituting a cause of action. This might have benefits, but it also encourages senseless battles over form—such as whether the pleader was being too specific by pleading "evidence" or too general by pleading "conclusions."

(2) *Issue Pleading.* The common-law approach required the pleadings to produce a single contested issue of law or fact. This asked too much of the pleading stage, which consequently became the center of legal attention, provided the vehicle for monumental abuse, and often ended up mired down in battles over technicalities.

Under modern pleading, most of the former functions of pleadings have been largely shifted forward into the stages of disclosure, discovery, pretrial conference, summary judgment, and trial. The motivating theory is that these later stages can more efficiently and fairly handle such functions as fully revealing facts and narrowing issues, and thus the whole system can better deliver a proper decision on the merits. Yet federal pleadings are still sometimes asked to do significantly more than give notice, as evidenced by the courts' entertaining contests over whether the pleadings reveal an absence of legal basis for claim or defense. In reality, such attempts to retain additional functions of pleadings most often seem counterproductive from the system's point of view. Nevertheless, the Supreme Court itself has just created an inexplicable new task for pleadings. In *Bell Atl. Corp. v. Twombly*, 127 S.Ct. 1955 (2007), it imposed a plausibility test on the pleading stage, in the hope of controlling access to the courts and their discovery devices. Such a move will prove momentous *if* it is not cut back by the Court.

b. Form of Pleadings

The Appendix of Forms to the Federal Rules of Civil Procedure [hereinafter Federal Forms] contains illustrative documents that clarify the Rules' formal requirements. See Rule 84. Those requirements can be enforced by the opponent's motion invoking the applicable Rule, but they are rather lenient requirements.

1) Caption

Rule 10(a) requires every pleading to have a caption setting forth the court, the title of the action, the file number, and the kind of pleading.

2) Paragraphs

Rule 10(b) provides that pleadings must be divided into "numbered paragraphs, each limited as far as practicable to a single set of circumstances." Such a qualified provision leaves paragraphing as a lenient requirement, suggesting only that the pleader should act as a reasonable person trying to be lucid.

3) Separate Counts and Defenses

Rule 10(b) also provides that each claim "founded on a separate transaction or occurrence" and each defense other than a denial must be stated in a separate count or defense if "doing so would promote clarity." This qualification, of course, diminishes the mandatory nature of the Rule. Moreover, Rule 8(d)(2) permits two or more statements of the same claim or defense "either in a single count or defense or in separate ones." All this leaves the use of separate counts or defenses pretty much up to the pleader. See also Rule 18(a).

4) Signing

Rule 11 requires an attorney, or if there is no attorney then the party, to sign each pleading. The signature certifies that to the best of the signer's knowledge, information, and belief formed after reasonable inquiry there is good ground in fact and law to support it and that it is not interposed for improper purpose. Rule 11 thus embodies an important albeit vague screening obligation. Courts eventually took to applying its sanctions with such enthusiasm as to prompt toning down the Rule by amendment in 1993.

5) Verification

Rule 11 does not require pleadings to be verified (i.e., sworn or the equivalent under 28 U.S.C.A. § 1746), although a few special federal provisions do require verification (e.g., Rule 23.1(b) requires a plaintiff's verification of the complaint in a shareholders' derivative action). In contrast, some states widely require the formality of verified pleadings, despite its ineffectiveness.

c. **Contents of Pleadings**

The purposes of pleadings dictate their contents. Pleadings should be simple, direct, and brief; and attacks on their contents should seldom succeed.

1) Burden of Allegation

Plaintiff is required to assert his position on certain matters in order to raise those matters, while defendant is required to assert her position on certain other matters in order to insert them into the case. This allocation of the burden of allegation for any particular kind of case accords with impulses of convenience, fairness, good policy, and apparent logic. Although that sounds vague, in practice the pleader can usually find clear guides as to burden in court rules, form books, statutes, and precedents.

2) Relevance

The pleader should allege only what is relevant under the applicable substantive and procedural law, sticking to the elements of matters on which he has the burden of allegation. He should avoid redundant, immaterial, impertinent, or scandalous matter. Likewise, he should avoid alleging matters on which his opponent has the burden of allegation. Such irrelevancies will often be ignored, but they can put things in issue that would not otherwise be in issue, cure defects in the opponent's position, suggest defects in the pleader's position, tip the pleader's hand, box the pleader in later on, waste energy in pleading skirmishes, or require time and money later to correct.

3) Detail

The Federal Rules require little detail in pleadings. The pleader must give a somewhat particularized mention of the elements of his claims or defenses and their factual circumstances, but only particularized enough to give fair notice and establish plausibility. Too much detail can cause trouble for the pleader, just as irrelevancies do. The desired level of short and plain generality is suggested by Rule 8(d)(1) ("Each allegation must be simple, concise, and direct. No technical form is required.") and Rule 8(e) ("Pleadings must be construed so as to do justice."). However, to serve the notice-giving purpose of pleadings, Rule 9 does require somewhat greater particularity in raising the defense of lack of capacity to litigate, in pleading fraud or mistake, in denying performance or occurrence of a condition precedent, and in claiming special damage.

d. Flexibility of Pleadings

The federal model tries to avoid technical restrictions on the pleader's staking out a position.

1) Alternative and Inconsistent Pleading

A pleader may state his single or multiple claims or defenses "alternatively [either-or] or hypothetically [if-then]" and "regardless of consistency," as Federal Rule 8(d) and other Rules provide and Federal Form 12 illustrates. This allows someone who is not sure of the provable facts or applicable law to proceed. He need not investigate the case fully nor have a single legal theory of the pleadings. However, Rule 8(d) implicitly incorporates the pleading obligations of Rule 11.

2) Multiple Claims and Parties

As just suggested, the Federal Rules liberally provide for multiclaim and multiparty litigation. Those provisions are explored in Part Four below.

e. Governing Law

As for most of the mechanics of civil procedure, federal law governs the mechanics of pleadings in any federal action, including diversity actions.

That is, how to plead is answered by federal law. However, what ultimately constitutes claim and defense—the elements of claim and defense—is under *Erie* governed by state law on state-created claims. Similarly, federal law governs the burden of allegation, but state law governs the burden of proof on issues to which state law applies. All this is treated in Part Five below.

2. STEPS IN PLEADING STAGE

Unlike the more traditional procedural models, modern pleading involves few steps: the plaintiff's complaint, the defendant's response in the form of motion and/or answer, and rather rarely the plaintiff's motion, reply, and/or answer.

See Federal Rule 7 (note that a motion is technically not a pleading; for more on motions attacking pleadings, see Rules 6(c), 12(i), and 43(c)).

a. Complaint

This document informs the court and defendant of the plaintiff's grievance and request for redress. A sample complaint for negligence follows, composed from Federal Forms 1, 2, 7, and 11:

UNITED STATES DISTRICT COURT FOR THE
SOUTHERN DISTRICT OF NEW YORK

Civil Action No. _____

A. B., Plaintiff)
      v.) *Complaint*
C. D., Defendant)

1. The plaintiff is a citizen of the State of Connecticut. The defendant is a citizen of the State of New York. The amount in controversy, without interest and costs, exceeds the sum or value specified by 28 U.S.C.A. § 1332.

2. On June 1, 2009, in a public highway called Boylston Street in Boston, Massachusetts, the defendant negligently drove a motor vehicle against the plaintiff who was then crossing said highway.

3. As a result, the plaintiff was physically injured, lost wages or income, suffered physical and mental pain, and incurred medical expenses of $1000.

Therefore, the plaintiff demands judgment against the defendant for $200,000, plus costs.

_____
Date

Signed:

_____

Attorney for Plaintiff

Printed name: _____
Address: _____
Telephone number: _____
E-mail address: _____

1) Jurisdictional Allegation

As can be seen in the sample, the body of a federal complaint consists of three basic parts, the first of which is an affirmative allegation of subject-matter jurisdiction. Rule 8(a)(1) requires "a short and plain statement of the grounds for the court's jurisdiction." The federal courts' approach to this requirement is generally pretty strict. But see 28 U.S.C.A. § 1653 (amendment). In state courts of general jurisdiction there is usually no need for such a paragraph on jurisdiction, but the federal requirement is typical of courts of limited jurisdiction. (See Chapter VIII below.)

2) Statement of Claim

The heart of the complaint is the statement of claim, which appears as paragraphs 2 and 3 in the sample. Rule 8(a)(2) requires "a short and plain statement of the claim showing that the pleader is entitled to relief." States following more traditional procedural models might require much more elaborate pleading.

3) Demand for Relief

Finally, Rule 8(a)(3) requires "a demand for the relief sought, which may include relief in the alternative or different types of relief." However, this demand usually does not box the pleader in, because Rule 54(c) provides that every "final judgment should grant the relief to which each party is entitled, even if the party has not demanded that relief in its pleadings"—except that any "default judgment must not differ in kind from, or exceed in amount, what is demanded in the pleadings." Thus, the court is free to do justice, but cannot unfairly surprise a defaulting defendant. In the various states, practices regarding demand for judgment range from enforcing strictly the demand to prohibiting a pleaded demand.

b. Motion and/or Answer

Under Rule 12(a), defendant must respond, usually within 20 days after service of the summons and complaint upon her. See also Rule 6 (time periods). Otherwise, defendant risks losing by default under Rule 55. There are *five important groups of responses*. Defendant may present some or all by motion or answer, as illustrated in Federal Forms 40 and 30; making such a pre-answer motion extends the time to answer. This scheme leaves considerable room for tactics; but to avoid waiver of some of the responses, defendant must observe carefully the complicated prescriptions of Rule 12, which attempts to curb the delay, harassment, and surprise of pleading abuses.

1) Objections

a) Types

First, Rule 12(e) allows defendant to require plaintiff to give "a more definite statement" if the complaint "is so vague or ambiguous that the party cannot reasonably prepare a response." Second, Rule 12(f) allows defendant to have the court strike from the complaint "any redundant, immaterial, impertinent, or scandalous matter" that causes her prejudice.

b) Presentation and Waiver

These rather uncommon and rarely successful objections are disposed of by motion before answer. Normally, they are waived if defendant omits them from her initial motion or if she answers. See Rule 12(e)–(g).

2) Disfavored Defenses

a) Types

Defendant may try to defeat the claim off the merits, by raising lack of territorial jurisdiction (Rule 12(b)(2)), improper venue

(12(b)(3)), defects in the form of the summons (12(b)(4)), or defects in the manner of transmitting notice (12(b)(5)). These defenses are discussed in Part Three below.

b)   Presentation and Waiver

Rule 12(b) permits defendant to raise these defenses by pre-answer motion or by answer. Normally, they are waived if defendant omits them (1) from her initial motion or (2) from the answer (including any amendment as a matter of course), whichever of the two defendant serves first. See Rule 12(h)(1).

3)   Defenses on the Merits

a)   Types

First, Rule 8(b) allows defendant to deny some or all of the plaintiff's allegations; she may make "specific denials" of designated portions of the complaint or a "qualified general denial" that denies everything not expressly admitted, or she may sometimes resort to the usually improper "general denial" of the whole complaint; she can plead a denial not only by directly denying on the basis of knowledge, but also by denying "upon information and belief" or, more frequently, by merely stating that she is without "knowledge or information" sufficient to form a belief. Second, Rule 8(c) allows defendant to assert affirmative defenses, i.e., new matter that would legally avoid liability even if the plaintiff's allegations were true.

b)   Presentation and Waiver

These defenses are properly raised by answer. Normally, they are waived if defendant omits them from the answer, unless the answer is amended to include them. See Rules 8(b)(6), 12(b).

4)   Favored Defenses

a)   Types

First, Rule 12(b)(6) allows defendant to challenge for "failure to state a claim upon which relief can be granted"; this defense, formerly called a demurrer, maintains that under the substantive law part or all of the complaint would result in no liability even if all the plaintiff's allegations were true; this is the usual avenue for challenging the legal sufficiency of the complaint, but under the lenient Federal Rules it should seldom succeed. Second, Rule 12(b)(7) allows defendant to challenge for "failure to join a [necessary or indispensable] party"; this defense is discussed in Part Four below. A successful challenge on either of these grounds often leads only to amendment of the complaint.

b) Presentation and Waiver

Rule 12(b) permits defendant to raise these defenses by motion or by answer. Rule 12(g) normally allows only one pre-answer motion under Rule 12; this means that these defenses should be raised in that pre-answer motion, in the answer, or in some post-answer motion discussed in Chapter IV–E below. Normally, these defenses are waived if defendant fails to raise them before the end of the trial. See Rule 12(h)(2).

5) Subject–Matter Jurisdiction Defense

a) Type

The issue of subject-matter jurisdiction, mentioned as a defense in Rule 12(b)(1), is treated with unique solicitude in federal court. During the action, any party may challenge subject-matter jurisdiction at any time, and the court must ever be ready to question its own subject-matter jurisdiction. This defense is discussed in Part Three below.

b) Presentation and Waiver

This defense may be raised in any fashion. Normally, this defense cannot be waived. See Rule 12(h)(3).

c. Motion, Reply, and/or Answer

Unlike the common-law and code models, federal pleading in a two-party lawsuit usually stops with the answer. The limited mission of modern pleading has then been accomplished. But there are two situations where there is the further step of the plaintiff's response.

1) Responding to Defenses

Assume that the defendant's answer includes defenses, but no counterclaims.

a) Motion

Usually within 20 days after service of the answer, plaintiff may move under Rule 12(f) to strike "any redundant, immaterial, impertinent, or scandalous matter" that causes him prejudice. Such a motion is uncommon and very rarely succeeds. Also, Rule 12(f) permits plaintiff to have the court strike from the answer "an insufficient defense." This poorly drafted provision is generally treated as authorizing a motion analogous to the defendant's 12(b)(6) motion.

b) Reply

Normally, plaintiff *neither must nor may reply* to an answer containing only defenses. Instead, Rule 8(b)(6) provides that the answer's allegations are automatically taken to be "denied or avoided." However, the court may order a reply under Rule 7(a)(7) in the interests of clarification, most likely on the defendant's motion. In such very rare case, under Rule 12(a)(1)(C), plaintiff usually has 20 days after service of the court's order to respond: plaintiff may in appropriate circumstances move under Rule 12(e) for a more definite statement, but should ultimately serve and file a reply denying or avoiding the new matter in the defendant's answer.

2) Responding to Counterclaims

Now assume that the defendant's answer contains one or more counterclaims, denominated as such. (See Chapter XIII below.) Plaintiff is then cast as a defendant with respect to the counter-claims. Under Rules 7(a)(3) and 12(a)(1)(B), plaintiff must respond to the counterclaims, usually within 20 days after service of the defendant's answer.

a) Motion

Plaintiff may move under Rule 12. This step is analogous to the defendant's motion against the complaint.

b) Answer

Similarly, plaintiff should ultimately answer the counterclaims. This step is analogous to the defendant's answer to the complaint.

3. AMENDMENTS

A hallmark of the federal pleading process is permitting amendments to the maximum extent consistent with the purposes of pleadings. Thus, a party can normally correct his pleading mistakes or amend on the basis of newly learned information.

See Federal Rule 15.

a. Amendments as a Matter of Course

Under Rule 15(a)(1), a party can amend his pleading once without applying to the court for permission if he acts promptly. He can do this at any time "before being served with a responsive pleading"; but if his pleading is one to which no responsive pleading is permitted, the party normally has only 20 days after serving his pleading.

Examples: (1) P serves his complaint. D moves in response. Thirty days later, P wishes to amend, hoping to moot D's pending motion. (Result: P can amend as a matter of course.)

(2) P serves his complaint. D answers without counter-claiming. Thirty days later, D seeks to amend. (Result: D must obtain leave of court or written consent of P.)

b. Other Amendments

Also under Rule 15(a)(2), if a party cannot amend as a matter of course, he must obtain the written consent of the adversary or move to obtain leave of court.

1) When Allowed

The Rule provides: "The court should freely give leave when justice so requires." The court will discretionarily balance (1) the *fault* of the movant in delaying and the *prejudice* to his interests in a full presentation of the merits that would be unavoidably caused by denying the amendment, against (2) any *fault* of the opponent in inducing the delay and the *prejudice* to her reliance interests (i.e., disadvantage attributable to the delay) that would be unavoidably caused by allowing the amendment, with the court also throwing onto the scales of the balance (3) considerations of *public interest* (which usually favor amendment). The burden of persuasion will be on the opponent of amendment. The court may grant leave to amend subject to conditions. There is no time limit on seeking amendment, although the chances of being allowed to amend usually decrease with the passage of time.

2) Special Situations

Thus, a party can amend his pleading at or after trial. Rule 15(b) treats the following two special situations of late amendments that fall within the general scope of Rule 15(a). Rule 15(b) thereby largely solves the ancient problem of fatal "variance" between pleading and proof, doing so by decreasing the significance of the pleadings. The background for understanding Rule 15(b) is the outmoded axiom that a claim or defense can be sustained after trial only if its essentials had been pleaded in full and also only if it has been fully proved in conformity with the pleadings.

a) Amendments to Meet Objections at Trial
    Rule 15(b)(1) covers the special situation of an amendment to circumvent the opponent's successful objection to trial evidence on the ground that the proffered evidence is irrelevant under the pleadings. This part of the Rule simply emphasizes that such a curative amendment is permissible under Rule 15(a)(2).

b) Amendments to Conform to Evidence at Trial
    Rule 15(b)(2) covers the different situation where the opponent failed to object fully to trial evidence that unambiguously went beyond the pleadings. When issues have been so tried by express or implied consent, this part of the Rule specially provides that the pleadings later will be treated as if the original pleadings included those issues and that they may even be actually so amended. Actual amendment would help, for example, to facilitate later application of res judicata.

c. **Relation Back of Amendments**
    Rule 15(c) addresses an amended pleading's effective date, which is primarily of importance for the statute of limitations. The amendment relates back if the applicable limitations law so provides. Also, Rule 15(c) provides an alternative federal provision for relation back: the amendment relates back to the date of the original pleading if "the amendment asserts a claim or defense that arose out of the conduct, transaction, or occurrence set out or attempted to be set out in the original pleading"; however, the amendment relates back with respect to a changed party-defendant only if, in addition, that new party received timely notice of the misdirected lawsuit.

d. **Supplemental Pleadings**
    To be distinguished from an amendment is a supplemental pleading under Rule 15(d), which is a pleading "setting out a transaction,

occurrence, or event that happened after the date of the pleading to be supplemented." Upon motion, the court may permit such a supplemental pleading.

B. DISCLOSURE

In 1993, amid much controversy, the rulemakers introduced a new stage called disclosure. In 2000, they had to cut it back. Now, elaborating on the pleaded facts, parties must disclose certain core information, without awaiting a discovery request.

See generally Wright's Hornbook § 83A.

1. PURPOSES

Disclosure aims at achieving some savings in time and expense, and also at moderating litigants' adversary behavior in the pretrial phase. Parties find the core information useful in virtually all cases. The information is all discoverable anyway. Disclosure essentially makes the obvious interrogatories automatic, so that parties just hand over the information without awaiting a discovery request.

2. SCOPE

According to Federal Rule 26(a), there are three distinct types of disclosure. However, the individual judge by order or the parties by stipulation may alter these disclosure obligations.

a. Initial Disclosures

Rule 26(a)(1)(A) requires disclosure, at the outset, of routine evidentiary and insurance matters that are reasonably available. These matters comprise (i) witnesses "likely to have discoverable information . . . that the disclosing party may use to support its claims or defenses, unless the use would be solely for impeachment," (ii) documents and things "that the disclosing party has in its possession, custody, or control and may use to support its claims or defenses, unless the use would be solely for impeachment," (iii) computation of claimed damages, and (iv) insurance agreements that might cover part or all of an eventual judgment. Rule 26(a)(1)(B) exempts certain special categories of cases from this requirement.

b. Expert Information

Rule 26(a)(2) requires a party to disclose, at a specified time, the identity of any expert who may be called at trial. Most of these experts must also deliver a detailed report, which must include all opinions to be expressed and the underlying reasons, as well as details about qualifications, compensation, and previous experience as a witness. A special duty to supplement is set forth in Rule 26(e)(2).

c.   Pretrial Disclosures

Rule 26(a)(3) requires disclosure, shortly before trial, of trial witness lists and the like regarding nonimpeachment evidence. In particular, the party must disclose trial exhibits, which allows airing evidentiary disputes in advance of trial.

3.   MECHANICS

Disclosure under the Federal Rules is meant to proceed in an atmosphere of cooperation.

a.   Form

All disclosures are to be in writing, signed, and served. Rule 26(a)(4). The pretrial disclosures under Rule 26(a)(3) must be promptly filed with the court, but the other disclosures, like most discovery items, must not be filed until used in the proceeding. Rule 5(d)(1).

b.   Certification

Rule 26(g) requires an attorney, or if there is no attorney then the party, to sign each disclosure under Rule 26(a)(1) or (3). The signature is a certification that to the best of the signer's knowledge, information, and belief formed after reasonable inquiry the disclosure is complete and correct as of the time it is made. Violations of the Rule are to be punished by sanctions.

c.   Supplementation

Rule 26(e)(1) says that a party is under a duty to supplement disclosures if the party learns that in some material respect the information disclosed is incomplete or incorrect, unless the other parties are aware of the additional information.

d.   Sanctions

After conferring with any nondisclosing party, a party may move under Rule 37(a) to compel disclosure and for appropriate sanctions. Also, Rule

37(c)(1) provides that a party who without substantial justification fails to make a mandatory disclosure, unless such failure is harmless, is subject to appropriate sanctions, which will usually prohibit use of the undisclosed evidence.

e. Conference

A key feature of the disclosure and discovery schemes lies in Rule 26(f): very early on, the attorneys and unrepresented parties normally must confer to consider the case and the disclosures, as well as attempt to develop a proposed discovery plan and then submit a written report to the court along the lines of Federal Form 52. A duty to participate in good faith is enforceable under Rule 37(f). Under Rule 26(d)(1), discovery normally cannot proceed until this conference takes place.

4. PROBLEMS

Overlaying a system of disclosure on the current pretrial system of the Federal Rules would seem to increase costs, as well as produce more satellite litigation. In addition, disclosure seems to clash with parts of that pretrial system, especially tending to undermine modern pleading. Although scholarly attacks on disclosure have tended to exaggerate these costs, empirical research discouragingly demonstrates that disclosure has little beneficial effect to offset them.

C. DISCOVERY

The pivotal feature of the federal procedural system is a significant discovery stage, or rather its availability. Its existence allows the de-emphasis on pleading and inevitably diminishes the trial's importance. Its extensiveness stands in marked contrast to discovery under more traditional procedural systems.

See generally Wright's Hornbook §§ 81–90.

1. GENERAL RULES

A number of policies and rules apply throughout the discovery stage in federal court.

a. Purposes of Discovery

Discovery allows a party to expand on the notice given by the pleadings and any disclosures. He thereby can clarify and narrow the issues and, especially, can investigate the facts and explore the evidence before trial.

This permits him to build his own case and feel out his opponent's case. Discovery can perform these functions better than elaborate pleadings would. But should the procedural system perform these functions at all? The primary motive behind pretrial airing of the case is to avoid an inaccurate or unfair outcome determined by the parties' relative capacities for pursuing private investigation and for surviving a blind trial. Discovery might also facilitate settlement; it might even allow the tried case to proceed more efficiently, as the trial stage becomes more predictable and orderly (and dull).

b. Scope of Discovery

The scope of discovery is very wide, according to Federal Rule 26(b). The same scope generally applies to all the various discovery devices.

1) General Standards

A party generally may discover any matter that is "relevant" and that is "nonprivileged." Rule 26(b)(1).

a) Relevance

The discovering party is free to seek any matter that is "relevant to any party's claim or defense." Moreover, for "good cause" shown, the court may order discovery of any matter that is "relevant to the subject matter involved in the action" (and thus perhaps relevant only to unasserted but possible claims or defenses). These two relevance standards are meant to be loose, encompassing all the issues possibly in the case and the evidence thereon. Furthermore, the "[r]elevant information need not be admissible at the trial if the discovery appears reasonably calculated to lead to the discovery of admissible evidence." Id. However, the party must seek to discover the matter for the reason that it bears on, or because it might reasonably lead to other matter that bears on, some issue that will or may be decided in the case. *Oppenheimer Fund, Inc. v. Sanders*, 437 U.S. 340, 98 S.Ct. 2380 (1978) (Rule 26(b)(1) does not authorize attempt to obtain class members' names and addresses for purpose of sending class-action notice).

b) Privilege

The reference to privilege incorporates the evidentiary rules of privilege applicable at trial. See Federal Rules of Evidence 1101(c), 501.

2) Additional Provisions

There are other policies and rules affecting the scope of discovery, some of which are expressed in the remainder of Rule 26(b).

a) Work Product

Hickman v. Taylor, 329 U.S. 495, 67 S.Ct. 385 (1947), recognized an important, broad, and complex principle further limiting the scope of discovery in two ways: (1) tangible materials, such as witness statements, that were prepared by or for a party or her representative in anticipation of any litigation or for any trial ("ordinary work product") can be discovered only upon a showing of substantial need and of inability without undue hardship to obtain the substantial equivalent; and (2) mental impressions, conclusions, opinions, or legal theories of the party's attorney or other representative concerning any litigation ("opinion work product") are even more strictly protected and indeed can perhaps never be discovered. However, these protections do not extend to prevent normal discovery of raw facts that happen to be embodied in undiscoverable work product. Rule 26(b)(3) codifies part of *Hickman*'s broad principle and leaves the rest undisturbed, except that Rule 26(b)(3)(C) permits any person to obtain his own statement without any special showing and Rules 33(a)(2) and 36(a)(1) permit some inquiry into opinions in the form of contentions. Protecting work product is thought to be critical to the workings of the adversary system.

b) Expert Information

Rule 26(b)(4) overrides Rule 26(b)(3) to provide a special rule for discovery from experts. This Rule on expert information is fairly permissive in allowing regulated discovery regarding experts whom a party may call as expert witnesses at trial, but much more restrictive with respect to discovery of facts known and opinions held by other experts who have been retained or specially employed in anticipation of litigation or preparation for trial. The party obtaining discovery may be ordered to pay fees and expenses. This Rule's approach permits thorough trial preparation, while minimizing the risk of freeloading.

c) E–Discovery

Today's big discovery problem, beyond doubt, involves the discovery of electronically stored information. Digital information certainly has its tricky facets, such as the dynamic and precarious form of its storage. But the central difficulty is simply its volume. The nature and volume of computer-based information mean that it will hold the key to winning or losing numberless cases, ranging from divorce suits to corporate megasuits, and often entail crushing effort and expense. Parties will engage in a fair amount of meeting and conferring, under Rules 16 and 26(f), about e-discovery. Discoverers will rely most heavily on Rule 33 interrogatories to acquire the necessary knowledge of the respondent's computer system, and then on requests for production under Rules 34 and 45 to get the actual computer-based information. Finally, the courts must wade in under Rules 26(c) and 37(a), all too often. The federal rulemakers started their serious study of this new problem in 2000. Meanwhile, courts gave ever increasing attention to the problem. Amendments worked through the rulemaking process to emerge in 2006 as new provisions on e-disclosure and e-discovery. Rules 16, 26, 33, 34, 37, and 45, among others, underwent amendment to codify the formerly disparate practices ordained by case law and local rules.

d) Other Restrictions

When the court intervenes in the discovery process, as pursuant to a motion for a protective order or for an order compelling discovery, it may regulate or limit discovery. On this case-by-case basis, it will vindicate implicit policies, such as the uncodified part of the work-product doctrine or policies emanating from the First Amendment.

c. Mechanics of Discovery

Discovery under the Federal Rules is meant to work almost wholly by action of the parties, without intervention by the court. Nevertheless, to remedy abuse or recalcitrance, anyone involved in the process should be able to invoke the court's assistance in a situation of need.

Bear in mind that the individual judge by order or the parties by Rule 29 stipulation may alter most of the discovery Rules.

1) Signing

Rule 26(g) requires an attorney, or if there is no attorney then the party, to sign each discovery request or response. The signature is a certification of reasonableness, with violations of the Rule to be punished by sanctions.

2) Requests to Discover

A party may initiate any of the discovery devices without addressing the court, except where he seeks to invoke the broader relevance standard under Rule 26(b)(1); where he seeks discovery before the parties' conference under Rule 26(f); where under Rule 27 he seeks discovery before commencement of an action or pending appeal in order to perpetuate evidence; or where under Rule 35 he seeks a physical or mental examination. (See also Rules 30(a)(2) and 31(a)(2) on leave of court required for certain depositions, and Rules 30(d)(1) and 33(a)(1) on leave of court required for lengthy depositions and excessive interrogatories.)

3) Discovery Responses

The respondent (1) may comply with the request for discovery, (2) may seek the court's protection, or (3) may refuse to comply. If the discovering party is dissatisfied with the course followed, he may seek sanctions from the court. Thus, either side may choose to get the court involved.

a) Supplementation

Rule 26(e)(1) says that the responding party is under a duty to supplement her response to an interrogatory, request for production, or request for admission if the party learns that the response is in some material respect incomplete or incorrect, unless the other parties are aware of the additional information.

b) Protective Orders

Rule 26(c)(1) allows the respondent, or any party, to curb abuse by getting the court involved. The party or person must first confer with affected parties. Then the court may upon motion regulate or limit discovery "to protect a party or person from annoyance, embarrassment, oppression, or undue burden or expense." The court has broad power to issue such a protective order, often discretionarily and flexibly shaping it to meet the problem at hand; indeed, the court may act on its own initiative under Rule 26(b)(2). Alternatively, the court may deny the motion and instead issue an order compelling discovery under Rule 26(c)(4). (See also Rule 30(d)(3) on controlling oral depositions in progress.)

c) Sanctions

First, when the discovering party meets recalcitrance, he usually must *confer* with the recalcitrant party or person. Second, if that fails, he must go to court under Rule 37(a) to move for an *order compelling discovery*, unless the court has already entered an equivalent order (e.g., an order under Rule 35) or unless there has been a gross failure to respond that is directly sanctionable (i.e., a party's failure to appear for deposition, to serve any answers or objections to interrogatories, or to serve any written response to a request for inspection or a person's failure to obey a subpoena, as provided in Rules 37(d) and 45(e)). In ruling on such motions, courts will decide whether discovery should be ordered or denied, and on what terms and conditions. Third, in case of further need for relief, the discovering party must go to court to obtain a *sanction* under Rule 37(b), such as having disputed facts treated as established, obtaining a dismissal or default, having failure to obey an order treated as contempt, or obtaining reimbursement of reasonable expenses. Courts have long restricted themselves to occasional and light remedial sanctions in the discovery process, but they now seem increasingly tough in imposing sanctions as deterrents. (See also Rules 36(a)(3) and 37(c)(2) on sanctions for failure to admit.)

d) **Procedural Incidents of Court Action**
   Skirmishing for protective orders or sanctions takes place in the court in which the action is pending, except that with regard to a deposition it might take place in the court in the district where the deposition is being taken and with regard to a subpoena it might take place in the court from which the subpoena issued. The burden of persuasion is normally on the person resisting discovery.

4) **Discovery Expenses**
   The expenses incurred in discovery can be enormous. Normally, they fall ultimately on the party who initially incurred them; for example, the discovering party pays the small cost of preparing interrogatories, and the responding party pays the huge cost of answering. However, the court may eventually award certain, relatively insignificant discovery expenses as costs to the party who prevails in the lawsuit. More significantly, the Rules have ample provisions for shifting discovery expenses as a condition of approving discovery (see, e.g., Rule 26(c)); for ordering parties, deponents, or counsel to reimburse anyone's reasonable expenses, including

attorney's fees, incurred in successfully invoking the court's assistance in a discovery dispute or resisting such an attempt (see, e.g., Rule 37(a)(5)); and for requiring reimbursement of reasonable expenses as a discovery sanction (see, e.g., Rule 37(d)(3)).

5) Use of Discovery Products

The parties generally may use the products of discovery as evidence in the trial only so far as those products are admissible under the Federal Rules of Evidence—and generally the scope of admissibility is obviously more restricted than the scope of discovery itself. However, the use of depositions, which are so like trial testimony, receives special treatment in Rule 32(a): the Rule specifies that the rules of evidence need only be applied as though "the deponent were present and testifying," provided that the use of the deposition falls within one of the situations listed in Rule 32(a)(2)–(4) or (6) and thus justifies this avoidance of the normal hearsay rule.

d. Problems of Discovery

Questions persist regarding the desirability of the federal model's extensive discovery, at least when one moves out of the world of theory and into the reality of litigation. That is, doubts remain whether the benefits of discovery outweigh its costs. Surprise at trial might sometimes act as a promoter of truth, and the discovery weapon sometimes allows browbeating of the opponent. Certainly, the time and money involved can be staggering. Nevertheless, given that most people agree that discovery is and should be here to stay, perhaps the most effective control on its costs (and therefore the most fruitful avenue for reform) is more active supervision by the court.

2. SPECIFIC DEVICES

The Federal Rules provide six major types of discovery devices. Unless otherwise ordered, the parties may use one or more of these devices repeatedly, and in any sequence or simultaneously. See Rule 26(d)(2). However, Rules 30(a)(2)(A) and 31(a)(2)(A) now limit each side to 10 depositions and prohibit redeposition of the same person, in the absence of leave of court or agreement of the parties; Rule 30(d)(1) similarly limits an oral deposition to one day of seven hours; and Rule 33(a)(1) similarly limits each party's interrogatories served on any one party to 25, "including all discrete subparts."

a. Types

The litigator today must have a solid grasp of the various discovery tools and their relative value.

1) Oral Depositions

A deposition upon oral examination is a private proceeding initiated by any party for taking anyone's testimony as at trial—with oral direct examination, cross-examination, and so on. Typically, an oral deposition involves a sworn deponent, a reporter, and a bunch of lawyers sitting around a table in some lawyer's office. See Rule 30. Unlike trial, there is no judge; there is only a presiding officer, who is described in Rule 28 and who has no judicial powers; therefore, Rules 30(c)(2) and 32(b) and (d) exist to provide a mechanism for preserving evidentiary objections. Largely because of all the attorneys' time involved, an oral deposition is very expensive; but there is no substitute for pinning down a respondent or reaping other fruits of oral testimony.

2) Written Depositions

A deposition upon written questions resembles an oral deposition but with all the questions written out in advance. The presiding officer simply reads the questions to the sworn deponent and records the responses. See Rule 31. This inflexible device is seldom used; being less expensive to conduct than an oral deposition, a written deposition might be used in special situations such as where the device of interrogatories would suffice but is unavailable because the respondent is a nonparty.

3) Interrogatories

Interrogatories are simply written questions, each of which the responding party must answer in writing under oath, unless her attorney objects thereto with reasons in writing. See Rule 33. Answers to interrogatories tend to be studied and artfully evasive; but they very often provide a simple and inexpensive way to clarify the issues and to obtain evidence and leads to evidence, such as a list of eyewitnesses.

4) Production of Documents and Such

A written request to a party for production of any designated documents, electronically stored information, or tangible things (or for entry upon land or other property) within that party's possession, custody, or control provides a route for the discovering party to inspect, copy, test, or sample them. The responding party must serve a written response, either agreeing to comply or objecting with reasons. See Rule 34. Similarly, a nonparty may be compelled to produce by subpoena under Rule 45.

5) **Physical and Mental Examination**

Upon motion and for "good cause" shown, the court in which the action is pending may order a physical or mental examination of any party or a person in the custody or under the legal control of any party (e.g., a party's minor child), if the physical or mental condition of the person to be examined is "in controversy." See Rule 35. Because of concerns of privacy and risks of serious abuse, the court should use special care in exercising its discretion to order an examination. (See also Rule 35(b) on exchange of reports of findings.)

6) **Requests for Admission**

A written request to a party to admit, for purposes of the pending action only, the truth of matters set forth in the request (including genuineness of described documents) can lead to admissions that are *conclusive*—unless later the court on motion permits withdrawal or amendment of admissions. The responding party or her attorney must serve a written response, which will admit or deny each matter, explain why she cannot truthfully admit or deny it, or object thereto with reasons. See Rule 36. Although the format of this discovery device is rather inflexible and limited, it does offer a simple and inexpensive way to narrow the issues with binding effect.

b. **Summary**

The following chart summarizes critical information on the discovery tools:

	Oral Depositions	Written Depositions	Interrogatories	Production of Documents and Such	Physical and Mental Examination	Requests for Admission
Fed. R. Civ. P.	30	31	33	34	35	36
Availability	Any time, but Rule 27 requires order before action or pending appeal, and Rule 30(a)(2) and (d)(1) requires leave of court or stipulation for certain depositions	Any time, but Rule 27 requires order before action or pending appeal, and Rule 31(a)(2) requires leave of court or stipulation for certain depositions	Any time after filing complaint, but leave of court or stipulation required before Rule 26(f) conference or for more than 25 interrogatories	Any time, but leave of court or stipulation required before Rule 26(f) conference; for nonparties, see Rules 34(c) and 45; see also Rule 27	Any time, but only on court order; see also Rule 27	Any time after filing complaint, but leave of court or stipulation required before Rule 26(f) conference
Respondents	Any person, but use subpoena under Rule 45 for nonparties	Any person, but use subpoena under Rule 45 for nonparties	Parties (for nonparties, use deposition with subpoena)	Any person, but use subpoena under Rule 45 for nonparties	Parties and persons in custody of or under legal control of a party	Parties
Time Periods	Reasonable notice in writing to every other party; time required for review through delivery under Rule 30(e) and (f)	Notice, with written questions, to every other party; then 14 + 7 + 7 days for preparation of cross, redirect, and recross questions; time required for review through delivery under Rule 31(b) and (c)	30 days after service of interrogatories to answer or object	30 days after service of request to agree or object; for nonparties, see Rules 34(c) and 45	Notice of motion to examinee and to every other party	30 days after service of request to answer or object
Special Advantages	Quickly invoked; opposing lawyer cannot actively assist deponent; discovering lawyer can flexibly react to answers given; other advantages of oral testimony	Advantageous only in very special circumstances	Inexpensive and simple to prepare; useful for clarifying issues and for obtaining evidence leads	Serves particular purposes	Serves particular purposes	Fairly inexpensive and simple to prepare; useful for narrowing issues with binding effect and thus for fleshing out pleadings
Special Disadvantages	Very expensive	Expensive, although attorneys need not attend deposition; cumbersome; other disadvantages of written interrogation	Can be used only against parties; corporate respondent can choose any officer or agent to answer; disadvantages of written interrogation	Can result in a pile of paper or data	Expensive	Inflexible format and limited purposes

D. PRETRIAL CONFERENCE

The federal procedural system requires a tool to help move the case through the pretrial process and toward trial, and also to focus the case after the skeletal pleading stage and the dispersive effects of disclosure and discovery. The modern tool for accomplishing this is the judicially (or parajudicially) supervised pretrial conference.

The traditional conference was the loose pretrial procedure authorized by Federal Rule 16 in 1938. See generally Wright's Hornbook § 91. However, the 1983 and 1993 amendments radically expanded Rule 16 to provide for more conferences and to make the court's involvement therein a little more dictatorial in tone and structured in format and a lot more active in case management, thus rather basically and questionably affecting the role of the judge in the adversary system. Indicative of the change is the important new requirement in Rule 16(b) that in most cases, within about 100 days of commencement, the court after consultation must issue a "scheduling order" limiting the time for settling pleadings, filing motions, and completing discovery.

1. PURPOSES

A pretrial conference allows the court and the litigants to confer about the case, so moving it along to disposition and molding it for trial. Such a conference may lead to settlement. It should shape and condense the case, as by amending the pleadings, formulating and simplifying the issues, streamlining the proof, or handling any other of a wide variety of pretrial matters.

2. PROCEDURAL INCIDENTS

At any time after commencement of the action, the court in its discretion may direct the attorneys and unrepresented parties to appear before it for one or more pretrial conferences. The key feature (and perhaps the secret strength) of this procedure is that there is no uniform practice, but instead the practice varies from district to district, from judge to judge, and especially from case to case: (1) In the piddling case, the court may not hold any pretrial conference. (2) In selected, more difficult cases—typically—the court will call one pretrial conference shortly before trial; local rules will require the litigants to engage in an extensive written exchange of views beforehand, and they will have to attend the conference further to reveal fully and fairly their positions and plans; but that conference will properly tend—with some courts' practices in notable disagreement—to be otherwise voluntary in tone and relatively simple, flexible, and informal in format. (3) In the "big case," the court today is likely to be much more active through a series of conferences.

3. ORDER

After a pretrial conference, the court must enter a binding but amendable order reciting the action taken at the conference. See Rule 16(f) on sanctions.

E. OTHER STEPS

Numerous other procedural steps can be taken in the pretrial period, the more important of which are described below. Do not slip into thinking that the various steps must all be taken or that they must always be taken in some fixed order.

1. PROVISIONAL REMEDIES

The claimant may seek temporary relief to protect himself from loss or injury while his action is pending. The point is to preserve or sometimes to alter the status quo in the short run, so that intervening events will not frustrate any final relief that may eventually be granted. There are two major kinds of such temporary relief.

a. Seizure of Property

If plaintiff seeks a money judgment, he has an interest in ensuring that the defendant's assets will still be there to satisfy any eventual judgment. Accordingly, the law provides security by way of seizure of the defendant's real or personal property at the outset of or during the lawsuit.

1) Procedural Incidents

In federal court, Federal Rule 64 authorizes all pre-judgment seizure remedies available under the law of the state in which the district court is held, except that any existing federal statute governs to the extent applicable. Thus, federal practice varies from state to state. States provide for such remedies where circumstances suggest a sufficient need for security, as where defendant has left the jurisdiction. States provide for such remedies in various manners, such as "attachment" (legal process directing seizure of the defendant's property that is in the hands of defendant) and "garnishment" (legal process subjecting to the plaintiff's claim the defendant's property that is in the hands of a third person, or "garnishee," or freezing a debt owed defendant by the garnishee).

2) Constitutional Aspects

The drastic effects of these remedies can raise questions of fundamental fairness. The constraints of due process on this procedure are explored in connection with the discussion of notice in Chapter X.

b. Injunctive Relief

Plaintiff may have an immediate interest in making defendant do or not do some act, in order to avoid frustrating any permanent relief. Accordingly, the court may grant interim injunctive relief—which binds defendant and those persons in active concert or participation with her, provided that the party or person to be bound has received actual notice of the court's action. See Federal Rule 65, which imposes typically severe limitations on this drastic relief, such as requiring plaintiff to give security. There are two kinds of such injunctive relief.

1) **Temporary Restraining Order**

   The court may first grant a request for relief that is of very short duration, doing so *without a hearing* and sometimes even without advance notice to defendant. Plaintiff may obtain such a "temporary restraining order" upon a showing of immediate irreparable harm. A "t.r.o." is typically a stopgap in expectation of a preliminary injunction.

2) **Preliminary Injunction**

   In order to minimize expected costs, the court may grant a motion for a "preliminary injunction" that can last until final judgment, but only after notice and *hearing*. Granting this discretionary remedy to prevent possible irreparable harm involves measuring the *likelihood of the plaintiff's ultimate success on the merits*, with the requisite probability of success decreasing as the *balance of the plaintiff's and the defendant's equities and the public interest* tilts more decidedly in favor of interim relief.

2. SUMMARY JUDGMENT AND OTHER STEPS THAT AVOID TRIAL

In addition to the motions attacking pleadings, which were discussed in connection with the pleading stage in Chapter IV–A above, there are various other steps that may avoid trial. Indeed, in most cases, trial is ultimately avoided in one of these ways.

a. Summary Judgment

This important tool for determining whether trial is necessary nicely complements the prevailing federal scheme of barebones pleading and extensive discovery.

See Federal Rule 56. See generally Edward J. Brunet & Martin H. Redish, Summary Judgment (3d ed. 2006); Wright's Hornbook § 99.

1) **Availability**

   The summary judgment device is broadly available: (1) Either a claimant or a defending party may move. (2) The motion may concern all or part of any claim; Rule 56(d) expressly treats "partial summary adjudication." (3) The motion may be made on the pleadings alone; or it may be supported by affidavits, products of discovery, and other factual materials, all of which can be used to pierce the pleadings. (4) A defending party may move at any time, either before or after the pleadings close, as Rule 56(b) specifies; a claimant may move at any time after the defending party serves a summary judgment motion or after the expiration of 20 days following commencement of the action, as Rule 56(a) specifies.

2) Standard

Summary judgment will be given to a movant "entitled to judgment as a matter of law" if "there is no genuine issue as to any material fact." Rule 56(c). Summary judgment thus allows the court to decide legal disputes, without trial, when there are no genuine and material factual disputes. The principal inquiry on the motion is whether factual disputes truly exist—never how to resolve factual disputes that do exist. If there is a real factual dispute, the motion must be denied. In determining whether there is a genuine issue as to any fact, the court construes all factual matters in the light reasonably most favorable to the party opposing the motion and then asks whether reasonable minds could differ. (This test is essentially that test applicable on the trial motion for judgment as a matter of law.) However, the judge in actuality can almost always choose to deny a summary judgment motion and proceed to trial. See also Rule 56(f). Or the judge can grant summary judgment in favor of the party opposing the motion, or even so act sua sponte in the absence of a motion, if the party is fairly entitled thereto and the other party has received adequate notice.

3) Procedural Incidents

The procedure aims at revealing whether factual disputes truly exist.

a) Support

Just as the movant can support his motion, the opponent is free to submit affidavits, products of discovery, and other factual materials in opposition. The court may also consult materials in the case on file with the court. However, only information that would be admissible at trial is considered on a summary judgment motion.

b) Burden

The movant has the burden of persuasion that summary judgment should be granted to him. However, if the movant supports his motion sufficiently to make a prima facie showing that summary judgment should be granted, then the opponent normally cannot rest upon her pleading but must produce a response or suffer summary judgment. See Rule 56(e)(2).

4) Judgment on the Pleadings Distinguished

Rule 12(c) authorizes any party to move for judgment on the pleadings, after the pleadings are closed but within such time as not to delay the trial. The court will grant such judgment to a movant entitled to judgment under the law when the pleaded facts are read most favorably to the party opposing the motion. This device tests the legal sufficiency of the pleadings, but does not go behind those pleadings to the real facts. In brief, Rule 12(c) is a stunted version of Rule 56. In view of the many advantages of Rule 56, the litigant should virtually never have reason to resort to the common-law relic embodied in Rule 12(c).

a) Relation of Rule 12(c) to Rule 12(b)(6) and to Rule 12(f)

The motion for judgment on the pleadings is quite similar to the defendant's motion to dismiss under Rule 12(b)(6) for failure to state a claim and to the plaintiff's motion to strike under Rule 12(f) for failure to state a sufficient defense, which were discussed above in connection with the pleading stage. The major difference is timing. Indeed, the Rule 12(c) motion serves the purposes of these two motions when it later becomes available after the pleadings close, as Rule 12(h)(2)(B) makes clear. However, motions under Rule 12(c) and under Rule 12(f) may both be available at a given time, in which event use of Rule 12(c) is technically proper if judgment on the whole claim is sought and use of Rule 12(f) is technically proper if striking of fewer than all defenses to the claim is sought.

b) Conversion of Rule 12 Motions

On a motion under Rule 12(b)(6), (f), or (c), if materials outside the pleadings are presented to *and* not excluded by the court, the motion is treated as a summary judgment motion, as Rule 12(d) makes clear.

b. Other Steps That Avoid Trial

In addition to the above-discussed motions, there are four other steps that may avoid trial in federal court.

1) Voluntary Dismissal

A claimant generally may obtain dismissal of his action or claim by his filing a *notice of dismissal* early in the case, by all parties' signing a *stipulation of dismissal*, or by *court order* upon such terms and conditions as the court deems proper. Unless otherwise specified in the notice, stipulation, or order, any such dismissal is *without prejudice* to a new action—except that a notice of dismissal operates with prejudice when filed by a claimant who has in any federal or state court previously dismissed the same claim by notice of dismissal (the "two-dismissal" rule). See Federal Rule 41(a).

2) Involuntary Dismissal

A defending party may move for dismissal of an action or claim against her on the ground of the claimant's *failure to prosecute*, or *failure to comply* with a court order or rule. Unless otherwise specified by the court, any such dismissal is *with prejudice*. See Federal Rule 41(b). Also, the court may so act on its own initiative.

3) Default

If a party against whom a claim for relief is asserted has *failed to plead or otherwise defend*, the claimant may (1) get the court clerk (or the judge pursuant to implicit powers) to enter a default, and then (2) get the judge (or the court clerk when the act is strictly ministerial) to enter a default judgment. See Federal Rule 55. Also, the court may enter a default judgment for *failure to comply* with a court order or rule. See, e.g., Rule 37(b)(2)(A)(vi).

4) Settlement

The parties may agree to a *compromise*, and then usher the action or claim out of court by one of the preceding routes or by entry of a consent judgment. Thus, most lawsuits in fact do not make it all the way through the above-described pretrial practice. Indeed, most disputes do not even become lawsuits in the first place, as injured persons abandon or settle the overwhelming majority of grievances at some point along the line. First, from the viewpoint of the civil justice system, settlement is a critical need. Ours is a slow and expensive procedure. The system simply would not be able to adjudicate all cases filed. We depend on the parties' finding alternatives to using the system. Accordingly, reformers are constantly seeking ways to increase the settlement rate, which is a loose term that measures the percentage of filed cases not resulting in contested judgments but instead leaving the system, whether by abandonment, concession, or privately negotiated settlement or by alternative dispute resolution such as arbitration, mediation, and conciliation. Second, shifting from the viewpoint of the system to that of the disputants, settlement is also of critical importance. For them in the usual course, settlement *is* our system of justice. For their "trial" lawyers, negotiation of settlements—and pursuit of other alternatives to litigation—is what their profession primarily comprises.

3. MASTERS AND MAGISTRATE JUDGES

Another possible step in a lawsuit involves referring the case to a "parajudge," of which there are two kinds in the federal system.

a. Masters

The use of masters has ancient roots, and Federal Rule 53 now authorizes that use. Today the only kind of master is what was formerly termed a "special master," i.e., someone specially appointed by the district judge to help handle a particular action. The judge supposedly can appoint a master only in rare complicated cases where there is exceptional need, and the master must assist rather than displace the judge or jury. The judge gives the master specific assignments, most often involving ascertainment of facts. Ultimately, the master files a report with the court, but note that the master's factual findings in a nonjury case stand accepted unless clearly erroneous and in a jury case are normally admissible as evidence. Normally the master's compensation, fixed by the court, falls on the parties upon terms directed by the court.

b. Magistrate Judges

Congress created the corps of magistrates in 1968 and has since expanded their jurisdiction several times. See 28 U.S.C.A. §§ 631–639; Federal Rules 72–73. Magistrate judges are salaried judicial officers appointed for a term, a number being appointed for each district by the district judges of that district. In addition to a good deal of criminal work, magistrate judges exercise the following civil jurisdiction under § 636:

(1) a district judge may designate a magistrate judge to serve as a special master;

(2) a district judge may designate a magistrate judge to hear and determine any so-called nondispositive pretrial matter, examples

being some pleading motions and also discovery disputes and pretrial conferences; the judge will consider any party's objections to the magistrate's determination, setting aside any portion shown to be clearly erroneous or to be contrary to law;

(3) a district judge may designate a magistrate judge to conduct hearings, make proposed findings of fact, and recommend disposition with respect to a so-called dispositive pretrial matter, examples being motions for injunctive relief and for summary judgment; the judge must make a de novo determination (upon the record or after additional evidence) on those portions of the magistrate's findings and recommendation that any party objects to;

(4) upon consent of all the parties, the court clerk may refer to a specially designated magistrate judge all proceedings in any case, including trial of a jury or nonjury case and entry of judgment; appeal from the magistrate judge's judgment goes to the appropriate court of appeals; and

(5) district judges may assign to magistrate judges "such additional duties as are not inconsistent with the Constitution and laws of the United States."

Although this procedural innovation has enjoyed heavy use and proved generally successful, the broad extent of the magistrate judges' jurisdiction raises some unsettled constitutional questions of due process and separation of powers.

*

V

Trial

■ ANALYSIS

A. SCENARIO

Trial in federal court follows a relatively settled order by tradition. In large part, trial practice is not laid down by the Federal Rules, but is instead confided to the discretion of the trial judge. Trial practice is the special concern of such upperclass courses as Evidence and Trial Techniques. See generally Roger S. Haydock & John O. Sonsteng, Trial (3d ed. 2004).

1. PLAINTIFF'S CASE

Eventually, a lawsuit that has survived the pretrial gantlet will come to trial under local calendar rules adopted pursuant to Rule 40. At trial, plaintiff ordinarily goes first. The plaintiff's attorney usually makes an *opening statement* to explain what the issues are and what he proposes to prove—an introductory road-map for his case. The defendant's attorney commonly follows with her own opening statement, although she sometimes can but seldom will choose to delay this until the beginning of the defendant's case. Then, to prove his part of the case, the plaintiff's attorney calls his first witness, who is sworn and subjected to direct examination, cross-examination, and possibly redirect examination, recross-examination, and so on. This continues with other witnesses until the plaintiff's attorney rests his case.

a. Burden of Proof

The burden of proof dictates who must produce evidence and ultimately persuade the fact-finder on which elements of the case. Burden of proof encompasses two concepts:

(1) *Burden of Production*. This burden might require either party at a given time during trial to *produce* evidence on an element or suffer the judge's adverse determination on that element.

(2) *Burden of Persuasion*. This burden ultimately requires a certain party to *persuade* the fact-finder of the truth of an element or suffer an adverse determination on that element. The required degree of persuasion in a civil case is normally a "preponderance of the evidence," which requires only a showing of more-probable-than-not.

Usually, but not always, both the initial burden of production and the burden of persuasion are on the party with the burden of allegation, a concept discussed in Chapter IV–A above.

Example: In a federal jury case for negligence, plaintiff need not plead his own due care. However, if defendant carries the burden of allegation by pleading contributory negligence under Rule 8(c)(1), the applicable state law conceivably could allocate the initial burden of production and the burden of persuasion on this element to plaintiff. Then, at trial plaintiff must produce evidence of his own due care to avoid an adverse judgment as a matter of law. Assume that plaintiff comes forward with sufficient evidence and eventually gets to the jury. The jury believes that the evidence is evenly balanced on this issue of due care. (Result: the jury should find against plaintiff, because he must persuade the jury by a preponderance of the evidence that he exercised due care for his own safety.)

b. Rules of Evidence

The rules of evidence include the requirement of relevance and the exclusionary rules of incompetency, privilege, and hearsay. They also govern such matters as examination of witnesses and objections to evidence. In federal court, these rules are embodied in the Federal Rules of Evidence, a *statute* enacted in 1975. See generally Michael H. Graham, Handbook of Federal Evidence (6th ed. 2006); McCormick on Evidence (Kenneth S. Broun gen. ed., 6th ed. 2006). (In a nonjury trial, the judge tends to apply the rules of evidence less strictly than the judge would in a jury trial.)

2. MOTIONS

In a jury trial, when plaintiff rests, defendant may move for *judgment as a matter of law* under Rule 50(a), formerly called a directed verdict. This can be granted if, viewing the plaintiff's evidence in the light reasonably most favorable to plaintiff, a reasonable jury could not find for plaintiff. However, the judge can choose to deny the motion in order to let the trial proceed toward completion. Defendant waives no rights by so moving. (In a nonjury trial, defendant may instead move for *judgment on partial findings* under Rule 52(c). This can be granted if "a party has been fully heard on [a dispositive] issue in a nonjury trial and the court finds against the party on that issue"—a test that is easier to meet than the test for a directed verdict, because here defendant is merely asking the judge as fact-finder for favorable findings without further proof, rather than asking the judge to intervene by withdrawing an extremely weak case from the jury as fact-finder. That is, a judgment on partial findings means that plaintiff has not quite persuaded the judge in a nonjury trial, while a judgment as a matter of law means that plaintiff has not even produced enough evidence to reach the jury in a jury trial.)

3. DEFENDANT'S CASE

If the trial has not been short-circuited by the granting of such a motion, defendant may present her part of the case, either trying to meet the plaintiff's contentions or trying to prove new matter on which defendant has the burden of production. (In a nonjury trial, this stage does not significantly differ from the scenario of a jury trial.)

4. MOTIONS

In a jury trial, when defendant rests, plaintiff may move for judgment as a matter of law under Rule 50(a). Indeed, whenever one side rests, the other side may move for such a judgment. If not granted, plaintiff may then present *rebuttal evidence*, which should attempt to meet any new evidence presented by defendant as opposed to merely adding to the plaintiff's own evidence. Later, defendant may present *rejoinder evidence*, and so on. These phases narrow down in focus, as each is normally limited to meeting new evidence from the prior phase. When both sides finally rest at the close of all the evidence, either side may move for judgment as a matter of law under Rule 50(a). As usual, this can be granted *if, looking only at all the evidence that is favorable to the opponent of the motion but not incredible and also the unquestionable evidence that is favorable to the movant, the judge believes that a reasonable jury could not find for the opponent.* (In a nonjury trial, there can be equivalent motions for judgment on partial findings during this stage.)

5. SUBMISSION OF CASE

If the trial has still not been short-circuited, counsel usually make *closing arguments* that the evidence is on their side, with the plaintiff's attorney ordinarily speaking first and last. In a jury trial, after and/or before closing arguments, the judge gives oral *instructions* to the jury—the judge must determine and then instruct on the law, may summarize the evidence on the contested factual issues, and may but most often does not comment on the evidence by expressing with restraint personal views on its weight and credibility. Rule 51 allows counsel to submit beforehand written requests for specific instructions on the law; it also provides a procedure for specifically objecting, before the jury retires, to the judge's instructions. Then the jury retires to deliberate in isolation on a *verdict*, which will require deciding the contested factual issues. The judge as a matter of discretion will have chosen the kind of verdict, which might be:

(1) a general verdict, through which the jury simply finds in writing for plaintiff or defendant, in theory doing so by having applied the judge's instructions on the law to its own resolutions of the contested factual issues;

(2) a special verdict, "in the form of a special written finding on each issue of fact," under Rule 49(a); or

(3) a general verdict accompanied by answers to "written questions on one or more issues of fact that the jury must decide," under Rule 49(b).

The general verdict is the most common kind; the other two guide and constrain the jury and will better indicate what the jury decided, but might prevent the jury from doing "justice" by fiddling with the law and are so complicated to use that they require the detailed curative provisions of Rule 49. If the jury cannot agree, the judge will eventually discharge the jury and later retry the case with a new jury. If the jury reaches a verdict, the verdict will be returned in open court with the jury present and then be recorded, and the jury will be discharged. See generally Wright's Hornbook § 94. (In a nonjury trial, in lieu of instructions and verdict, "the court must find the facts specially and state its conclusions of law separately." Rule 52(a)(1).)

6. MOTIONS

After decision, judgment is normally entered in conformity therewith, as discussed in Chapter VI–A below. But other motions are still possible to change the outcome of the trial. In a jury trial, these are:

(1) *Judgment as a Matter of Law.* Rule 50(b) authorizes a motion to have the adverse verdict and any judgment thereon set aside and to have judgment entered in the movant's favor, provided that the movant has filed this motion no later than 10 days after entry of judgment and provided that the movant earlier had unsuccessfully moved for judgment as a matter of law under Rule 50(a). This *renewed motion for judgment as a matter of law,* formerly called a motion for judgment notwithstanding the verdict and sometimes called a motion for judgment n.o.v. from its Latin name, can be granted if the test for a directed verdict is met—a judge who grants judgment n.o.v. might have refused a directed verdict in order to let the jury trial run its course, thus possibly avoiding the need for intervention, and to get a jury verdict recorded, thus possibly avoiding the need for retrial after an appeal. However, on a motion for judgment n.o.v., a judge who believes the n.o.v. test is met can instead grant a new trial if that would better serve the ends of justice. See also Rule 50(d).

(2) *New Trial.* Rule 59(a) authorizes a motion to have the adverse verdict and any judgment thereon set aside and to hold a new trial, provided that the movant has filed this motion no later than 10 days after entry of judgment. This motion should be granted if the verdict is "against the weight of the evidence," i.e., *if, looking at all the evidence, the judge is clearly convinced that the jury was in error*—a test that is easier to meet than the test for judgment as a matter of law, but not so easy as to authorize the judge freely to substitute personal opinion for the jury's. Incidentally, the judge can grant a "partial new trial" if the verdict's infected issues are so distinct and separable from the rest of the case that retrial of them alone is possible without injustice; and where a verdict goes against the weight of the evidence by awarding excessive damages to plaintiff, the judge can grant a new trial that plaintiff can avoid by agreeing to a "remittitur" of the damages in excess of the highest amount that would have survived a new trial motion. Additionally, there are other entirely distinct grounds for a new trial. Indeed, Rule 59(a)(1)(A) authorizes a new trial upon motion wherever required to prevent injustice; and within the 10 days a new trial can even be ordered on the court's own initiative, as Rule 59(d) specifies. In particular, there can be a new trial on such grounds as non-harmless *error* by the judge or *misconduct* by the participants in the course of the trial, subject to the requirement that ordinarily there must have been an objection at the time of the error or misconduct; or there can be a new trial on the ground of *newly discovered evidence*.

These two "ten-day motions" may be and usually are made together. The four possible decisions are treated in Rule 50(c) and (e):

(1) *Deny n.o.v.; Deny New Trial.* This decision upholds judgment in accordance with the verdict.

(2) *Deny n.o.v.; Grant New Trial.* This decision leads directly to a retrial.

(3) *Grant n.o.v.; Grant New Trial.* This decision means that a judgment contrary to the verdict will be entered. If that judgment is reversed on appeal, however, there will ordinarily be a new trial in accordance with the trial court's grant of a new trial, which was *conditional* on such reversal. The judge in so ruling was saying: "If I turn out to be wrong in granting judgment n.o.v., I would still believe that a new trial is proper."

(4) *Grant n.o.v.; Deny New Trial.* This decision means that a judgment contrary to the verdict will be entered. If that judgment is reversed on

appeal, however, a judgment in accordance with the verdict will ordinarily be entered, given the trial court's *conditional* denial of a new trial.

See generally Wright's Hornbook § 95. (In a nonjury trial, the roughly analogous ten-day motions are a motion to amend findings under Rule 52(b) and a motion for a new trial under Rule 59(a)(1)(B).) The following graph suggests the critical differences among the various important motions:

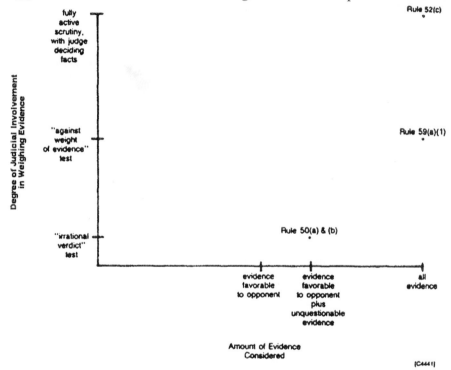

B. JURY AND JUDGE

Many of the complications of trial practice result from the presence of a jury as the fact-finder, and from its interaction with the judge.

1. TRIAL BY JURY

In federal court, there are jury trials as well as some nonjury or "bench" trials. The basic scenarios in these two kinds of trial are similar. (The unique features of nonjury trial were described parenthetically throughout Chapter V–A above. See generally id. § 96.) But several aspects of the jury merit special attention.

a. Formal Characteristics of a Jury

Traditionally a federal civil jury numbered *twelve* members—but now a federal district court may seat as few as six according to *Colgrove v.*

Battin, 413 U.S. 149, 93 S.Ct. 2448 (1973), and Federal Rule 48. Traditionally a federal civil jury's verdict must be *unanimous*, but the parties may stipulate otherwise under Rule 48—the Rule still follows this approach to unanimity, but significantly the Supreme Court has held in a series of cases that there is no constitutional impediment to a limited degree of nonunanimity in state criminal trials.

b. Selection of a Jury

Generally speaking, a panel of jurors is summoned from the body of citizens. See 28 U.S.C.A. §§ 1861–1869. From this panel, the jurors for a particular civil trial are tentatively drawn by lot. These jurors are then subjected to a "voir dire" examination under Federal Rule 47(a), and federal judges usually follow the more desirable practice of conducting this examination themselves. On the basis of the examination or other information, a party may challenge any individual juror or a panel of jurors "for cause," with the court determining whether bias or other grounds for disqualification exist. Also, an individual juror may be excluded by one of either party's typically three "peremptory challenges" under 28 U.S.C.A. § 1870; the manner of exercising these largely arbitrary challenges is a matter of local rule or practice. By continuing this whole process, an impartial and qualified trial jury is eventually selected and then sworn.

c. Right to Trial by Jury

An important question is when trial by jury is allowed. See generally Wright's Hornbook § 92.

1) Sources of Jury Right

In federal court, there will be trial by jury on those contested factual issues:

(1) that are triable of right by a jury under the Seventh Amendment to the Federal Constitution, which provides: "In suits at common law, where the value in controversy shall exceed twenty dollars, the right of trial by jury shall be preserved . . . . ";

(2) that are triable of right by a jury under some federal statute, such as the Jones Act covering certain actions by seamen; or

(3) on which the court, in its discretion with the express or implicit consent of both parties, orders a trial by jury under Federal Rule 39(c)(2).

So there are constitutional and statutory rights, as well as the equivalent possibility of jury trial by consent. Note that allowance of trial by jury is determined on an issue-by-issue basis.

a) Trial by Judge

If an issue does not fall within one of the above-described three categories, it will be tried by the judge. That is, federal courts respect a complementary court-created right to trial by judge, in the absence of contrary constitutional or statutory command. However, the court, in its discretion upon motion or on its own initiative, may try any such issue with the assistance of an *advisory jury* under Rule 39(c)(1). This ancient device is not the same as a jury of right; the judge ultimately must decide the issue as in a nonjury trial, and the judge may accept or reject the advisory jury's finding.

b) Loss of Jury Right

Even if an issue does fall within one of the above-described three categories, it may still be tried by the judge, with or without an advisory jury, as the result of either of two rules:

(1) there is a *waiver* of a constitutional or statutory right to trial by jury if neither party makes a timely written demand for trial by jury on the issue as provided in Rule 38(b)–(d), although the court in its discretion upon motion may relieve such waiver as provided in Rule 39(b); or

(2) the parties may consent to *withdraw* a demand for jury trial, as Rules 38(d) and 39(a)(1) provide.

2) Meaning of Constitutional Jury Right

The biggest problem in this federal scheme is determining the scope of the Seventh Amendment's prohibition on legislative and judicial infringement of the jury right.

a) Historical Test

The starting point is the idea that the Seventh Amendment preserves the common-law jury right prevailing in England in 1791, when the Seventh Amendment was adopted. *First*, this protection rather loosely preserves the procedural incidents of jury trial, such as the number of jurors, but only to the extent necessary to preserve the substance and not the form of common-law trial by jury: the modern jury need only operate substantially the same as the common-law jury. *Second*, this protection rather demandingly preserves the waivable right to go to a jury on all contested factual issues that would have been triable to a common-law jury: this problem of the kinds of issues that go to a jury today is indeed the subject of expansive constitutional interpretation, as explained below. *Third*, the Seventh Amendment goes on to provide that "no fact tried by a jury, shall be otherwise re-examined in any Court of the United States, than according to the rules of the common law": courts today must find a historical antecedent to authorize any review, at the trial or appellate level, of a jury's fact-finding.

b) Problems of Historical Test

It is especially difficult to determine which contested factual issues would have gone to a common-law jury in 1791. Few people now master legal history. Moreover, the law/equity line was not clearly delineated in 1791 and, indeed, was as always in the process of shifting over time. Furthermore, the procedural setting was then so different: on the one hand, many factors other than jury trial affected the old system's allocation of jurisdiction between law and equity and also the parties' choice of courts between law and equity, so it is strange now to make the single consequence of jury right turn on what was then a many-factored decision; on the other hand, we have a *merged procedural system* today with very different procedures, so it is artificial now to recreate the decision between law and equity. It is very uncertain how the changed circumstances should be taken into account in recreating history—at the least the cases now indicate that any historical judicial discretion in choosing between law and equity should be exercised in light of modern realities. In short, the historical test perhaps should not and almost certainly cannot be applied in a pure form any longer, a situation that revives the tension between the popular reverence for the jury and the elitist distaste for the jury.

c) Modified Historical Test

Today, the initial inquiry is whether a contested factual issue arises in a case such that the issue would have been triable of right to a common-law jury, in which event there is a constitutional jury right thereon.

Examples: (1) P sues D in a negligence action for damages. (Result: jury right.)

(2) P sues D in a suit for an injunction. (Result: no jury right.)

Most cases are easily handled under this historical approach, especially where the case presents a single claim for relief. But there are some tough cases in the gray area between the common-law and equity poles, especially where the historical approach is particularly difficult to apply, or leads to some sophisticated exception to the jury right, or is particularly ambivalent in outcome. Under the Supreme Court's decisions, the Seventh Amendment's protection currently tends to reach these gray cases, making it unclear just how much of the historical approach remains in the gray zone. Consider these five major problems:

(1) *New Claims.* Consider first a modern claim that did not exist in the old days. A federal court looks for a historical analogue in light of the nature of the new claim's right and remedy, and it gives a jury right whenever the common law plausibly supplied that analogue. See *Curtis v. Loether*, 415 U.S. 189, 94 S.Ct. 1005 (1974). Recent cases lay special stress on the form of relief, so that damages claims tend to be classified as legal.

(2) *Joinder of Legal and Equitable Claims.* If plaintiff seeks legal and equitable relief cumulatively (or if plaintiff and defendant by claim and by defense or counterclaim seek legal and equitable relief), a federal court allows both plaintiff and defendant a jury right on the legal issues. If an issue is common to the legal and equitable relief, the jury right includes having the jury rather than the judge first reach that issue. The judicial tendency is to ignore subtle historical distinctions—such as the discretionary clean-up doctrine and the old requirements of trying certain equitable issues first—that would limit the jury right of either party. See *Dairy Queen, Inc. v. Wood*, 369 U.S. 469, 82 S.Ct. 894 (1962); *Beacon Theatres, Inc. v. Westover*, 359 U.S. 500, 79 S.Ct. 948 (1959).

(3) *Alternative Remedies.* If plaintiff seeks legal and equitable remedies that are available only alternatively, the lower federal courts seem to give plaintiff and defendant a jury right on the legal and common issues. The tendency is to opt for this simple solution and thus to avoid the incredible complications of recreating this historical situation in a modern procedural setting.

(4) *Equitable Devices.* If a party uses some procedural device that was previously available only in equity—such as interpleader, class action, shareholders' derivative action, intervention, or declaratory judgment—a federal court simply overlooks the device and gives a jury right on legal issues in the underlying claim. This practice might represent a dynamic view that the constitutionally protected realm of the common law has expanded to handle more kinds of cases than in 1791. Or this practice might represent a technique of viewing each issue in isolation, rather than in its contextual setting as part of a case. Either view obliterates the constraints of history. See *Ross v. Bernhard*, 396 U.S. 531, 90 S.Ct. 733 (1970) (also offhandedly suggesting that whether an issue should go to a jury turns in part on the functionality of using a jury).

(5) *Complex Cases.* Some lower federal courts have taken the freewheeling modified historical test and turned it against the jury right, denying a jury right for highly complex but otherwise legal cases. It is currently a subject of dispute, but ultimately doubtful, whether the Seventh Amendment's dictate can be circumvented on the ground of complexity, either because the issues thereby somehow become equitable or because trial by an uncomprehending jury would violate due process.

d. State Practice

State jury practice is widely similar to federal, but it need not be. Very importantly, the Seventh Amendment is not incorporated or implicit in Fourteenth Amendment due process, hence does not apply to the states, and so does not constrain state civil trials. Indeed, the states generally have not followed the Supreme Court's modern expansion of the jury right. However, federal jury practice may occasionally apply in state courts under the reverse-*Erie* doctrine. See *Dice v. Akron, C. & Y.R.R.*, 342 U.S. 359, 72 S.Ct. 312 (1952) (FELA case). On the other hand, state jury practice should generally not apply in federal courts under the *Erie* doctrine. (See Part Five below.)

2. JUDICIAL CONTROLS

As this Chapter V has demonstrated, a critical feature of trial practice is the interaction of judge and jury.

a. Federal Practice

Following the common-law tradition, federal practice leans toward maximizing judicial control of the jury, through such devices as the trial judge's:

(1) prescribing much of trial practice as a matter of discretion;

(2) administering exclusionary and other rules of evidence;

(3) deciding issues of law;

(4) deciding judgment as a matter of law and new trial motions;

(5) giving instructions after rather than before closing arguments;

(6) summarizing and commenting on the evidence; and

(7) using a special verdict or a general verdict with written questions.

However, federal judges often choose not to use all their powers of control.

b. State Practice

Some states aggrandize the role of the jury vis-à-vis the judge and allow it much freer rein, as by the common state prohibition of judicial comment on the evidence.

*

VI

Judgment

■ ANALYSIS

A. ENTRY OF JUDGMENT

The outcome of litigation, reached with or without trial, finds expression in a judgment. More specifically, in federal court, Federal Rule 58 requires a *formal* and *prompt* expression of the outcome in a judgment. Federal Forms 70 and 71 give examples of a judgment—which should be simple and usually must be a separate document. Various time periods (as for taking an appeal) begin running upon entry of the judgment—which can be accomplished in one of two ways:

(1) on a simple verdict or decision, the court clerk promptly prepares, signs, and enters the judgment in the docket book, unless the judge otherwise orders; or

(2) when the outcome is more complicated, the judge promptly approves the form of judgment, and then the court clerk enters it.

For correcting errors, Rule 59(e) authorizes a motion to alter or amend the judgment, filed not later than 10 days after entry. Insignificant mistakes may be corrected at any time under Rule 60(a).

B. KINDS OF RELIEF

Very significant are the kinds of final relief that American courts can give in their judgments. See generally Dan B. Dobbs, Dobbs Law of Remedies (2d ed. 1993). There are two principal categories and several subdivisions thereof, all of which may be given in a single lawsuit pursuant to the applicable substantive law. For explanatory purposes, assume that plaintiff has sued defendant on a single claim for relief.

1. COERCIVE RELIEF
Courts generally can give active relief that the government will enforce. This includes relief formerly associated with both common-law judgments and equity decrees.

a. Legal Relief
There are three types of traditionally legal-type relief, which comes in the form of an award to the prevailing party rather than an order to the losing party.

1) Damages
A court can award plaintiff money damages, including:

(1) actual damages—as fixed by an out-of-pocket, benefit-of-the-bargain, or restitutionary measure—or, alternatively, nominal damages;

(2) punitive damages, in some situations; and

(3) interest on damages, sometimes pre-judgment and always post-judgment.

2) Restoration of Property

A court can award plaintiff the restoration of his real or personal property taken and wrongfully withheld by defendant.

3) Costs

Finally, a court normally awards costs to the prevailing party, either plaintiff or defendant, as part of any judgment. In federal court, Federal Rule 54(d)(1) and 28 U.S.C.A. § 1920 are the central provisions. Costs normally are taxed by the court clerk, whose determinations may upon motion be reviewed by the judge. Costs normally include certain litigation fees and expenses, such as docket fees. Costs normally do not include attorney's fees, which are usually by far the biggest expense; however, this so-called American rule is subject to some significant exceptions, as particular statutes, court rules, and judicial doctrines call for reimbursement of attorney's fees.

b. Equitable Relief

By traditionally equitable-type relief, a court can order defendant to do or not to do something, as by an injunction or an order of specific performance. These discretionary remedies are available when the legal remedies are inadequate.

2. DECLARATORY RELIEF

Courts generally can give passive relief that declares legal relationships.

a. Actions for Declaratory Judgment

Through this largely modern creation, a court can declare the rights and other legal relations of the parties. A potential plaintiff or defendant may bring an action for such a declaration. In federal court, in a case otherwise within federal jurisdiction, this sort of remedy is authorized and governed by 28 U.S.C.A. §§ 2201 and 2202 and Federal Rule 57; but as always, to fall within the constitutional limits of Article III, the dispute must be advanced enough to constitute an actual controversy. See generally Wright's Hornbook § 100.

b. Declarative Effects of Other Judgments

Other judgments, most obviously many judgments other than in personam judgments and also any judgment for defendant, have effects like those of a declaratory judgment.

C. ENFORCEMENT OF JUDGMENT

Of great practical importance is the subject of enforcement of judgments. A lawyer may spend much time in such post-judgment activity. Devices must be available to ensure enforcement of judgments, but these tools must comport with the constitutional requirements of equal protection and due process. The successful plaintiff (or any other prevailing party) seeks local enforcement in the court that rendered judgment. (Interstate and international enforcement of judgments is treated in Chapter XXII below.)

1. LEGAL COERCIVE RELIEF

Legal-type relief awards something to plaintiff, and it is up to plaintiff to enforce the judgment if defendant does not voluntarily satisfy the judgment. The mode of enforcement is cumbersome. The usual tool for enforcing a federal legal-type judgment is a "writ of execution," obtained from the court clerk and directing a marshal to seize literally or figuratively the defendant's property within the state.

Consider in particular the very common judgment for the payment of money. The governing Federal Rule 69(a)(1) states as a general matter that the procedure for enforcement thereof "must accord with the procedure of the state where the district court is located," except that any existing federal statute governs to the extent applicable. That state law provides a maze of enforcement tools. See, e.g., David D. Siegel, New York Practice ch. 18 (4th ed. 2005).

a. Discovery

In connection with a federal judgment for the payment of money, Rule 69(a)(2) specifically provides that plaintiff may use the federal discovery devices or any state post-judgment discovery devices to identify and locate the defendant's assets.

b. Execution

Rule 69(a)(1) also provides: "A money judgment is enforced by a writ of execution, unless the court directs otherwise." The court clerk will deliver the writ to the marshal, and plaintiff usually will tell the marshal about the identity and location of the defendant's property. Following state law, the marshal (or deputy marshal) typically will levy upon so much of the defendant's nonexempt property as is necessary to pay the judgment—and will eventually sell that property if necessary, use the proceeds to cover the marshal's fees and expenses and to satisfy the plaintiff's judgment, and then give any remainder to defendant. Such execution extends even to authorizing the marshal to levy upon a debt owed defendant by a third person.

c. Supplementary Proceedings

Rule 69(a)(1) implies that if execution on such a judgment is not fully successful, the judge may permit plaintiff to use any additional enforcement devices that are available under state law and which are termed "supplementary proceedings." For example, most states provide a means for compelling defendant or a third person to appear before a judge to undergo sworn examination and for obtaining a court order that commands the person to take steps to satisfy the judgment. Such court orders include a turnover order and an installment payment order. Such orders are essentially equitable relief.

2. EQUITABLE COERCIVE RELIEF

Equitable-type relief consists of a court order that operates directly upon defendant. In case of disobedience, the court will usually enforce its order through contempt proceedings.

a. Civil Contempt

Civil contempt proceedings benefit plaintiff, by (1) a compensatory payment from defendant to plaintiff or (2) a compulsive sanction of imprisoning defendant until she complies or imposing fines conditional on continued noncompliance.

b. Criminal Contempt

Criminal contempt proceedings punish defendant for disobedience of a court order, by a fixed jail term or an unconditional fine.

c. Other Enforcement Tools

Among other enforcement tools, there are now some provisions for using legal enforcement techniques to enforce an equitable judgment.

For example, Federal Rule 70 provides, among other things, for enforcing a judgment ordering defendant to do a specific act by the court's directing the act to be done by some other person appointed by the court. Note also that the above-discussed Rule 69(a)(1) applies to an equitable judgment ordering defendant to pay money, thus making a writ of execution the usual tool for enforcement thereof.

D. RELIEF FROM JUDGMENT

The subject of obtaining relief from judgment, as where a judgment was obtained by fraud, is treated in Chapter XVII–C below—along with a study of the effects of a judgment in subsequent civil litigation.

VII

Appeal

■ ANALYSIS

A. **Appealability**
   1. Routes to Court of Appeals
   2. Routes to Supreme Court
B. **Reviewability**
   1. Standards of Review
   2. Appellate Procedure

A. APPEALABILITY

An "appealable" decision is one that can receive immediate appellate review. A party can take an appealable decision of a federal district court possibly through *two levels* of appellate review. First, there is an appeal to the appropriate court of appeals—the primary function of this appeal is *correctness review*, which mainly tries to satisfy a litigant's desire for the correct result and which implies at least one appeal of statutory right in some court in every case. Second, there may be review by the Supreme Court—the primary function here is *institutional review*, which mainly tries to serve the systemic need for overview of the judicial lawmaking branch and which implies largely discretionary review in a single court only in important cases. Reform of many aspects of this scheme is always under consideration.

1. ROUTES TO COURT OF APPEALS

The basic jurisdictional rule, drawn from the common law, says that only final decisions of a district court are appealable to the court of appeals—but drawing on the tradition of equity, the courts and Congress have created a series of exceptions to make some other decisions appealable. The overriding idea is to strike an optimal balance primarily between the general desire for the net efficiency of delaying appeal to the end of the case and the specific need for the net fairness of immediate appellate review.

a. Final Decisions

The final decision rule finds expression in 28 U.S.C.A. § 1291. If the district court has fully treated the case, except for award of costs and enforcement of judgment, then its judgment is appealable. If not, as where the district court has granted a new trial, there is normally no immediate appeal. But the courts have played with this meaning of "final decision." See generally Wright's Hornbook § 101.

1) Collateral Order Doctrine

There are several judge-made doctrines that treat certain categories of orders in the course of an action as final decisions under § 1291. See 15A Wright, Miller & Cooper § 3910 ("Hardship: Orders Transferring Property"), § 3912 ("Death Knell Orders"), 15B id. § 3917 (certain "Contempt Orders"). The most important is the collateral order doctrine recognized in *Cohen v. Beneficial Indus. Loan Corp.*, 337 U.S. 541, 69 S.Ct. 1221 (1949) (denial of defendant's motion to require security for bringing suit). For a type of order to be appealable thereunder, (1) the order must conclusively determine an issue, (2) that issue must be separate from the merits of the action, and (3) the important order must be effectively unreviewable on later appeal from a final judgment and thus impose the risk of irreparable injury. Any attempt at rigidly defining a category, such as this doctrine, is inevitably *inaccurate* in that it allows some unnecessary appeals and fails to reach other needy cases. Moreover, this particular category proves *uncertain* in application, especially as the appellate courts deform it in order to come to the optimal result on appealability; and thus this doctrine breeds wasteful disputes at the threshold of the court of appeals.

2) **Ad Hoc Approach**

Very rarely, the court of appeals treats an appealed order as a final decision under § 1291 simply because the needs for immediate appellate review are deemed strong relative to the reasons behind the final decision rule. See, e.g., *Gillespie v. United States Steel Corp.*, 379 U.S. 148, 85 S.Ct. 308 (1964). Obviously, this free-form approach multiplies wasteful threshold disputes on appealability. Naturally, the appellate courts then yearn to reduce the approach to a narrowly defined category.

3) **Rule 54(b)**

In multi-claim and multi-party litigation, the district court may under Federal Rule 54(b) render an appealable ruling that disposes of fewer than all of the claims or parties by directing entry of a final judgment on that part of the case "if the court expressly determines that there is no just reason for delay." That is, within the Rule's limits, the district court can in its informed discretion authorize appeal of certain decisions under § 1291—thus readily picking out appropriate rulings for appeal and labeling them with certainty as being appealable. Note that here the parties may waive the right to appellate review by failure to take a timely appeal from a Rule 54(b) judgment.

b. **Interlocutory Decisions**

In addition to the above-discussed masked exceptions to the final decision rule, there are four explicit exceptions that directly allow review of avowedly interlocutory decisions. See generally Wright's Hornbook § 102.

1) **28 U.S.C.A. § 1292(a)**

This statute carves out a number of categories of interlocutory decisions for immediate appeal. Most importantly, § 1292(a)(1) allows immediate appeal of decisions concerning injunctions. Even here, there are remarkable disputes about what does and does not fall within this category.

2) **Mandamus**

In a case that ultimately could be within the court of appeals' jurisdiction—and upon a clear and indisputable showing that the district court has usurped power, disregarded a duty to exercise power, or perhaps just abused its discretion—the court of appeals may under 28 U.S.C.A. § 1651(a) immediately review and correct the district court's action or inaction by granting a petition for a writ of mandamus. Currently, the appellate courts are attempting to restrict this irregular and extraordinary, but essentially ad hoc, means of review to a more narrowly defined category.

3) **28 U.S.C.A. § 1292(b)**

This statute permits an immediate appeal of an interlocutory decision (1) if the district court in its discretion has certified that the decision "involves a controlling question of law" on which there exists "substantial ground for difference of opinion" and also that an immediate appeal "may materially advance the ultimate termination of the litigation" and (2) if the court of appeals in its discretion agrees to hear the appeal. Because both the district court and the court of appeals must agree to allow such an appeal, appeals under § 1292(b) are uncommon.

4) **28 U.S.C.A. § 1292(e)**

This statute, added in 1992, authorizes the Supreme Court to prescribe Federal Rules that would allow immediate appeal of types of interlocutory decisions. So far, the Supreme Court in 1998 promulgated Rule 23(f), by which the court of appeals in its discretion may permit an immediate appeal from an order granting or denying class certification.

2. ROUTES TO SUPREME COURT

Under 28 U.S.C.A. § 1254, there are two routes from a court of appeals to the Supreme Court. See generally Wright's Hornbook § 106. See also id. § 105 (direct review of district-court decisions by Supreme Court in special circumstances).

a. Certiorari

The usual route is under § 1254(1)—a petition for a writ of certiorari. Any party can so petition at any time after the case reaches the court of appeals. Granting a petition means only that the Supreme Court will review the case; but the Court grants a petition only where there are special and important systemic reasons for review. Review by certiorari is thus a matter of discretion, not right.

b. Certification

The court of appeals under § 1254(2) theoretically may, but very rarely does, certify at any time any question of law as to which instructions are desired.

B. REVIEWABILITY

A "reviewable" issue is one that the appellate court will consider on appeal from a trial-court decision. Ordinarily, to be reviewable an act by the trial court that supposedly infects the decision must have been objected to at the time of the act, must appear on the record, and must be asserted on appeal. Moreover, the appellate court simply will not review certain issues; for example, on appeal from final judgment it will not examine the denial of the defendant's motion for judgment as a matter of law at the close of the plaintiff's case if defendant "waived" the point by proceeding with her own evidence. Finally, the alleged error must not have been harmless, as 28 U.S.C.A. § 2111 specifies for the federal courts.

1. STANDARDS OF REVIEW

There are basically three degrees of scrutiny that the appellate court applies in reviewing these issues. The applicable degree of scrutiny is fixed by a complex balancing of the needs for appellate review of the issue (such as controlling possible abuses by the trial judge and maintaining uniformity of the law) against the policies that favor limited review (such as conserving resources and respecting the fact-finder).

a. Nondeferential Review

The appellate court makes a virtually fresh determination of questions of law. As always, the law/fact distinction is fuzzy and chameleonic. But legal questions here include allegedly erroneous instructions on the law to the jury and also the judge's decision on a motion for judgment as a matter of law at the close of all the evidence.

b. Middle–Tier Review

The appellate court shows deference on most determinations for which presence on the trial-court scene was important. The appellate court does not disturb such a determination unless it is clearly convinced there was error.

1) Clearly Erroneous Test

Fact-findings by a judge in a nonjury trial stand "unless clearly erroneous, and the reviewing court must give due regard to the trial court's opportunity to judge the witnesses' credibility." Federal Rule 52(a)(6).

2) Abuse of Discretion Test

Discretionary rulings, such as a decision on a new trial motion based on misconduct of counsel, stand unless there was an "abuse of discretion."

c. Highly Restricted Review

The appellate court intrudes on other determinations only in the most extreme situations. Thus, a denial of a new trial motion based on the weight of the evidence—where the court of appeals is reviewing the trial judge's approving review of the sacrosanct jury's verdict—should very rarely be disturbed.

2. APPELLATE PROCEDURE

Appeal does not entail a retrial of the case, but a rather academic reconsideration of the reviewable issues in search of prejudicial error.

a. Court of Appeals

Procedure in the courts of appeals is largely governed by the Federal Rules of Appellate Procedure and local circuit rules. Speaking generally, the party appealing an appealable decision must timely file a simple *notice of appeal* with the clerk of the district court—note that this is the sole jurisdictional step, but remember that appeal can be waived. With the help of counsel, that clerk then assembles and transmits the *record* to the court of appeals, where the clerk of the court of appeals files the record. A panel of three judges hears the appeal on the record and on the *briefs* of counsel; usually there is also oral argument. The panel then affirms, reverses, or modifies the decision by majority vote. See generally

Gregory A. Castanias & Robert H. Klonoff, Federal Appellate Practice and Procedure in a Nutshell (2008); Wright's Hornbook § 104.

b. Supreme Court

Procedure in the Supreme Court is largely governed by the Rules of the Supreme Court of the United States. Speaking generally, the Court decides, on the basis of a first round of papers timely submitted, whether to consider fully the issues presented. If four or more Justices wish full consideration, the issues are briefed on the merits and heard on oral argument. The Court then affirms, reverses, or modifies the decision by majority vote. See generally Robert L. Stern, Eugene Gressman, Stephen M. Shapiro & Kenneth S. Geller, Supreme Court Practice (8th ed. 2002); Wright's Hornbook § 108.

c. Stays

The pendency of an appeal usually stays proceedings in the court below. Also, there are complex provisions for staying enforcement of the judgment prior to the conclusion of the appeal stage. See Federal Rule 62; Federal Rule of Appellate Procedure 8; 28 U.S.C.A. § 1651(a). Some such stays of enforcement are automatic, but many rest successively in the discretion of the district court, the court of appeals or a judge thereof, and a Justice of the Supreme Court or the whole Court. Usually, such a stay is conditioned upon the applicant's giving a bond.

REVIEW QUESTIONS

Questions (1)–(5): P sold machinery to D. Although D took delivery of the machinery, he failed to pay. So P sues him for breach of contract in a diversity action in federal court.

1. **T or F**   Federal pleading rules govern.

2. **T or F**   A complaint simply stating that D owes P $115,000 for goods sold and delivered to D on August 19 of last year is sufficient.

3. **T or F**   If D moves to dismiss for insufficiency of process and fails on that motion, he may raise a defense of lack of jurisdiction over his person in the answer.

4. **T or F**   If D moves to dismiss for insufficiency of process and fails on that motion, he may raise a defense of lack of subject-matter jurisdiction in the answer.

5. **T or F**   In D's answer, he denies that P delivered the machinery. P must respond to this defense in a reply.

Questions (6)–(9): Paul, a landlord, rented to Donna Dart. She failed to pay her rent due on May 1. Paul files an action and serves her in April of the following year, seeking to recover the month's rent owed. He sues in a state court that follows the Federal Rules model.

6. **T or F**   Assume that Donna was properly served, but the complaint named "Dora Dart" as defendant. If after the one-year statute of limitations runs Paul amends the complaint to read "Donna Dart," the action will not be time-barred.

7. **T or F**   If Paul served Donna on April 28 and she moved to dismiss on May 2, he may not amend his complaint on May 3 without leave of court.

8. **T or F**   If Paul seeks to discover material that would not be admissible in evidence at trial, Donna need not comply.

9. **T or F**   Paul will probably not be able to compel Donna to submit to a physical examination.

Questions (10)–(13): P and D are running for the same elective office. On television, D says that P has a loathsome disease. P sues D for defamation in a state court that follows the Federal Rules model.

10. **T or F** Assume that after P presents her case to the jury, D moves for judgment as a matter of law. The motion can be granted if, viewing P's evidence in the light reasonably most favorable to her, a reasonable jury could not find for her.

11. **T or F** After D presents his case to the jury, P may not move for judgment as a matter of law.

12. **T or F** If at the close of all the evidence D again moves for judgment as a matter of law, he will prevail if, looking at all the evidence, the judge is clearly convinced that the jury should not find for P.

13. **T or F** If instead D does not move for judgment as a matter of law before or at the close of all the evidence, and if the jury irrationally finds for P, D then can make a renewed motion for judgment as a matter of law.

Questions (14)–(15): Dave and Paula own adjoining plots of land. Dave begins digging a well and accidentally floods Paula's property. Paula files suit against Dave in an appropriate federal district court, the requirements of diversity jurisdiction being satisfied.

14. Which of the following is most accurate?

   a.   If Paula seeks an injunction, she will be entitled to a jury trial.

   b.   If she seeks money damages, she will not be entitled to a jury trial.

   c.   If she seeks both money damages and an injunction, she will not be entitled to a jury trial.

   d.   If she seeks both money damages and an injunction, she will be entitled to a jury trial.

   e.   If she fails to make a timely written demand for trial by jury, there will be no jury trial.

15. Paula is awarded $15,000 in damages. Which of the following is most accurate?

   a.   To enforce her judgment, she must now bring an action upon the judgment.

    b.   She may not use federal discovery devices to locate Dave's assets.

    c.   A United States marshal or deputy marshal will, if necessary, enforce her judgment.

    d.   Even if Dave continues to refuse to pay, he cannot be held in civil contempt.

Questions (16)–(17): D kicks P. Later P sues D to recover for his personal injuries, bringing the action in an appropriate federal district court.

16.   To whom of the following is an immediate appeal available?

    a.   A witness, who is jailed for refusing to testify.

    b.   D, if the judge overrules her hearsay objection.

    c.   P, if the judge denies his motion to dismiss.

17.   Upon judgment for D after a nonjury trial, P appeals. Which of the following may the court of appeals do?

    a.   Reject erroneous findings of fact by the judge.

    b.   Reject erroneous conclusions of law by the judge.

    c.   Order P and D to testify before the court of appeals if the record is unclear.

    d.   Order a directed verdict for P.

18.   Prepare an essay in response to this question:

Pip sues Dion for breach of a construction contract in the United States District Court for the District of Taylor, asking specific performance of the contract or, alternatively, damages for breach of the contract. Jurisdiction rests on diversity of citizenship, and the matter in controversy greatly exceeds the jurisdictional amount.

The law of the State of Taylor provides for jury trial in all suits seeking any remedy for breach of contract and requires a unanimous verdict by a six-person jury. A federal local rule for the District of Taylor provides that any verdict in a civil case in which there is a right to jury trial be "by a jury of twelve, seven of whom must concur to render a verdict, unless otherwise stipulated pursuant to Federal Rule 48."

Pip makes a timely written demand for trial by jury. He very much wants a jury and wants one that has to act unanimously. Dion does not. Pip is perfectly willing to litigate these procedural questions to the hilt. Will Pip's jury wishes come true?

*

PART THREE

Authority to Adjudicate

■ ANALYSIS

*

VIII

Subject–Matter Jurisdiction

■ ANALYSIS

A. INTRODUCTION TO SUBJECT–MATTER JURISDICTION

For a court properly to undertake a civil adjudication, the court must have jurisdiction over the subject matter. That is, it must have, under applicable constitutional and statutory provisions, *authority to adjudicate the type of controversy before the court.*

1. ENDS

In delineating this requirement, constitutions and statutes divide functions among the organs of government, thus accommodating federal and state authority, separating courts from the other governmental branches, and differentiating one court from another. Accordingly, the requirement of jurisdiction over the subject matter is taken very seriously, generating the commonly repeated rules (1) that the parties cannot confer subject-matter jurisdiction by consent, collusion, waiver, or estoppel and (2) that the court must ever be ready to question its own subject-matter jurisdiction.

2. MEANS

Constitutions and statutes specify the scope of the courts' subject-matter jurisdiction in various terms. For example, a particular court might be empowered to hear patent cases or be excluded from hearing cases against the government involving more than $10,000. However, unlike territorial authority to adjudicate, subject-matter jurisdiction is defined in essentially nongeographic terms.

B. STATE COURTS

A state may organize its judicial branch as it wishes. There are courts of *original jurisdiction*, where an action may be initiated—and one to three levels of courts of *appellate jurisdiction*, where a judgment of a lower court may be reviewed. The state constitution and statutes prescribe the subject-matter jurisdiction of these courts, although federal statutes do impose certain limits described below.

1. GENERAL VERSUS LIMITED JURISDICTION

Among the courts of original jurisdiction in the typical state, there will be one set of courts of *general jurisdiction*, with courthouses all over the state. Such a court can hear any type of action, unless specifically prohibited by constitution or statute. There will also be several sets of courts of *limited jurisdiction*. These inferior courts can hear only those types of actions that are specifically consigned to them, such as small claims or probate matters.

2. EXCLUSIVE VERSUS CONCURRENT JURISDICTION

State courts entertain most of this nation's judicial business. A great deal of this business can be handled only by state courts, because the subject-matter jurisdiction of the federal courts is sharply limited.

Example: P of New York wishes to sue D of New York for $160,000, alleging injuries incurred in a traffic accident. (Result: P must sue in a state court.)

Among the cases that the federal courts can hear, most can also be heard in state courts. The federal and state courts have *concurrent jurisdiction* in these cases.

Example: P of New York wishes to sue D of Massachusetts for $160,000, alleging injuries incurred in a traffic accident. (Result: P may choose between state and federal court.)

Among the cases that the federal courts can hear, a few are restricted by federal statute to the federal courts. Thus, the federal courts have *exclusive jurisdiction* in these cases.

Example: P wishes to sue D for patent infringement. (Result: P must sue in a federal court.) 28 U.S.C.A. § 1338(a).

C. FEDERAL COURTS

Article III of the Federal Constitution establishes the Supreme Court of the United States, and Articles I and III give Congress the power to establish lower federal courts as it sees fit. See generally Wright's Hornbook §§ 2–5. In addition to a number of territorial and other specialized federal courts, the federal system today comprises a three-tiered pyramid of courts:

(1) *District Courts.* The United States District Courts are the principal federal courts of original jurisdiction. There is such a district court for each of 91 districts, with one to four districts within each state, the District of Columbia, and Puerto Rico. The judges of each district normally sit singly. The district court exercises subject-matter jurisdiction to be described below.

(2) *Courts of Appeals.* The United States Courts of Appeals are at the next higher level. There is such a court of appeals for each of 12 regional circuits, as shown on the following map. The judges of each circuit normally sit in panels of three. The court of appeals, as its foremost duty, exercises appellate

jurisdiction over the district courts in the circuit (28 U.S.C.A. §§ 1291–1292). Additionally, there is a thirteenth court of appeals named the United States Court of Appeals for the Federal Circuit, which similarly hears appeals from a number of specialized tribunals and also hears appeals from all district courts in cases involving certain special areas such as patents or certain claims against the United States (28 U.S.C.A. § 1295).

(3) *Supreme Court*. The Supreme Court is at the summit. There is one Supreme Court in Washington, D.C. Its nine Justices normally sit as a group. The Supreme Court, most significantly, exercises a small original jurisdiction (28 U.S.C.A. § 1251), appellate jurisdiction for important cases coming up from the federal courts of appeals (28 U.S.C.A. § 1254), and appellate jurisdiction for important federal questions decided by the highest state courts (28 U.S.C.A. § 1257).

Article III, as modified by the Eleventh Amendment, marks the outer boundary of federal subject-matter jurisdiction. It extends the federal judicial power to certain types of cases defined in terms of the nature of the claim (e.g., admiralty jurisdiction) or the status of the parties (e.g., controversies to which the United States is a party). See generally Wright's Hornbook § 8. Moreover, Articles I and III give Congress a fairly free hand in allocating to the federal courts or withholding from them the jurisdiction delimited by Article III. Congress has invoked this authority through a whole series of jurisdictional statutes. See generally id. § 10. Thus, for a case to come within the jurisdiction of a federal court, the case normally must fall (1) within some congressional authorization and (2) within the bounds of the Constitution. In sum, the federal courts are courts of limited jurisdiction, according with the basic principle of American federalism whereby the federal government is a government of limited powers. See generally id. § 7.

1. FEDERAL QUESTIONS

Most importantly, Article III extends the federal judicial power to cases "arising under" the Constitution, federal statutory or common law, or treaties. Congress has acted thereunder to vest original jurisdiction for such cases in the district courts, both by the general provision in 28 U.S.C.A. § 1331 and by a string of special statutes.

a. Constitutional Provision

The constitutional phrase of "arising under" sweepingly embraces all cases that include a federal "ingredient." See *Osborn v. Bank of the United States*, 22 U.S. 738 (1824) (Marshall, C.J.) (constitutional language autho-

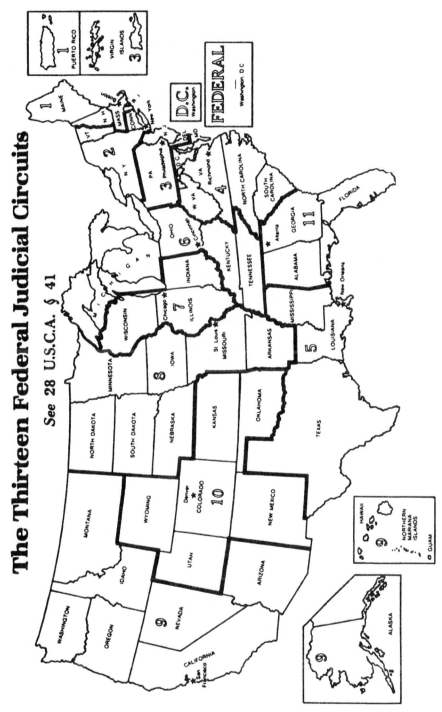

The Thirteen Federal Judicial Circuits

See 28 U.S.C.A. § 41

rized Congress to bestow federal jurisdiction over all actions brought by the federally chartered bank, because any such action would at least have as an ingredient the minor federal question of whether the bank under its charter has the power to sue). This broad reading of the

Constitution means that Congress has wide power to bestow federal question jurisdiction on the federal courts, even where the federal element in a case is slight and not really in issue. But remember, for a case to come within district-court jurisdiction, Congress must have exercised its power in an applicable jurisdictional statute.

b. Statutory Provisions

1)   28 U.S.C.A. § 1331

This statute uses almost the same language as the Constitution, but it has been read much more narrowly. In order to keep themselves from being overwhelmed by a flood of cases having a mere federal ingredient, the federal courts have read three major restrictions into the statutory phrase of "arising under."

a)   Adequate Federal Element

It is clear that the statute, as construed, requires the case to have more than a federal ingredient. It is not clear how much more. A common but sometimes inaccurate formulation is that federal law must create the claim. A more accurate formulation is necessarily less definite: an important element of plaintiff's claim must be of federal origin. See generally Wright's Hornbook § 17.

b)   Well–Pleaded Complaint Rule

The federal element must also be such as would appear on the face of a properly pleaded complaint. The reasons for this difficult and obstructive rule are rather weak: (1) by making jurisdiction determinable at the very outset, the rule saves the time and money that would be wasted in litigating a case ultimately dismissed on jurisdictional grounds; (2) the rule gives plaintiff certainty as to jurisdiction, because it avoids the situation where defendant could veto jurisdiction by omitting the expected federal question from her response; and (3) the rule ensures that conceptually the court has power to require a response from defendant. See generally id. § 18.

Example: Plaintiffs sued a railroad for specific performance of an agreement to issue free passes, which the railroad allegedly refused to issue because a subsequent federal statute prohibited the giving of free passes. Plaintiffs further alleged that the statute was inapplicable or unconstitutional. (Result: no federal question jurisdiction, because the federal questions appear only in relation to an improperly anticipated defense.) *Louisville & N.R.R. v. Mottley*, 211 U.S. 149, 29 S.Ct. 42 (1908).

c) Substantiality Rule

The basis of the federal claim must be nonfrivolous, in order to avoid dismissal on jurisdictional grounds. See generally 13B Wright, Miller & Cooper § 3564.

2) Special Statutes

Note that § 1331 neither covers the whole range of the federal question clause in the Constitution nor makes the federal jurisdiction exclusive. However, if applicable, one of the special federal question statutes might avoid some of the restrictions read into § 1331, or might impose other restrictions, or might make the jurisdiction exclusive. Many of these special statutes are found in title 28 of U.S.C.A., such as § 1338 (patents and the like); others are scattered elsewhere, such as 15 U.S.C.A. §§ 15 and 26 (antitrust actions).

2. DIVERSITY OF CITIZENSHIP

Article III extends the federal judicial power to controversies between citizens of different states ("diversity jurisdiction") and those between state citizens and foreign citizens ("alienage jurisdiction"). Congress has acted thereunder to vest original jurisdiction for such cases in the district courts, both by the general provision in 28 U.S.C.A. § 1332(a) and by special statutes such as the interpleader statute in 28 U.S.C.A. § 1335. However, Congress has restricted the federal jurisdiction by imposing jurisdictional amount requirements on most such cases.

a. Constitutional Provision

The Constitution requires only "partial (or minimal) diversity," which is satisfied in any action that involves a state citizen as a party when any opposing party is of different citizenship. See *State Farm Fire & Cas. Co. v. Tashire*, 386 U.S. 523, 87 S.Ct. 1199 (1967) (interpleader). Thus, Congress has broad power to bestow diversity and alienage jurisdiction on the federal courts.

b. Statutory Provisions

Congress has neither bestowed on the federal courts the whole constitutional range of diversity and alienage jurisdiction nor made the federal jurisdiction exclusive.

1) 28 U.S.C.A. § 1332(a)

This statute bestows federal jurisdiction, where the matter in controversy exceeds $75,000, for actions (1) between citizens of different states, with or without foreign citizens as additional parties on either or both sides, and (2) between state citizens and foreign citizens. This general statute is much criticized, largely on the ground that it has outlived its traditional justification of providing a federal forum to avoid state-court bias against litigants from other states. See generally Wright's Hornbook § 23.

a) Complete Diversity

Reading the statutory language more narrowly than the almost identical constitutional language, the Supreme Court has held that the statute requires "complete diversity." That is, no two opposing parties can be citizens of the same state. See *Strawbridge v. Curtiss*, 7 U.S. 267 (1806) (Marshall, C.J.).

Example: P–1 of New York and P–2 of California sue D–1 of New Mexico and D–2 of California. (Result: no diversity jurisdiction, because citizens of the same state are on opposing sides of the action.)

b) Realignment of Parties

In determining jurisdiction, the court does not treat as conclusive the pleadings' alignment of the parties as plaintiffs and defendants. Instead, the court will realign the parties for jurisdictional purposes according to the ultimate interest of each. See *City of Indianapolis v. Chase Nat'l Bank*, 314 U.S. 63, 62 S.Ct. 15 (1941). Realignment may either create or defeat jurisdiction.

c) Devices to Create Jurisdiction

In order to get a case into federal court, a potential plaintiff will sometimes assign his claim to someone whose citizenship is different from the defendant's, or use some analogous tactic. However, such tactics will often fail. See *Kramer v. Caribbean*

Mills, Inc., 394 U.S. 823, 89 S.Ct. 1487 (1969). First, courts ignore the citizenship of any named party whose interest at stake is strictly nominal, such as a purely formal obligee. Second, 28 U.S.C.A. § 1359 says to ignore the citizenship of any party "improperly or collusively" named. In applying § 1359, courts look for a motive to manufacture federal jurisdiction. But as the named party's interest at stake becomes more substantial, the motive necessary for triggering § 1359 must increasingly be a blatant one. Indeed, if the named party has a very real or even exclusive interest, and bears no resemblance whatsoever to a straw party, then his or her citizenship is considered, as motive in naming the party again becomes irrelevant. A complete and absolute transfer of interest will thus affect jurisdiction.

d) **Devices to Defeat Jurisdiction**

In order to prevent defendant from removing the action to federal court (see Section C–3 below), a potential plaintiff will sometimes try to destroy complete diversity by joining a party whose state citizenship is the same as an opposing party's. If the joined party is not nominal, this device will often work, because there is no general equivalent of 28 U.S.C.A. § 1359 that would prohibit obstruction of federal jurisdiction. Nevertheless, some courts of late have invoked an inherent power to reject artificial devices that would defeat jurisdiction, shaping the so-called fraudulent joinder doctrine into a kind of converse § 1359.

e) **Meaning of Citizenship**

Citizenship is determined as of the time when jurisdiction was invoked.

Examples: (1) P, a citizen of New York, wishes to sue D, a citizen of New York, for $160,000 in damages from an automobile accident. To create diversity, P validly establishes a new domicile in New Jersey. P then sues in federal court. (Result: diversity jurisdiction exists.)

(2) Subsequently, the same P moves again, establishing a new domicile back in New York. (Result: diversity jurisdiction is not ousted.)

For an individual, state citizenship requires the person (1) to be a U.S. citizen (or have the equivalent status of permanent resident alien) and (2) to be domiciled in the state; however, foreign citizenship requires the person only to be a citizen of the foreign country under its laws. Accordingly, an American domiciled abroad or a person without any national citizenship status does not come within the crudely written jurisdictional statute, and so cannot sue or be sued in federal court based on the diversity statute. A person has only one such domicile at a time; to acquire a new domicile, a person must (1) be physically present in the new place (2) with the intention to make his home there indefinitely. *For a corporation*, the usual reading of the definition in § 1332(c)(1) makes an American corporation a citizen (1) of every state by which it has been incorporated and also (2) of the one state in which it has its principal place of business, if its principal place of business is in America; under that statute, courts used to treat a foreign corporation as a citizen only of the country of incorporation, but they are today shifting toward treating it as a citizen also of its principal place of business. Determining the principal place of business is a factual question that requires looking at the locale of both the corporate activities and its management, although giving somewhat more weight to the former factor. *For an unincorporated association*, the courts treat it like a group of individuals and so deem it a citizen of every state and country of which one of its members is a citizen. Such a rule sharply diminishes the chance that federal jurisdiction will exist. However, a class action covering the association's members may offer an avenue into federal court, because only the citizenships of the named representatives are considered and not the citizenships of all class members. See generally Wright's Hornbook §§ 24, 26–28.

f) Exceptions to 28 U.S.C.A. § 1332

Neither domestic relations cases nor probate proceedings come within the statute. These exceptions, which judges carved out long ago and which they preserve because of a desire not to interfere in matters better left to state courts, give rise to difficult definitional problems. See generally Wright's Hornbook § 25.

2) 28 U.S.C.A. § 1335

This statute bestows federal jurisdiction, where the amount in controversy equals or exceeds $500, for interpleader actions involving claimants that include a state citizen and someone of different citizenship. (See the discussion of multi-party litigation in Chapter XIV below.) Using the federal courts to adjudicate special kinds of cases involving dispersed parties, such as interpleader actions, represents a good use of the constitutional authorization of diversity and alienage jurisdiction.

3) 28 U.S.C.A. § 1369

A less well-executed attempt to handle complex litigation in federal court came in the Multiparty, Multiforum Trial Jurisdiction Act of 2002. It now appears in 28 U.S.C.A. § 1369 ("original jurisdiction of any civil action involving minimal diversity between adverse parties that arises from a single accident, where at least 75 natural persons have died in the accident at a discrete location" with dispersed defendants or events), § 1391(g) (venue "in any district in which any defendant resides or in which a substantial part of the accident giving rise to the action took place"), § 1441(e) (removal), § 1697 (nationwide process), and § 1785 (nationwide subpoenas).

4) 28 U.S.C.A. § 1332(d)

An important extension of jurisdiction came in the Class Action Fairness Act of 2005, which covers interstate class actions, with the expressed intent of defeating plaintiff lawyers' manipulation of state courts by funneling more class actions away from the state courts and into the federal courts. By 28 U.S.C.A. § 1332(d), Congress bestowed original jurisdiction on the federal district courts for sizable multistate class actions, generally if there is minimal diversity between any plaintiff member of the class and any defendant and if the plaintiff class contains at least 100 members and their claims aggregated together exceed $5 million. By 28 U.S.C.A. § 1453, Congress further provided that any defendant alone can remove such a class action from state court to the local federal district court.

c. **Jurisdictional Amount**

Various statutes impose a jurisdictional amount requirement, but by far the most important is the requirement in 28 U.S.C.A. § 1332(a) that "the matter *in controversy exceeds the sum or value of $75,000, exclusive of interest and costs." See 14B Wright, Miller & Cooper § 3701. The purpose of such a requirement is to keep petty controversies out of the federal courts. However, what it seems to do best is to create litigation over how it should be applied.*

1) **Test Applied**

To satisfy this jurisdictional amount requirement, if plaintiff pleads a claim for more than $75,000 against defendant, the party invoking federal jurisdiction must be able to show that the plaintiff's judgment could legally exceed $75,000 under the applicable law. The amount in controversy is measured under the state of affairs that existed when the action was commenced in or removed to federal court.

Example: Invoking diversity jurisdiction, P sues D on a $75,000 interest-free promissory note, seeking the $75,000 debt plus $500,000 in punitive damages. D challenges jurisdiction. (Result: dismissal if punitive damages in contract actions are not recoverable under the applicable law, because then the award of damages could not legally exceed $75,000.)

This test is called the legal-certainty test, because an allegation in excess of $75,000 survives challenge unless there is *legal* certainty that damages will not exceed $75,000. *Saint Paul Mercury Indem. Co. v. Red Cab Co.*, 303 U.S. 283, 58 S.Ct. 586 (1938). The test is very easily passed, especially in unliquidated tort cases, because jurisdiction exists even though a recovery over $75,000 is on the *facts* highly unlikely. Some courts will at an early stage dismiss occasional cases in which requested damages are very flagrantly exaggerated, but all tests routinely more rigorous than the legal-certainty test have proved impractical. See generally Wright's Hornbook §§ 33–35.

a) **Interest and Costs**

In applying this jurisdictional amount requirement, the court will not include any interest on the underlying claim or any court costs expected to be awarded in the instant suit. However, problem cases exist here.

Example: P sues D for $76,000 in interest owing on P's loan to D. (Result: jurisdictional amount exists. See *Brown v. Webster*, 156 U.S. 328, 15 S.Ct. 377 (1895) (plaintiff could count any interest sought as part of the claim for damages, but not "interest as such").)

b) Injunctive and Declaratory Relief

When plaintiff seeks relief other than money damages, the court must look to the dollar value of the objective of the suit. For example, if plaintiff sues to overturn a statute regulating his business, the amount in controversy would be the difference between the business's value regulated and unregulated.

c) Collateral and Future Effects

In applying this jurisdictional amount requirement, the court will include only the *direct* value of judgment *on the claim* before the court; the court will not include side effects of the judgment sought, such as penalties for noncompliance with the judgment or even the value of collateral estoppel effects when the judgment could be used in other actions. Within the bounds of the claim, the court will value requested relief establishing future rights or dispelling future duties by roughly subjecting the relief to usual valuation techniques, which take into account time and probabilities. However, on such matters the courts do demonstrate unlimited confusion.

> *Example:* P sues D to establish a contractual right to a life annuity, the expected present value of which is $76,000. (Result: jurisdictional amount exists.)

d) Viewpoint for Valuation

The courts show more confusion on how to apply the test when the value of the requested relief to plaintiff is apparently different from its cost to defendant, as where a shipowner sues to remove the defendant's bridge. Among the possible solutions, most courts seem to choose the "plaintiff-viewpoint rule," looking only at the value to plaintiff. Perhaps a more logical approach would look to the smaller of the plaintiff's value and the defendant's cost, with the idea that the parties could theoretically strike a bargain at that smaller amount; but this approach has no case support.

e) Costs Sanction

In 1958 Congress authorized a costs sanction, giving the courts discretionary power to impose court costs on any plaintiff who has invoked diversity jurisdiction but has recovered less than the jurisdictional amount. 28 U.S.C.A. § 1332(b). This has proved ineffective, because the courts use the power rarely and because "court costs" are usually minuscule.

2) Aggregation of Claims

Consider now this problem: When can the amounts in controversy on two or more joined claims be added together to satisfy this jurisdictional amount requirement?

a) Claims Between Same Parties

All claims asserted by one plaintiff against the same defendant may be aggregated, regardless of the relation among the claims.

Example: P sues D for $36,000 on a contract claim, and P joins an unrelated tort claim against D for $40,000. (Result: jurisdictional amount exists.)

b) Claims Involving Different Parties

Claims asserted by multiple plaintiffs against the same defendant, or claims asserted by the same plaintiff against multiple defendants, cannot be aggregated. But an exception here allows aggregation of claims that assert a "common and undivided interest," which represents a small category of ancient lineage that is virtually undefinable and can only be delineated by example (e.g., an estate's distributees suing defendant who allegedly converted the estate). Suffice it to say that this exception requires much more than relatedness among the claims. See 14B Wright, Miller & Cooper § 3704.

Example: Invoking diversity jurisdiction, P–1 and P–2 sue D for $51,000 and $58,000 respectively, on claims arising out of the same automobile accident. D challenges jurisdiction. (Result: dismissal, because P–1 and P–2 cannot aggregate.)

The same rule applies to class actions. So, for a plaintiff-class action based on diversity jurisdiction, class members with separate and distinct claims cannot aggregate to satisfy the jurisdictional amount requirement. See *Snyder v. Harris*, 394 U.S. 332, 89 S.Ct. 1053 (1969).

c) A Better Approach

Both of the established rules above are undesirable. A more sensible rule would allow aggregation if and only if the claims are related.

3) Counterclaims

Consider now the problem of whether the amount in controversy on a counterclaim can be considered in applying this jurisdictional amount requirement to the main claim. The courts show yet more confusion in approaching this question in its varied factual settings, leaving it unsettled. The best approach under the current statutory scheme is to ignore the counterclaim in so applying the jurisdictional amount requirement.

Example: Invoking diversity jurisdiction, P sues D for $35,000 for damages from an automobile accident. D counterclaims for $48,000, alleging damages from the same automobile accident. The court raises the jurisdictional issue. (Result: dismissal.)

If, however, the counterclaim falls into that small category of "common-law compulsory counterclaims" (see Chapter XVIII–C below), then in the author's view the counterclaim helps to define the amount of the main claim and should be so considered. See *Horton v. Liberty Mut. Ins. Co.*, 367 U.S. 348, 81 S.Ct. 1570 (1961) (jurisdictional amount, then $10,000, exists where workers' compensation insurer sues to set aside administrative award of $1050 and claims no liability, and workman counterclaims for his full claim of $14,035).

3. REMOVAL

Although the Constitution makes no mention of removal of cases from state court to federal court, Congress has used its Article I powers to provide for such removal from state trial courts to the district courts of specified cases within the federal judicial power. The basic statute is 28 U.S.C.A. § 1441.

a. General Rules

Under § 1441(a), only a *defendant* can remove, and *all* served defendants must seek removal together.

Examples: (1) P sued D in state court. D asserted a counterclaim that would have been within the federal original jurisdiction. P sought to remove. (Result: P cannot remove, because P is not formally a defendant.) *Shamrock Oil & Gas Corp. v. Sheets*, 313 U.S. 100, 61 S.Ct. 868 (1941).

(2) P joins D–1 and D–2 as joint tortfeasors in a state-court case. The case would have been within the federal original jurisdiction. D–1 seeks to remove. (Result: D–1 alone cannot remove.)

Moreover, defendants can remove only on the basis of the claims against them, and not on the basis of any counterclaims asserted by them. Upon removal, the whole case goes to the federal district court for the district in which the particular state courthouse is located.

b. Removable Actions

Defendants can remove from state court (1) pursuant to § 1441 any civil action against them that is *within the district courts' original jurisdiction*, subject to the exceptions noted immediately below, and (2) certain other cases that are outside said original jurisdiction, although within the bounds of Article III, such as those cases specified in 28 U.S.C.A. § 1442 (federal officers sued) and § 1443 (certain civil rights matters).

1) Nonremovability Statutes

Certain cases that might be within the federal original jurisdiction are nevertheless declared by various statutes to be nonremovable, thus protecting plaintiffs' choice of a state forum. E.g., 28 U.S.C.A. § 1445(a) (FELA cases), § 1445(c) (workmen's compensation cases).

2) Diversity of Citizenship

An important exception to § 1441(a)'s removability of *cases not founded on a federal question* appears in § 1441(b), whereby defendants cannot remove a case *if any served defendant is a citizen of the forum state*. The idea here is that such defendants have no need to escape from local bias in the state court, although strangely no comparable limitation restricts plaintiffs when invoking the federal courts' original jurisdiction.

Example: P, a citizen of New York, joins D–1, a citizen of New Jersey, and D–2, a citizen of Pennsylvania, as defendants in a New Jersey state court, asking $160,000 from each. Defendants seek to remove. (Result: defendants cannot remove, unless the case is founded on a federal question.)

c.   Separate and Independent Claims

Some hope for circumventing the restrictions on removal appears to lie in § 1441(c). That narrow and difficult statute provides for defendants' removal of a federal question claim when joined by plaintiffs with a separate and independent claim that would otherwise be nonremovable. Given such joinder, the entire case becomes removable, but the district court may remand those matters as to which state law predominates. See generally Wright's Hornbook § 39.

d.   Removal Procedure

Congress has specified the mechanics of removal in 28 U.S.C.A. §§ 1446–1450.

1)   Defendants' Steps

Defendants must seek removal promptly, normally within 30 days of receipt of the complaint. Defendants file in the local federal district court a notice of removal, subject to Federal Rule 11 and setting forth the grounds that justify removal. Next, defendants give notification of the filing to plaintiffs and to the state court. Removal is then complete.

2)   Judicial Steps

After this activity solely on the part of defendants, the state court can proceed no further. The action is now in the federal court, and under Federal Rule 81(c) the action will be treated henceforth like a normal federal action. See also § 1448 (service of process). If the action has been improperly removed, the federal court will *remand* it to the state court. Such a remand order is generally not appealable or reviewable, so the case would then resume in the state court.

4.   SUPPLEMENTAL JURISDICTION

Although the Constitution and the jurisdictional statutes did not expressly authorize the federal district courts to hear claims related to pending claims within the federal jurisdiction, the courts generally read Article III and those statutes to permit so hearing whole cases when desirable. In 1990, Congress codified this doctrine in 28 U.S.C.A. § 1367.

a.   Pendent Jurisdiction

This doctrine evolved from an ancient core of necessity: a court of original jurisdiction must have the power to entertain all of a case's elements that need to be resolved in order to render judgment on a claim. Such power for the district courts exists, whether those elements are federal or state in nature, with justification for this and related powers lying in the constitutional reference to jurisdiction over "cases" rather than merely over certain issues and also in the statutory references to "civil actions." However, under "pendent jurisdiction" the district courts reached much farther into the states' domain in pursuit of fairness, convenience, and efficiency: given jurisdiction over a federal question claim, the district court can entertain a plaintiff's parallel state claim that does not independently satisfy federal jurisdictional requirements. See generally Wright's Hornbook § 19.

Example: P sued D in district court on (1) a federal claim for infringement of the copyright in a play and (2) a state claim for unfair competition in unauthorized use of the play. (Result: court can exercise jurisdiction over the pendent state claim.) *Hurn v. Oursler*, 289 U.S. 238, 53 S.Ct. 586 (1933) (*Hurn*'s particular result now codified in 28 U.S.C.A. § 1338(b)).

1) General Rule

UMW v. Gibbs, 383 U.S. 715, 86 S.Ct. 1130 (1966), set out the modern law of pendent jurisdiction. *Gibbs* imposed tests of both power and discretion.

a) Power

For the district court to have the power to entertain the state claim, the federal question claim and the state claim must be closely enough related to constitute one "case" in the constitutional sense. *Gibbs* seemingly defined this by requiring that (1) the two "claims must derive from a common nucleus of operative fact" and (2) they must be such that plaintiff "would ordinarily be expected to try them . . . in one judicial proceeding." And *Aldinger v. Howard*, 427 U.S. 1, 96 S.Ct. 2413 (1976), expressed the further point that the district court's power can be constricted by Congress. Pendent jurisdiction is impermissible if expressly prohibited by statute, although in fact Congress generally has not chosen to prohibit it. Instead, § 1367(a) now broadly codifies this judicial power.

b) Discretion

Under *Gibbs*, the district court will not exercise this power when "considerations of judicial economy, convenience and fairness to litigants" and "of comity" on balance argue against federal jurisdiction. The court in its discretion will decline to exercise pendent jurisdiction, for example, when "state issues substantially predominate" or sometimes when the federal question claim is dismissed at an early stage. So, the court's discretion cuts back on its broad power. Now § 1367(c) codifies this discretion.

2) Pendent Parties

Pendent jurisdiction extends to a state claim against a different party, subject as always to the court's discretion.

Example: P sues D–1 in district court on a federal question claim. Can the court exercise pendent jurisdiction in that action over a closely related state claim that P has against D–2? (Result: the court has this power.)

3) Venue and Territorial Jurisdiction

The normal rules of territorial jurisdiction and venue apply; but note that one such rule (see Chapter IX–B below) gives personal jurisdiction with respect to any claim added to a pending action, if defendant has appeared in the action and if determining the additional claim concurrently with that action would not be unreasonable.

b. Ancillary Jurisdiction

This doctrine drew on a related notion of necessity: a court of original jurisdiction should have the power to entertain certain matters incidental to the main claim, such as conflicting claims to property under the court's control. The district courts should be able to deal with a whole "case," including some claims not by themselves within the courts' jurisdiction. However, under "ancillary jurisdiction" the district courts reached much farther in pursuit of fairness, convenience, and efficiency: given jurisdiction over the main claim, the district court can entertain counterclaims, crossclaims, and other claims that do not independently satisfy federal jurisdictional requirements. See generally Wright's Hornbook § 9.

Example: P sued D in district court on a federal antitrust claim, and D asserted a related state counterclaim. (Result: court can exercise jurisdiction over the ancillary state counterclaim.) *Moore v. N.Y. Cotton Exchange*, 270 U.S. 593, 46 S.Ct. 367 (1926) (incidental claim must bear "logical relationship" to main claim).

1) **General Rule**

Owen Equip. & Erection Co. v. Kroger, 437 U.S. 365, 98 S.Ct. 2396 (1978), suggested the modern law of ancillary jurisdiction.

a) **Theory**

Seemingly like *Gibbs*, *Owen* required *power* to exist under the Constitution (claims must arise from "common nucleus of operative fact") and not be negated by statute, and *Owen* also allowed the district court in its *discretion* to decline to exercise ancillary jurisdiction. However, § 1367(b) today broadly negates power with respect to claims added by plaintiffs.

b) **Practice**

The courts have adopted an unfortunately rigid approach, working out wooden rules to decide the propriety of ancillary jurisdiction. The following claims come within ancillary jurisdiction:

(1) compulsory counterclaims under Federal Rule 13(a);

(2) crossclaims under Rule 13(g);

(3) intervention of right under Rule 24(a), unless the intervenor is intervening as a plaintiff in a diversity case or unless the intervenor would have been an indispensable party under Rule 19(b);

(4) impleader claims under Rule 14(a)(1); and

(5) third-party defendants' claims against plaintiffs under Rule 14(a)(2)(D).

The doctrine does not cover:

(1) permissive counterclaims under Rule 13(b);

(2) permissive intervention under Rule 24(b), unless the intervenor is a class member intervening in a class action; or

(3) plaintiffs' claims against third-party defendants under Rule 14(a)(3), when the main claim rests on diversity jurisdiction.

2) Ancillary Parties

Ancillary jurisdiction permits a defendant to assert a compulsory counterclaim or a crossclaim that involves new parties under Federal Rule 13(h). However, ancillary jurisdiction does not permit a plaintiff suing in diversity to join a claim against a different defendant that would otherwise be beyond the federal jurisdiction.

> *Example:* Invoking diversity jurisdiction, P of New York sues D–1 of Vermont for $160,000. Can the district court exercise ancillary jurisdiction in that action over a closely re-lated state claim that P has against D–2 of New York for $170,000? (Result: no jurisdiction over claim against D–2, because 28 U.S.C.A. § 1332(a) and its requirement of complete diversity implicitly prohibit ancillary juris-diction here.)

Again, such wooden rules are likely either too broad or too narrow from the viewpoint of desirable policy. Nevertheless, in the Supreme Court's sole foray into supplemental jurisdiction, it chose to read § 1367(b)'s prohibition rigidly: it rejected clear legislative intent in favor of explicit statutory wording, holding that the statute did not prohibit the use of supplemental jurisdiction to satisfy the jurisdic-tional amount requirement for multiple plaintiffs joined under Rule 20 or 23 who are suing a single defendant. *Exxon Mobil Corp. v. Allapattah Servs., Inc.*, 545 U.S. 546, 125 S.Ct. 2611 (2005). Still, supplemental jurisdiction does not exist if the case does not satisfy the complete diversity rule or if the multiple plaintiffs are suing multiple defendants.

3) Venue and Territorial Jurisdiction

If the district court exercises ancillary jurisdiction, then the doctrine of "ancillary venue" steps in to overcome any defense of improper venue. On the other hand, the normal rules of territorial jurisdiction apply.

c. Synthesis: Supplemental Jurisdiction

The doctrines of pendent and ancillary jurisdiction exhibited a similar evolution and theory. They shared a common ancient origin, although later American courts came to speak of them separately. Then their realms began to overlap, and their precedents were becoming interchangeable. Now Congress has combined them in its statutory brand of "supplemental jurisdiction." The future should see them truly merge into a doctrine giving the federal courts broad constitutional and statutory power over the whole "case" and relying on the judicial exercise of discretion in accord with good policy to restrain that broad power. Of course, there will be a generally wider scope of such supplemental jurisdiction in the classic pendent areas than in the classic ancillary areas, but this follows from the realization that good policy calls for different degrees of restraint in different situations.

d. Role of Discretion in Jurisdiction

Note that the federal courts here have discretion to define their own jurisdiction within broad bounds of power. This is not atypical. After all, the judicial branch in effect has discretion regarding the scope of federal question jurisdiction too: the Supreme Court reads the Constitution broadly as requiring only a federal ingredient, but reads the statutes more narrowly as imposing such fluid limits as almost to free itself to define the scope of federal question jurisdiction on the basis of pragmatic considerations. Moreover, judicial discretion plays a large role in the doctrines of limitation that have grown up from the constitutional requirement of "case or controversy," including such doctrines as ripeness and standing. See generally Wright's Hornbook §§ 12–15. Also, the doctrine of "abstention" calls sometimes for the federal courts, usually in deference to a state's interests, discretionarily to decline federal jurisdiction. See generally id. §§ 52–52A. Such matters are the subject of study in upperclass courses like Federal Courts.

IX

Territorial Authority to Adjudicate

■ ANALYSIS

A. INTRODUCTION TO TERRITORIAL AUTHORITY TO ADJUDICATE

For a court properly to undertake a civil adjudication, the court must have territorial authority to adjudicate. This requirement confines the *place of litigation*, putting restrictions on the court's authority to entertain litigation with nonlocal elements. The scope of territorial authority to adjudicate is defined in terms of the geographic relationship among the parties, the forum, and the litigation.

1. TERRITORIAL JURISDICTION AND VENUE

Territorial authority to adjudicate comprises both territorial jurisdiction and venue. See generally Kevin M. Clermont, Civil Procedure: Territorial Jurisdiction and Venue (1999).

a. Territorial Jurisdiction

This concept, sometimes termed "judicial jurisdiction," "amenability," or "nexus," comprises the more important rules of territorial authority to adjudicate. Indeed, territorial jurisdiction rests heavily on the Federal Constitution. Accordingly, those territorial restrictions on state courts deriving from the Due Process Clause will be first considered. Later, in Chapter IX–C below, consideration will be given to the other territorial restrictions on state courts, and to how all this applies to federal courts.

b. Venue

This lesser but related concept is sometimes difficult to distinguish from territorial jurisdiction. Venue will also be considered in Chapter IX–C below.

2. CURRENT DUE PROCESS DOCTRINE

The principal limitation on a state court's territorial jurisdiction is the Due Process Clause of the Fourteenth Amendment to the Federal Constitution. The ever-evolving due process doctrine now requires the categorization of the action and then the application of both the power and the unreasonableness tests.

a. Categorization—Introductory Definitions

Plaintiff brings an action in state court, thus implicitly asserting that the state has territorial jurisdiction. If defendant challenges this assertion, the courts must pass on jurisdiction, ultimately subjecting it to constitutional scrutiny. Under the Due Process Clause, the action must initially be categorized in terms of the target of the action so that the jurisdictional tests may be appropriately applied. In *Pennoyer v. Neff*, 95 U.S. 714 (1878), the Supreme Court laid the theoretical foundation for categorizing actions.

1) In Personam

Jurisdiction in personam, or "personal jurisdiction," can result in a judgment imposing a personal liability or obligation upon defendant in favor of plaintiff or, more generally, diminishing the personal rights of a party in favor of another party. This is the most common kind of territorial jurisdiction. For example, a successful tort action resting on personal jurisdiction subjects all of the defendant's nonexempt assets to execution. For another example, a suit for an injunction requires jurisdiction in personam and subjects defendant to the court's contempt sanctions.

2) In Rem

Jurisdiction in rem usually involves an action against a thing, but can be stretched to cases treating status as a thing.

a) Pure In Rem

Jurisdiction in rem can result in a judgment affecting the interests of *all* persons in a designated thing, or "res." Theoretically and formally, the action is against the thing. No personal liability or obligation results. Examples of proceedings in rem include actions to register title to land, forfeiture actions, admiralty proceedings to enforce a maritime lien upon a vessel, and probate proceedings to settle an estate.

b) Jurisdiction over Status

This type of jurisdiction, which is best classified as a subtype of in rem jurisdiction, can result in a judgment establishing or terminating a status, such as a family relationship or citizenship. By so treating the status as a thing, the state may determine status. For example, the state where the plaintiff spouse resides may grant a divorce; but note that the state could not impose support obligations without personal jurisdiction over the defendant spouse.

3) Quasi In Rem

Jurisdiction quasi in rem can result in a judgment affecting only the interests of *particular* persons in a designated thing. The difference between in rem jurisdiction and this category is that here state law does not authorize a judgment affecting the interests of all persons in the world. Although a proceeding quasi in rem is formally brought against the named defendants, only their interests in the thing are at stake. There are two distinct varieties of proceedings quasi in rem.

a) Subtype One

In subtype one, plaintiff seeks to establish a pre-existing interest in the thing as against defendant's interest. Examples include actions to partition land, to quiet title, and to foreclose a mortgage.

b) Subtype Two

This subtype of quasi in rem jurisdiction, sometimes termed "attachment jurisdiction," fundamentally differs from in rem and subtype one of quasi in rem. In subtype two, plaintiff seeks to apply the defendant's property to the satisfaction of a claim against defendant that is *unrelated* to the property. For example, a New York plaintiff might obtain jurisdiction in a New York state court for a tort claim arising from an auto accident in Japan by garnishing a New York bank account belonging to the French defendant; if successful, plaintiff would apply the bank account to awarded court costs and then to the satisfaction of his claim.

b. **Jurisdictional Tests—Introductory Definitions**

As the Supreme Court finally made clear in *World–Wide Volkswagen Corp. v. Woodson*, 444 U.S. 286, 100 S.Ct. 559 (1980), due process dictates both that the forum state must have *power* over the target of the action (be it a person or a thing) *and* that litigating the action there must be *reasonable*. And the Court in *Burger King Corp. v. Rudzewicz*, 471 U.S. 462, 105 S.Ct. 2174 (1985), further clarified that while plaintiff has the burden of persuasion as to power, it is up to defendant to show unreasonableness.

1) Power

The power test originated in the notion that a state had exclusive authority over persons and things present within its territorial boundaries. See *Pennoyer v. Neff*, 95 U.S. 714 (1878). Changes in society doomed such a wooden approach, as the Court explained in

Int'l Shoe Co. v. Washington, 326 U.S. 310, 66 S.Ct. 154 (1945) (replacing physical-power approach with "minimum contacts" formulation). Today several bases of power other than presence exist, some representing power only in a metaphorical sense. For instance, power exists over a defendant who has purposefully availed herself "of the privilege of conducting activities within the forum State, thus invoking the benefits and protections of its laws." *Hanson v. Denckla*, 357 U.S. 235, 253, 78 S.Ct. 1228, 1240 (1958). Other bases are listed in Chapter IX–B below, where the due process doctrine is applied. The common element in specifying the various bases of power is the narrow focus on whether the relation of the target of the action to the forum state constitutes "minimum contacts," as opposed to a broader inquiry that would take account of the plaintiff's and the public's interests. However, the current rationale for the power test is foggy.

2) Unreasonableness

The *International Shoe* case not only expanded the old notion of power, but also gave birth to an additional test of reasonableness by its reference to the requirement of "fair play and substantial justice." *McGee v. Int'l Life Ins. Co.*, 355 U.S. 220, 78 S.Ct. 199 (1957), further indicated that the reasonableness issue involved balancing the defendant's, the plaintiff's, and the public's interests. Examples of relevant interests include the convenience of litigating in the forum state, the availability of an alternative forum, and the state's interest in adjudicating the dispute. The chosen forum need not be the ideal forum, but the forum must not be an unreasonable one in light of all these interests in the litigation. This very flexible, and hence rather uncertain, methodology directly addresses the pertinent concern of fundamental unfairness in the broadest sense.

3. FUTURE DUE PROCESS DOCTRINE

Several commentators argue that the due process doctrine should evolve into a much simpler formulation that merely asks whether the state court's exercise of territorial jurisdiction is reasonable.

a. Jurisdictional Test

The highly complicated power test proves essentially undefinable, tending to disintegrate into a test that asks whether it is "reasonable to exercise power." Moreover, the power test has a weak justificatory rationale. Any valid concerns underlying it could be taken into account as part of a multifactored reasonableness test. And this could be achieved without the arguably undesirable denials of jurisdiction that the inflexible power test now yields. Accordingly, reformers call for the demise of the power test and the triumph of reasonableness as the sole due process test for territorial jurisdiction.

b. Categorization

The traditional categorization of proceedings in terms of the target of the action is necessary for the power test, because that test translates as power over *whom* or *what*. This is so despite the undeniable fact that all actions really affect the interests of people. However, categorization is unnecessary for determining reasonableness. A reasonableness test is the same for all types of proceedings, although the varying effects of the different kinds of judgment naturally enter into the wide-ranging consideration of reasonableness. Thus, there might be circumstances where it would be reasonable to cut off a nonresident's interest in local land, but where it would not be reasonable to render a money judgment against her. Yet there is no need to call the former in rem and the latter in personam. In sum, eliminating the power test in favor of a reasonableness test would obviate the need for categorization.

c. The *Mullane* Case

The Supreme Court adopted this law of the future in *Mullane v. Central Hanover Bank & Trust Co.*, 339 U.S. 306, 312, 70 S.Ct. 652, 656 (1950). At issue was New York's territorial jurisdiction to conduct a judicial settlement of accounts by the trustee of a New York common trust fund, a statutory proceeding that would cut off all resident and nonresident beneficiaries' rights against the trustee for improper management during the period covered by the accounting. The Court refused to categorize, acting in the belief that due process did "not depend upon a classification for which the standards are so elusive and confused generally." And the Court found jurisdiction to be reasonable, especially in light of New York's interest in providing a means to close New York trusts. However, in subsequent years the Court abandoned this futuristic approach, leaving the *Mullane* case in uncertain health.

B. APPLICATION OF CURRENT DUE PROCESS DOCTRINE

Under today's law, first, categorize the action and, second, apply both the power and the unreasonableness tests. Applying this doctrine gives a better idea of the scope of state-court territorial jurisdiction.

1. IN PERSONAM

The due process tests for personal jurisdiction over individuals and corporations historically come from different lines of cases, but today are essentially the same.

a. Modern Analysis

In a case of in personam jurisdiction, usually the court will apply the power test before the unreasonableness test, power being the higher hurdle for most such cases. If the state has no power over defendant, there is no jurisdiction and therefore unreasonableness is irrelevant. If there is power, then the court must consider unreasonableness.

Note that normally, but not always, reasonableness of personal jurisdiction follows almost a fortiori from a finding of power, because reasonableness involves looking at a broader range of interests and these additional interests most often favor jurisdiction. Consider these examples in which, respectively, (1) power is lacking, (2) power and reasonableness both exist, and (3) reasonableness is lacking.

Examples: (1) While passing through Oklahoma on a move from New York to a new home in Arizona, plaintiffs had a car accident. They suffered burns allegedly resulting from their car's defective design. While still hospitalized in Oklahoma, they sued in state court there. They included as defendants the regional wholesale distributor for New York, New Jersey, and Connecticut and the retail dealer from whom they had bought the car, both those defendants being incorporated in New York and also having their place of business there. These two defendants' only connection with Oklahoma was selling the car involved in this accident. (Result: there is no jurisdiction over these two defendants. They did not have minimum contacts with Oklahoma, which therefore had no power over them. Admittedly, one could argue that these defendants sell cars predictably to be used in Oklahoma, plaintiffs have an interest in litigating at the scene of the accident, and Oklahoma has an interest in enforcing its highway safety laws. And one could further argue that all this makes jurisdiction reasonable. However, reasonableness is irrelevant if there is no power.) *World–Wide Volkswagen Corp. v. Woodson*, 444 U.S. 286, 100 S.Ct. 559 (1980).

(2) Same as (1), except the issue is jurisdiction over two other corporate defendants, the car's German manufacturer and its American importer incorporated in New Jersey. (Result: personal jurisdiction is constitutional. By their active purposes to serve the market for cars in Oklahoma, these two defendants subjected themselves to that state's power. The exercise of jurisdiction over them would also not be unreasonable.)

(3) Plaintiff was severely injured in a motorcycle accident in California, allegedly caused by the explosion of the cycle's defective rear tire. In California state court he sued the Taiwanese manufacturer of the tube, which impleaded the Japanese manufacturer of the tube's valve. The main claim settled, leaving only the indemnity claim. The valve manufacturer made valves in Japan and sold some of them in Taiwan to the tube manufacturer, who sold tubes throughout the world including California. (Result: there is no jurisdiction over the valve manufacturer. Although power might exist, jurisdiction would be unreasonable, considering the severe burdens of defending in a foreign legal system, the slight interests of the third-party plaintiff and California in the exercise of jurisdiction, and the international interests in not subjecting this alien corporation to an indemnification offshoot of an American product liability action.) *Asahi Metal Indus. Co. v. Superior Court*, 480 U.S. 102, 107 S.Ct. 1026 (1987).

b. Scope of Jurisdiction

All of the relationships between defendant and the forum state that are sufficient to establish the state's power fall into several basic types. These are the primary bases of power. Of course, to survive due process scrutiny, any exercise of jurisdiction must not fail the more free-form test of unreasonableness. Nevertheless, cataloguing the primary bases of power is an expressive means for mapping the bounds on state-court personal jurisdiction.

1) General Jurisdiction

Some of these bases of power rest on strong contacts between defendant and the forum state, giving the state power to adjudicate any personal claim whether or not related to those contacts. Thus, one says these bases support "general jurisdiction."

a) Presence

This ancient basis gives the state power to adjudicate any personal claim if defendant is served with process within the state's territorial limits. Thus, even momentary presence of defendant creates power to adjudicate a claim totally unrelated to that presence. See *Grace v. MacArthur*, 170 F.Supp. 442 (E.D.Ark.1959) (valid service on defendant flying over state).

Example: D, a Minnesotan driving to Maine for a vacation, stops at a gas station in Vermont. While waiting in line there, D assaults P, who is a businessman from Ohio. P sues D in an Ohio state court, managing to serve D with process when D stops for the night in Ohio on a later trip to New York. (Result: such "transient jurisdiction" is constitutional.)

Burnham v. Superior Court, 495 U.S. 604, 110 S.Ct. 2105 (1990), seems to suggest that transient jurisdiction merely by its historical pedigree satisfies any reasonableness test. (Despite former attempts fictitiously to apply the "presence" concept to corporations, the view today is that this basis meaningfully refers only to jurisdiction over individuals, since only individuals can be physically present.)

b) Domicile

This basis gives the state power to adjudicate any personal claim if defendant is domiciled in the state when served with process. "The state which accords him privileges and affords protection to him and his property by virtue of his domicile may also exact reciprocal duties." *Milliken v. Meyer*, 311 U.S. 457, 463, 61 S.Ct. 339, 343 (1940).

Example: P sues D in Minnesota, where D is domiciled, for an assault that occurred in Vermont. (Result: personal jurisdiction is constitutional. Note that the claim is unrelated to D's contacts with Minnesota.)

Some support exists for stretching this basis of power to reach defendants who were domiciliaries only when the claim arose or to reach defendants who are mere residents as opposed to domiciliaries. (For corporations, the analogy to state of domicile is state of incorporation.)

2) Specific Jurisdiction

Other of these bases of power rest on lesser contacts between defendant and the forum state, giving the state power to adjudicate only those personal claims related to the contacts. Thus, these bases support "specific jurisdiction."

a) Consent

An individual or corporate defendant may consent to personal jurisdiction, thereby creating a basis of power defined by the terms of the consent. The possibility of the defendant's limiting the consent justifies classifying the consent basis under the label of specific jurisdiction. Defendant may express consent in a number of ways. Defendant may consent *before* suit is brought, as in the common provision in business contracts consenting to a particular state's jurisdiction, or as pursuant to the common statutory requirement that anyone seeking a license to do business in a state must appoint a local agent to accept service of process. Alternatively, defendant may consent *after* suit is brought, as by accepting or waiving service of process, or as by choosing not to object to personal jurisdiction.

> *Example:* Michigan farmers leased equipment from a New York corporation under a standard printed lease. By one of the lease's terms, the farmers appointed a New York woman, whom they did not know personally, as their agent to accept service in connection with any litigation under the lease. A dispute arose, the corporation sued in New York by serving the woman, and she forwarded the process to the farmers. (Result: personal jurisdiction for lease dispute is constitutional.) *Nat'l Equip. Rental, Ltd. v. Szukhent*, 375 U.S. 311, 84 S.Ct. 411 (1964) (suit in federal court).

In the past, the courts stretched the "consent" basis into various *fictitious* forms, in order to uphold jurisdiction where it was highly desirable but where the then-prevailing jurisdictional theory did not yet extend. This is probably no longer necessary or proper. Thus, the better view is that only *actual* consent is a valid basis of power.

> *Example:* A nonresident motorist had an accident in Massachusetts. He later left the state. The accident then spawned a suit against him in Massachusetts. (Result: personal jurisdiction for tort action is constitutional. In *Hess v. Pawloski*, 274 U.S. 352, 47 S.Ct. 632 (1927), the Court upheld jurisdiction under a Massachusetts statute that deemed driving on the state's roads to be "implied consent" to jurisdiction for litigation arising from an accident on those roads. Today the same result would be achieved, but the basis of power would be the "state-directed act.")

b) State–directed Acts

This relatively new and very vibrant basis of power gives the state power over an individual or corporation that has committed certain acts directed at the state, but the power extends only to those personal claims arising out of those acts. However, *Int'l Shoe Co. v. Washington*, 326 U.S. 310, 66 S.Ct. 154 (1945), made the point that as the level of the defendant's state-directed activity increases, the state's power extends to claims less related to that activity.

Important Examples: (1) *Tortious Acts.* Plaintiff sued Wisconsin defendant in Illinois, alleging that defendant while unloading his truck in Illinois negligently injured plaintiff. (Result: personal jurisdiction for negligence action is constitutional.) *Nelson v. Miller*, 11 Ill.2d 378, 143 N.E.2d 673 (1957).

(2) *Business Activity.* In California, a California woman sued a Texas insurance company to recover on a policy on her son's life, where the defendant's only contacts with California were mailing this solitary insurance contract to the son residing in that state and accepting premiums mailed by him from there. (Result: personal jurisdiction for recovery action is constitutional.) *McGee v. Int'l Life Ins. Co.*, 355 U.S. 220, 78 S.Ct. 199 (1957). Compare *Burger King Corp. v. Rudzewicz*, 471 U.S. 462, 105 S.Ct.

2174 (1985) (same result for Florida franchisor's federal action in Florida against breaching Michigan franchisee), with *Perkins v. Benguet Consol. Mining Co.*, 342 U.S. 437, 72 S.Ct. 413 (1952) (defendant's activities so extensive in forum state as to support jurisdiction in action unrelated to those activities, thus blurring the distinction between specific and general jurisdiction).

(3) *Property Ownership, Use, or Possession.* Plaintiff sued New Jersey defendant in Pennsylvania for injuries sustained on the defendant's Pennsylvania property. (Result: personal jurisdiction for tort action is constitutional.) *Dubin v. City of Philadelphia*, 34 Pa.D. & C. 61 (C.P.1938).

(4) *Litigating Acts.* Nonresident P sued D in California. D brought a counterclaim arising out of the same transaction. (Result: personal jurisdiction over P for the counterclaim is constitutional. More generally, a state has power over anyone who has appeared in a pending action in a court of the state and may exercise it when determining the additional claim concurrently with that action would not be unreasonable.) *Adam v. Saenger*, 303 U.S. 59, 58 S.Ct. 454 (1938).

These examples should not give the idea that anything goes. The Supreme Court has sometimes found the defendant's activity too slight to bestow power on the state, as in the above *World–Wide Volkswagen* case.

Examples: (1) A Delaware trustee had no contact with Florida other than remitting trust income to the trust's settlor after she moved there and receiving her occasional instructions from there. After her death, her legatees sued in Florida to attack the validity of the Delaware trust. (Result: no jurisdiction over trustee.) *Hanson v. Denckla*, 357 U.S. 235, 78 S.Ct. 1228 (1958).

(2) A New York husband had no contact with California, but his estranged wife and children had moved there with his consent. She sued him in California for child support. (Result: no jurisdiction over husband.) *Kulko v. Superior Court*, 436 U.S. 84, 98 S.Ct. 1690 (1978).

Drawing the line is difficult. *International Shoe* did the pioneering theoretical work; the *Kulko* case sought refinement by phrasing this power test as "whether the 'quality and nature' of the defendant's activity is such that it is 'reasonable' and 'fair' to require him to conduct his defense in that State." (This is yet another example of how fairness or reasonableness notions creep into the power test.) And however phrased, the test in application turns on a close inspection of the facts and circumstances peculiar to the case. At any rate, the following graph structurally embodies the power rationale of *International Shoe*, *Kulko*, and other recent cases, and further tries to plot the results of the major Supreme Court cases on this subject, with the hatched area representing the zone beyond the due process limit on state-court power:

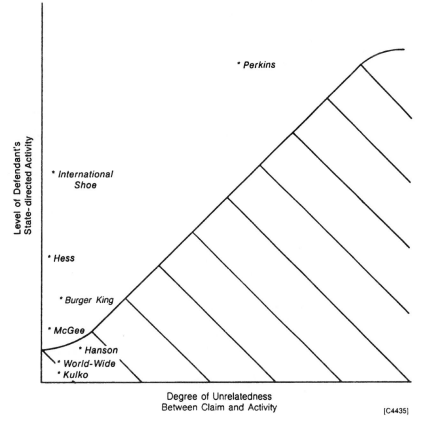

[C4435]

2. IN REM

Consider separately pure in rem and jurisdiction over status.

a. Pure In Rem

To satisfy the power test, a proceeding in rem normally must be brought where the thing is. Unreasonableness will thus be the key test under the modern law.

1) Scope of Jurisdiction

Jurisdiction in rem, if exercised at the thing's location or "situs," will not be unreasonable when litigating there is fair to the persons whose property interests in the thing are to be affected and when the state has an interest in adjudicating the dispute. Since an in rem action involves conflicting claims to the property itself, most likely reasonableness follows because those claims indicate that the claimants expected to benefit from the situs state's protection of their property interests, because important records and witnesses are in the state, and because the state has an interest in maintaining the marketability of property within its borders and in peacefully resolving disputes concerning that property.

Example: Massachusetts provided by statute for a proceeding to register title to any land within the state. The proceeding would determine the interests in that land of all persons in the world. (Result: jurisdiction so to clear title against all the world is constitutional, because such jurisdiction in rem is fair and highly desirable.) *Tyler v. Judges of the Court of Registration*, 175 Mass. 71, 55 N.E. 812, writ of error dismissed, 179 U.S. 405, 21 S.Ct. 206 (1900).

2) Problem of Seizure

A pervasive problem concerning nonpersonal jurisdiction is the threshold necessity of officially seizing the thing, as by attachment. Despite some cases' intimations to the contrary, the better view is that there is no *constitutional* requirement of actual seizure. It suffices to phrase the complaint in such a way as to direct the action clearly against the thing.

b. Jurisdiction over Status

To satisfy the power test, jurisdiction over status must be exercised where the status is located; a status can be sited in any state to which one party in the relationship has a significant connection. The exercise of jurisdiction must not be unreasonable.

Example: Husband leaves his home in New York and goes to Idaho, which has more permissive grounds for divorce. Having established his domicile in Idaho, he sues there for divorce. Wife defaults. (Result: jurisdiction for divorce is constitutional.)

3. QUASI IN REM

Consider separately its two subtypes.

a. Subtype One

To satisfy the power test, this kind of jurisdiction normally must be exercised where the thing is. Unreasonableness will be the key test.

1) Scope of Jurisdiction

Subtype one of jurisdiction quasi in rem, if exercised at the situs, will not be unreasonable when the balance of interests of defendant, of plaintiff, and of the public favors jurisdiction.

Example: Plaintiff sues nonresident defendant in New York to partition New York real estate, which plaintiff and defendant own jointly. (Result: jurisdiction over the land is constitutional, because such jurisdiction in New York is reasonable.)

2) Problem of Reification

Another pervasive problem concerning nonpersonal jurisdiction is the play in the process of identifying the thing in dispute and of attributing an in-state situs to it. This "reification process" is especially elastic when the res is an intangible, such as a debt evidenced by a writing. In passing on its own jurisdiction, a state might deem the res to be either the writing or the debt itself, and might consider the latter to be located where the debtor is present, where the debtor is domiciled, or elsewhere. There must be some limit, albeit ill-defined, on the state's ability to expand its own jurisdiction by stretching reification. The current approach would apparently ask, as a special aspect of the jurisdictional inquiry, whether the state unreasonably performed this reification process.

b. Subtype Two

To satisfy the power test, this kind of jurisdiction normally must be exercised where the thing is. Unreasonableness will be the key test, here being particularly difficult to satisfy.

1) Scope of Jurisdiction

Subtype two of jurisdiction quasi in rem was formerly quite useful. If plaintiff had any claim against defendant but failed to acquire jurisdiction over her, plaintiff could proceed against any of the defendant's property within the state, such as a bank account. Defendant usually defaulted, and the resulting judgment allowed plaintiff to apply the property to satisfy the claim. Plaintiff could later sue on any unsatisfied portion of the claim, either in personam or again by this subtype of quasi in rem against other property. See *Harris v. Balk*, 198 U.S. 215, 25 S.Ct. 625 (1905) (plaintiff could constitutionally invoke this subtype of jurisdiction over debt owing from third person to defendant, thus pursuing unrelated claim against defendant by garnishment of debt where third person was temporarily present). However, in *Shaffer v. Heitner*, 433 U.S. 186, 97 S.Ct. 2569 (1977), the Supreme Court overturned *Harris* by making clear that nonpersonal jurisdiction must pass the reasonableness test. The result is that this subtype of quasi in rem jurisdiction is now available only in four, rather special situations.

Important Examples: (1) Ohio plaintiff sues by attaching Iowa defendant's land in New York in order to *secure* a judgment being sought by plaintiff in California for personal injuries stemming from a traffic accident with defendant in California. (Result: attachment jurisdiction in New York is constitutional.)

(2) Ohio plaintiff sues by attaching Iowa defendant's land in New York in order to *enforce* a judgment already rendered for plaintiff in California for personal injuries stemming from a traffic accident with defendant in California. (Result: attachment jurisdiction in New York is constitutional.)

(3) Ohio plaintiff sues by attaching Iowa defendant's land in New York in order to *recover* for his personal injuries stemming from a traffic accident with defendant in New York. (Result: attachment jurisdiction in New York is constitutional. *If a state could constitutionally exercise personal jurisdiction*, it may choose to allow plaintiff instead to cast his suit in the form of this subtype of quasi in rem jurisdiction, although arguably the Constitution prohibits actual seizure solely for this unnecessary formalism.)

(4) Ohio plaintiff sues by attaching French defendant's land in New York in order to *recover* for his personal injuries stemming from a

traffic accident with defendant in Japan. (Result: attachment jurisdiction in New York is thought to be constitutional, assuming personal jurisdiction is not available in any other American forum. This is an example of so-called jurisdiction by necessity, in which *the unavailability of an alternative American forum* arguably allows jurisdiction to squeak by the unreasonableness test.)

2) Problem of Categorization

Still another pervasive problem is the play in the process of categorizing an action as the preliminary step in applying the appropriate constitutional standard. A state could avoid the jurisdictional tests for personal jurisdiction by considering the suit to be quasi in rem. Conversely, a state could avoid the jurisdictional tests for jurisdiction over things by proceeding in personam. There must be some limit on the state's ability to expand its own jurisdiction by distorting the categorization process. The current approach would apparently ask whether the state unreasonably categorized the action.

Examples: (1) Plaintiff sought to assert in Delaware a shareholders' derivative suit against nonresident officers and directors of a Delaware corporation by going after their shares in the corporation. Plaintiff alleged mismanagement occurring in Oregon. Delaware authorized suit as an exercise of subtype two of quasi in rem jurisdiction. (Result: jurisdiction in Delaware is unconstitutional. The state's only apparent purpose in categorizing the suit as attachment jurisdiction was to evade the restrictions on personal jurisdiction, and this purpose was not a reasonable one. Accordingly, in applying the constitutional standard, the state had to categorize the suit as personal jurisdiction, which was unavailable in the circumstances because Delaware had no power over defendants.) *Shaffer v. Heitner*, 433 U.S. 186, 97 S.Ct. 2569 (1977). See also *Rush v. Savchuk*, 444 U.S. 320, 100 S.Ct. 571 (1980) (striking down Minnesota's categorization of an action as subtype two of quasi in rem jurisdiction, where resident plaintiff injured in an out-of-state auto accident sought to garnish nonresident defendant's liability insurance on the ground that the insurer did business in Minnesota).

(2) Plaintiff sues Connecticut defendant in Connecticut to partition land in New York. (Result: jurisdiction in Connecticut is unconstitutional. This action must meet the jurisdictional tests for subtype one of quasi in rem, but there is no power over the land.)

C. OTHER LIMITATIONS ON TERRITORIAL AUTHORITY TO ADJUDICATE

Looking beyond the Due Process Clause, restrictions on the territorial jurisdiction of courts may be found in other federal law, international law, state law, and agreements among the parties. In the interests of orderly restraint, any jurisdictional inquiry by a court should proceed in two steps: (1) whether the asserted jurisdiction falls within the restrictions imposed other than by the Due Process Clause and, if so, (2) whether the asserted jurisdiction passes muster under the Due Process Clause.

1. LIMITS ON STATE TRIAL COURTS

a. Federal Law

1) Federal Constitution

As already noted, the principal limitation on state-court territorial jurisdiction is the Due Process Clause of the Fourteenth Amendment. Some authorities argue that other provisions of the Federal Constitution impose independent restrictions on territorial jurisdiction applicable in certain unusual circumstances. The better view is that the policies behind these other provisions enter into the balance of interests under due process's unreasonableness test, thus only indirectly restricting jurisdiction.

a) First Amendment

An assertion of state-court jurisdiction might offend the policies underlying our First Amendment freedoms, binding on the states through the Fourteenth Amendment.

Example: The defendant's only contacts with the District of Columbia are its dealings with a federal regulatory agency. An independent contractor employed by defendant to handle those dealings sues there for fees. (Result: jurisdiction is unconstitutional, in view of the First Amendment right to petition for redress of grievances. This illustrates the fledgling "government contacts" principle. The idea is that by doing nothing more than dealing with the government, one does not expose oneself to suit at the seat of government.) *Environmental Research Int'l, Inc. v. Lockwood Greene Eng'rs, Inc.*, 355 A.2d 808 (D.C.1976).

However, the Supreme Court has warned against an activist approach here, ruling that free press policies do not impede jurisdiction for libel actions. *Calder v. Jones*, 465 U.S. 783, 104 S.Ct. 1482 (1984).

b) Commerce Clause
In rare circumstances, an assertion of state-court jurisdiction might similarly offend the policies against burdening interstate and foreign commerce.

2) Federal Statutes
Congress has the constitutional power to regulate state-court territorial jurisdiction. It has done so only in a couple of statutes like the National Bank Act, 12 U.S.C.A. § 94, which dictates the locality where certain actions involving a national bank can be brought.

3) Other Federal Law
Federal jurisdictional law might sometimes apply in state courts under the reverse-*Erie* doctrine.

b. International Law
Consider a suit against a French woman. In the absence of a specific treaty, international law imposes no significant restrictions on state-court territorial jurisdiction beyond those restrictions already imposed by the Due Process Clause of the Fourteenth Amendment.

c. State Law

1) State Constitutions
Some restriction on state-court territorial jurisdiction might be found inserted in a state constitution.

2) Long–Arm Statutes
For separation-of-powers reasons, the states generally hold that a state court must be authorized by state statute to exercise the

various bases of jurisdictional power, except for the bases of presence and consent which were recognized at common law. Accordingly, the states have enacted statutes, often termed "long-arm" statutes, to extend their territorial jurisdiction. However, a state is not required to extend its jurisdiction all the way to constitutionally permissible limits. See generally Robert C. Casad & William B. Richman, Jurisdiction in Civil Actions (3d ed. 1998).

Of great practical importance is the fact that to the extent these statutes fall short of authorizing all the jurisdiction permitted by the Federal Constitution, these statutes serve in effect to restrict state-court jurisdiction.

Examples: (1) One basic type of state statutory scheme culminates in a long-arm provision extending jurisdiction over defendant far enough to permit suit on claims arising from certain listed activities by defendant within the state, such as transacting business, committing a tortious act, and owning, using, or possessing real property. E.g., N.Y.C.P.L.R. § 302. There is no jurisdiction in New York unless the case falls within a statutory provision, and unless the provision so construed is within the Due Process Clause.

(2) A variation on this basic type of statutory scheme reads just like New York's, but the state courts have so stretched the statutory wording that jurisdiction actually extends to the limits imposed by the Due Process Clause. E.g., Minn.Stat. § 543.19.

(3) A second basic type expressly authorizes jurisdiction wherever consistent with the Due Process Clause. E.g., Cal.Civ.Proc.Code § 410.10. This candid and conceptually straightforward approach maximizes reach, and also simplifies legislative drafting and ensures that the statutory scheme keeps in step with evolving notions of due process. But this vague type of statute is relatively difficult to apply, and also converts every jurisdictional issue into a constitutional question and squanders the legislative opportunity to rationalize jurisdiction.

(4) A variation on this second basic type of statutory scheme contains a catch-all due process provision like

California's, but also, in an attempt to provide some suggestive guidance to the courts, includes as alternatives a list of jurisdiction-bestowing activities like New York's statute. E.g., Ill.Comp.Stat. ch. 735, § 5/2–209.

3) Other Doctrines of Self–Restraint

State courts have developed a number of doctrines that further restrict their exercise of territorial jurisdiction. In some instances, these doctrines are now embodied in state statutes.

Note that as reasonableness has developed into a constitutional requirement, some of these doctrines of self-restraint may have acquired a constitutional underpinning.

a) Fraud or Force

In most states, a court will not exercise power over a person or thing if that power has been acquired by fraud or unlawful force.

Example: Plaintiff lures defendant into Florida with fraudulent promises of a candlelit dinner and more, and then serves defendant with process at the Miami airport. (Result: at least in the absence of some basis other than this presence, Florida court will not exercise jurisdiction.)

Today the unreasonableness test will most likely mandate the same result achieved under the older fraud and force rules.

b) Immunity

Many states grant immunity from service of process to witnesses, counsel, and parties when present in the state for attendance at litigation and during a reasonable time coming and going. Similarly, a state will not exercise power over a chattel sent into the state for use as evidence.

Example: A witness comes to Florida to testify at a criminal trial, and during the trial is served with process in an unrelated civil action. (Result: at least in the absence of some basis other than this presence, Florida court will not exercise jurisdiction.)

Granting immunity facilitates judicial administration. For example, it encourages the attendance of witnesses.

c) Forum Non Conveniens

Most states have adopted this important doctrine, by which a state court may discretionarily decline existing territorial jurisdiction if the court is a seriously inappropriate forum and if a substantially more appropriate forum is available to plaintiff.

> *Example:* Virginia plaintiff brought suit in New York against a Pennsylvania corporation qualified to do business in both New York and Virginia, alleging negligence that caused the plaintiff's warehouse in Virginia to burn. Defendant moved for dismissal, arguing that Virginia was the appropriate place for trial. (Result: dismissal.) *Gulf Oil Corp. v. Gilbert*, 330 U.S. 501, 67 S.Ct. 839 (1947) (suit in federal court). See also *Piper Aircraft Co. v. Reyno*, 454 U.S. 235, 102 S.Ct. 252 (1981) (shift to doctrine of convenience).

There are several important rules here: (1) Forum non conveniens may be invoked on the defendant's motion or on the court's own motion. (2) In passing on the motion, the court must give the plaintiff's choice of forum great weight, but the interests of the parties and the public for and against litigating elsewhere enter the balance. Examples of relevant factors include residence of the parties, relative ease of access to sources of proof, and which state's law will apply. (3) If the court grants the motion, the remedy is ultimately dismissal, either outright or conditional upon defendant's waiving defenses (such as personal jurisdiction or the statute of limitations) that would impede suit in the more appropriate forum.

d) Door–closing Statutes

Certain state statutes denying court access are closely related to forum non conveniens. For example, a statute might close the courthouse doors to any suit between nonresidents on a claim arising outside the state.

4) Venue Restrictions

Related to all these limits on state-court territorial jurisdiction are state venue restrictions, which most often are defined as those rules of territorial authority to adjudicate that specify as proper fora only certain courts within a state having territorial jurisdiction. Thus, state-court territorial jurisdiction comprises interstate rules, while state-court venue is intrastate.

a) Venue Statutes

The state legislature distributes judicial business among the counties or other state subdivisions by means of a statutory venue scheme. This scheme turns on such grounds as where the claim arose or where defendant or plaintiff resides or does business. The venue scheme varies from state to state, but is seldom a monument to good policy or intelligent drafting.

b) Local Actions

Most states perpetuate an ancient, confusing, and unsound judge-made doctrine that overrides the usual venue statutes and requires any of a rather arbitrary group of actions to be brought in the county or other subdivision where the subject matter of the action is located. These "local actions" contrast with "transitory actions," which can be brought anywhere the usual rules of territorial jurisdiction and venue are satisfied. Local actions usually include proceedings in rem and those within subtype one of quasi in rem, as well as certain personal actions such as trespass to land, negligent damage to land, and abatement of nuisance. Note that if the subject matter of a local action is not located within the state, this venue doctrine restricts territorial authority to adjudicate on an interstate level.

c) Territorial Jurisdiction Versus Venue

The accepted interstate-intrastate distinction is not very meaningful. A sounder and more fruitful doctrinal distinction would view territorial jurisdiction as those mandatory limits flowing from the Federal Constitution, while considering venue to encompass all the other limitations both interstate and intrastate in nature. In this view, venue appears as a scheme that aims in an integrated fashion at the convenient, efficient, and otherwise desirable distribution of judicial business among and within the states, and as a scheme that is not immune to reform by legislative or judicial reworking or refinement.

d. **Agreements Among Parties**

The parties may consent in advance to state-court territorial jurisdiction not otherwise existing, and they may waive in advance the restrictions of state-court venue and the other doctrines of self-restraint. Most states under modern law will usually give effect to such agreements, apparently subject to ordinary contract law and the requirement that the forum not be an unconscionable one.

Conversely, the parties generally may, by agreement, restrict any potential litigation to one or more courts among the fora otherwise permissible under the law of state-court territorial authority to adjudicate.

Example: In a contract providing that a German corporation (G) would tow from Louisiana to Italy an oil rig belonging to an American corporation (T) based in Texas, G and T agreed that any dispute would be heard in a London court known for its neutrality and expertise in such matters. After a storm damaged the rig under tow, G put into port in Florida. T sued G in Florida, but G invoked the "forum-selection clause." (Result: dismissal.) *The Bremen v. Zapata Off–Shore Co.,* 407 U.S. 1, 92 S.Ct. 1907 (1972) (suit in federal court). See also *Carnival Cruise Lines v. Shute,* 499 U.S. 585, 111 S.Ct. 1522 (1991) (further shift toward contract paradigm).

2. LIMITS ON FEDERAL DISTRICT COURTS

a. Federal Law

1) Federal Constitution
The principal constitutional limitation on a federal court's territorial jurisdiction is the Due Process Clause of the Fifth Amendment. Although clear case law is very scanty, it seems that this Clause operates analogously to the Fourteenth Amendment's Clause. Thus, here due process requires the categorization of the action and then the application of both the power and the unreasonableness tests.

a) Power
The federal court must have power over the target of the action. But here power requires only "minimum contacts" *with the United States.* Thus, this power test is an impediment only in international cases.

b) Unreasonableness
The particular district must not be fundamentally unfair in light of all the interests of defendant, plaintiff, and the public

concerning the litigation. This is the same test of "fair play and substantial justice" that applies to state courts, although very rarely results would differ because suit in a federal *district* court affects the relevant interests practically in a marginally different way than does suit in *state* court.

c) Other Constitutional Provisions

Just as for state courts, the First Amendment possibly may restrict federal-court territorial jurisdiction.

2) Jurisdictional Statutes and Rules

Congress and the Supreme Court, the latter acting as Congress's rulemaker, have authorized varying degrees of federal-court territorial jurisdiction in a confusing complex of provisions treating service of process. First, the idea of service of process must be here reintroduced. Second, the structure of the federal service scheme must be sketched. Third, jurisdictional reach under each provision may then be considered.

a) Service of Process

The rules of service concern the means of officially notifying the interested persons that plaintiff has brought an action and of formally asserting power over the target of the action. Federal Rule 4(a) specifies the form of the summons. Rule 4(b) dictates that upon or after the plaintiff's filing a complaint, the court clerk must issue the summons. Rule 4(c) says that the summons must be served with a copy of the complaint, and then describes the persons authorized to effect service. Rule 4(e)–(j) deals with the "manner of service," i.e., the mechanics of delivering original process to different kinds of defendants. Also, Rule 4(*l*) treats proof of service, and Rule 4(m) sets a time limit for service. Since 1993, Rule 4(d) provides that a plaintiff suing an individual (who is neither a minor nor an incompetent), a corporation, or an unincorporated association can mail a notice to a defendant requesting a waiver of service: if defendant complies, the suit can proceed without the need for the rather expensive formality of service; if defendant fails to comply, plaintiff needs to arrange for service of process, but defendant normally will have to pay the expenses of that service.

b) **Structure of Service Provisions**

Federal Rule 4 goes on to deal with a variety of service situations.

Important Examples: (1) *Rule 4(k)(1)(A)*. This is read to cover all ordinary situations of service.

(2) *Rule 4(k)(1)(B)*. This special alternative treats service within the United States and *within a 100–mile radius of the particular federal courthouse*. Note that it *applies only to additional parties being brought in under Rules 14 and 19*. This "100–mile bulge" provision facilitates complex litigation in metropolitan areas.

(3) *Rule 4(k)(1)(C)*. This incorporates by reference any special federal service statute, such as the securities long-arm statute.

(4) *Rule 4(k)(2)*. This narrow alternative applies in *federal law* actions, but *only to defendants who are beyond the jurisdiction of every single state*.

(5) *Rule 4(n)(1)*. 28 U.S.C.A. § 1655 is a special federal service provision within Rule 4(n)(1). It provides for service in federal proceedings *in rem* and those within *subtype one of quasi in rem*.

(6) *Rule 4(n)(2)*. This also treats service in nonpersonal proceedings, sometimes offering an alternative to 28 U.S.C.A. § 1655. Rule 4(n)(2) incorporates by reference the forum state's service provisions for proceedings *in rem* and *quasi in rem*.

c) **Territorial Jurisdiction Under Service Provisions**

Federal Rule 4 thus provides the structure for specifying the "circumstances of service," i.e., the situations where service will be effective in asserting territorial jurisdiction.

Important Examples: (1) *Rule 4(k)(1)(A)*. This Rule itself specifies that state law governs the circumstances of service thereunder, whether the claim is federally created or state-created. Thus, the federal court can reach only as far as the forum state could under its long-arm statutes and under the Fourteenth Amendment.

(2) *Rule 4(k)(1)(B)*. Currently, there are numerous possible views on how to read this Rule with respect to federal-court

reach. The best but disputed view is that if the additional party is served within the bulge, then the only restrictions on reach are the Fifth Amendment limits on the federal court. For illustration, if a third-party defendant in an action in the Southern District of New York is personally served in Hackensack, New Jersey, the only questions will be whether she has minimum contacts with the United States and whether it is unreasonable to hear the impleader claim in the Southern District.

(3) *Rule 4(k)(1)(C).* Here federal-court reach turns on the particular federal service statute. The reach extends to the Fifth Amendment limits, unless the statute otherwise indicates.

(4) *Rule 4(k)(2).* Federal reach here extends to the Fifth Amendment limits, so that defendant must have minimum contacts with the United States, and the particular district must not be an unreasonable forum.

(5) *Rule 4(n)(1).* 28 U.S.C.A. § 1655 requires the res to be in the district where the federal court sits.

(6) *Rule 4(n)(2).* This Rule requires the res to be in the district where the federal court sits, and provides that state law further governs the circumstances of service thereunder.

d) Summary

Federal courts generally exercise territorial jurisdiction only where authorized by Congress or its rulemaker. This authorization is implicitly or explicitly embodied in the variety of statutes and Rules treating federal service. For service under some of these provisions, federal law exclusively governs territorial jurisdiction. That federal law usually comprises only the Fifth Amendment due process standard. For service under the other provisions, the provision itself adopts state jurisdictional law. This means that the local state would have to be able to exercise jurisdiction under its long-arm statutes and under the Fourteenth Amendment.

Of great practical importance is the fact that to the extent these service provisions are construed to fall short of authorizing all the jurisdiction permitted by the Federal Constitution, these provisions serve in effect to restrict federal-court jurisdiction.

3) **Other Doctrines of Self–Restraint**
Just as state courts have done, federal courts have developed a number of doctrines that further restrict their exercise of territorial jurisdiction.

a) **Fraud or Force**
A federal court will not exercise jurisdiction acquired through fraud or unlawful force.

b) **Immunity**
Federal courts grant immunity from service of process to witnesses, counsel, and parties when in attendance at litigation and during a reasonable time coming and going. A similar rule exists for chattels used as evidence.

c) **Forum Non Conveniens**
A federal court may discretionarily decline existing territorial jurisdiction if the court is a seriously inappropriate forum, if a substantially more appropriate *foreign or state* forum is available to plaintiff, and if transfer of venue to a more convenient federal forum (a procedure described below) is not an adequate remedy. Although the *Erie* question here is not settled, the better view is that federal law governs forum non conveniens in federal court.

Application of federal law here conforms with the general rule that federal courts do not look to state law concerning the other doctrines of self-restraint and venue.

4) **Venue Restrictions**
Related to all these limits on federal-court territorial jurisdiction are federal venue restrictions, which most often are rather arbitrarily defined as those rules of territorial authority to adjudicate that are not linked to service provisions but instead are separately prescribed.

Unlike most service provisions, venue rules distribute judicial business on a district-by-district level. See generally Wright's Hornbook § 42. (Many districts are subdivided into divisions for local judicial administration.)

a) **General Venue Statute**
Under 28 U.S.C.A. § 1391, venue lies in a district where (1) any defendant resides if all defendants reside in the same state or (2)

where a substantial part of the events or omissions giving rise to the claim occurred or a substantial part of property that is the subject of the action is situated. However, (3) the statute effectively waives this venue requirement in the rare circumstance when it would block suit in every federal court.

Example: In the Federal District of Utah, P–1 of North Dakota and P–2 of South Dakota sue D–1 of Wyoming and D–2 of Utah, based on a traffic accident in Salt Lake City. (Result: federal venue lies in Utah, but nowhere else.)

For an individual, the cases equate residence with the district in which the individual is domiciled as a U.S. citizen; thus, individuals have only one residence. *For a corporate defendant,* § 1391(c) expands residence to include any district where the corporation would be subject to personal jurisdiction. *For an unincorporated association,* the courts apply the rules that they had developed for corporations.

b) **Special Venue Statutes**

There are many federal statutes prescribing special rules for particular kinds of cases. They form a hopelessly complex pattern and raise countless interpretive problems. Most are read to supplement the choice of venue under 28 U.S.C.A. § 1391, but some are read as overriding § 1391.

Important Examples: (1) *Shareholders' Derivative Actions.* 28 U.S.C.A. § 1401 adds, as a permissible venue, "any judicial district where the corporation might have sued the same defendants."

(2) *Aliens.* Section 1391(d) virtually eliminates the venue requirement as to an alien defendant.

(3) *Interpleader Actions.* 28 U.S.C.A. § 1397 provides that statutory interpleader suits may be brought only in a district wherein any claimant resides, thus overriding § 1391(a) and (b).

(4) *Removed Actions.* 28 U.S.C.A. § 1441(a), which provides that the venue for a removed action is the district in which the particular state courthouse is located, overrides the rest of federal venue law.

c)   Local Actions

The federal courts perpetuate this doctrine, which was described above for state courts. The federal doctrine derives from case law, although it is now mentioned in 28 U.S.C.A. § 1392. The doctrine overrides the rest of federal venue law, except the removal statute. The doctrine requires local actions to be brought in the district where the subject matter of the action is located.

Example: Edward Livingston of New York sued Thomas Jefferson of Virginia in the Virginia federal court, alleging trespass to land in New Orleans. (Result: dismissal for improper venue. Venue lay only where the land was, even though Jefferson was not subject to service of process issuing from there.) *Livingston v. Jefferson*, 15 F.Cas. 660 (C.C.D.Va.1811) (No. 8411).

d)   Territorial Jurisdiction Versus Venue

Both Federal Rule 4 and 28 U.S.C.A. § 1391 crudely perform their common mission of distributing judicial business within the federal system in a convenient, efficient, and otherwise desirable manner. Classifying the former as jurisdiction and the latter as venue can be dangerous to the extent practical consequences ride on the distinction, and this misleading line also leaves the doctrines in-between as difficult to classify. So, just as for state courts, a sounder and more fruitful doctrinal distinction would view territorial jurisdiction as those mandatory limits flowing from the Federal Constitution, while considering venue to include all the lesser limitations. This might induce a reform whereby Congress would extend service to those constitutional limits and would simplify and rationalize the whole venue scheme.

5)   Transfer of Venue

Preempting most of forum non conveniens, Congress in 1948 authorized the discretionary transfer of a federal case to another federal district.

See generally Wright's Hornbook § 44.

a)   28 U.S.C.A. § 1404(a)

An action properly commenced in or removed to a district court may be transferred to a more convenient district. There are several important rules here: (1) Such transfer may be invoked on any party's motion or on the court's own motion. (2) In passing on the motion, the court considers all relevant interests, but will grant it on a lesser showing of relative convenience than is required under forum non conveniens. (3) If the court grants the motion, the remedy is transfer rather than dismissal. (4) Most importantly, under § 1404(a) transfer can be ordered only to a federal forum where the case "might have been brought." This provision has unfortunately been read to mean a district where plaintiff could originally have satisfied the federal requirements of territorial jurisdiction and venue over the defendant's objection. See *Hoffman v. Blaski*, 363 U.S. 335, 80 S.Ct. 1084 (1960).

b) **28 U.S.C.A. § 1406(a)**

There is another important, but quite different, transfer statute. Under § 1406(a) as construed, if a federal action fails to meet the requirements of either territorial jurisdiction or venue, or both, the court may "in the interest of justice" transfer the case to a proper federal district. See *Goldlawr, Inc. v. Heiman*, 369 U.S. 463, 82 S.Ct. 913 (1962). Thus, a misguided plaintiff might avoid dismissal after the statute of limitations has run. (Somewhat similarly, 28 U.S.C.A. § 1631 authorizes transfer from one federal court to another in order to cure a defect of subject-matter jurisdiction.)

c) **Choice of Law**

After transfer under 28 U.S.C.A. § 1404(a), the transferee court applies the law that the transferor court would have.

> *Example:* Plaintiffs sued in the Eastern District of Pennsylvania for wrongful deaths in an air crash in Boston. Defendants moved to transfer under § 1404(a) to the District of Massachusetts. What law would apply in the transferee court on, say, damages? (Result: if transfer were ordered, the District of Massachusetts would have to apply the law that the Pennsylvania federal court would have, which under the *Klaxon* rule would have been Pennsylvania state law.) *Van Dusen v. Barrack*, 376 U.S. 612, 639, 84 S.Ct. 805, 821 (1964) (such transfer is "but a change of courtrooms," not law).

After transfer under 28 U.S.C.A. § 1406(a) from an improper court to a proper court, however, the transferee court applies transferee law—except that the transferee's statute of limitations will be tolled by the initial filing if within the transferor's as well as the transferee's limitations period.

b. International Law

In the absence of a specific treaty, international law imposes no significant restrictions on federal-court territorial authority to adjudicate beyond those restrictions already imposed by the Due Process Clause of the Fifth Amendment.

c. State Law

As already noted, state jurisdictional law frequently applies in federal court, because the applicable federal statute or Rule incorporates that state law. The bottom line is this: as a result of such self-restraint by the federal government, a federal court usually reaches no farther than the forum state does, despite the constitutional authority to reach considerably farther.

d. Agreements Among Parties

Just as for state-court litigation, the parties generally may, by agreement, expand or restrict the choice among federal fora. Ultimately, however, 28 U.S.C.A. § 1404(a) or forum non conveniens can override such an agreement.

X

Notice

■ ANALYSIS

A. INTRODUCTION TO NOTICE

For a court properly to undertake a civil adjudication, the persons whose property or liberty interests are to be significantly affected must receive *adequate notice*. If any such person duly challenges the adequacy of notice, the courts must pass on whether the notice satisfied constitutional and other requirements.

B. CONSTITUTIONAL REQUIREMENT

State and federal courts can be treated together here, because the same requirement of procedural due process applies to the state courts under the Fourteenth Amendment to the Federal Constitution as applies to the federal courts under the Fifth Amendment. Moreover, the same requirement applies regardless of the category of territorial jurisdiction, be it jurisdiction in personam, in rem, or quasi in rem.

1. GENERAL RULE

For adjudication, due process requires fair notice of the pendency of the action to the affected person or her representative. Fair notice must be suitably formal in tenor and informative in content. Fair notice must be either (1) actual notice or (2) notice that is reasonably calculated to result in actual notice. Fair notice must afford a reasonable opportunity to be heard.

Example: A trustee of a common trust fund sued to get a judicial settlement of accounts. In accordance with statute, notice to the numerous trust beneficiaries was by publication in a newspaper. (Result: notice is insufficient under the Due Process Clause. Due diligence must be used in identifying and locating affected persons, and in these circumstances they then must be informed at least by ordinary mail. For those who cannot be identified or located, "constructive service" in the form of notice by publication suffices.) *Mullane v. Central Hanover Bank & Trust Co.,* 339 U.S. 306, 314, 70 S.Ct. 652, 657 (1950) (notice need not be perfect, but must be "reasonably calculated, under all the circumstances, to apprise interested parties of the pendency of the action").

2. NOTICE BEFORE SEIZING PROPERTY

Consider the situation where plaintiff seeks seizure of the defendant's property as security for an eventual judgment, as by attachment or garnishment under Federal Rule 64. According to fairly recent decisions by a divided Supreme Court, due process actively constrains this procedure. But many unsettled questions remain.

a. Leading Cases

The Supreme Court struck down the procedure employed in *Sniadach v. Family Fin. Corp.*, 395 U.S. 337, 89 S.Ct. 1820 (1969) (garnishment of wages), *Fuentes v. Shevin*, 407 U.S. 67, 92 S.Ct. 1983 (1972) (replevin of stove and stereo), and *North Georgia Finishing, Inc. v. Di–Chem, Inc.*, 419 U.S. 601, 95 S.Ct. 719 (1975) (garnishment of corporation's bank account). However, in *Mitchell v. W.T. Grant Co.*, 416 U.S. 600, 94 S.Ct. 1895 (1974) (sequestration of household goods in which plaintiff had pre-existing lien), the Court upheld a state procedure under which:

(1) plaintiff must state specific facts by affidavit supporting issuance of the writ of sequestration;

(2) plaintiff must file a bond sufficient to protect defendant against any damage resulting from wrongful issuance;

(3) a judge issues the writ;

(4) defendant is able immediately to seek dissolution of the writ, which must then be ordered unless plaintiff proves the grounds upon which the writ was issued; and

(5) defendant is able to regain possession upon posting a bond for 125% of the lesser of the value of the property or the amount of the claim.

Then in *Connecticut v. Doehr*, 501 U.S. 1, 111 S.Ct. 2105 (1991) (attachment of real estate), the Supreme Court, in striking down the state procedure, generalized that due process requires a procedural safeguard such as pre-seizure notice when the risk of harm without the safeguard substantially exceeds the cost of the safeguard.

b. General Rule

Fair notice and opportunity to be heard must be given (or at least the procedure of a *Mitchell*-like statute must be followed in the case of a pre-judgment seizure where plaintiff has a pre-existing interest in the property or where there are exigent circumstances) before governmental action may unduly impair a person's property interest. The required level of procedural protection usually depends on a balancing of the various interests involved: when the creditor's interest is relatively substantial (e.g., where plaintiff has a pre-existing lien on the property or where exigent circumstances endanger security), the Constitution requires only the procedure of a *Mitchell*-like statute.

c. Other Applications

This general rule has implications ranging far beyond pre-judgment seizures of property for security. Generally, those implications extend to the many other ways in which the government may temporarily alter legal rights. Specifically, they extend to seizures of property for purposes other than security.

1) Seizure for Jurisdictional Purposes

The rule for pre-judgment seizures of property for security should also apply when property is seized to provide power for the exercise of territorial jurisdiction, as in nonpersonal jurisdiction under Federal Rule 4(n)(2).

2) Post–Judgment Seizure

Apparently, defendant is entitled to less procedural protection when her property is seized to enforce an already rendered judgment, as by execution under Federal Rule 69. Perhaps the only requirement is fair and prompt post-execution notice and opportunity to be heard.

C. NONCONSTITUTIONAL REQUIREMENTS

The provisions for service of process further specify the manner of giving notice to parties.

1. MANNER OF SERVICE

The structure of service provisions was sketched in Chapter IX–C above, by using federal service for illustration. Here the manner of service will be elaborated, primarily by drawing examples from the federal procedure for service on defendants in personal actions. See generally Wright's Hornbook §§ 64–65.

a. Serving Individuals

Under Federal Rule 4(e)(2), a process server may serve an individual defendant by handing her a copy of the summons and the complaint (so-called personal delivery), or by leaving these papers at her dwelling house or usual place of abode with some person of suitable age and discretion who resides there or by delivering these papers to her agent authorized by appointment or by law to receive service of process (examples of so-called substituted service, i.e., service other than by personal delivery). A special rule for minors and incompetents appears in Rule 4(g).

b. Serving Corporations and Unincorporated Associations

Under Federal Rule 4(h)(1)(B), a process server may serve such a defendant by delivering a copy of the summons and the complaint to one of its officers or to its agent.

c. Serving Other Defendants

Federal Rule 4(i) and (j) makes special provision for serving governmental defendants. The many other service provisions cover other special cases. See, e.g., Rule 4(f) (service in foreign country). However, some merely diversify the manner of service for the ordinary cases. See, e.g., Rule 4(e)(1) (service under state law). Sometimes no service technique has been specified or no usual technique can be employed, as where a defendant has completely disappeared; the court can then permit "expedient service," which is service in such manner as the court directs.

d. Service Tactics

Process servers must sometimes be very ingenious or devious to serve a defendant. They can effect service by fraud, provided that the fraud does not undermine the notice-giving function of service and does not supply the only basis for territorial jurisdiction. On the one hand, they can gain access to defendant by disguising their identity, although they cannot in July serve process hidden in a gift-box with a do-not-open-until-Christmas note and they cannot establish jurisdiction by fraudulently luring defendant into the state. On the other hand, use of unlawful force in serving process is held to invalidate that service.

2. TECHNICAL REQUIREMENTS OF SERVICE

Local law may strictly enforce some of the nonconstitutional requirements for giving notice. For example, defendant may succeed in attacking notice if the summons inaccurately named her or if the manner of service did not precisely comply with the statutes and rules. However, the trend is away from an overly strict approach, with courts now ignoring such irregularities (1) where the party actually received suitably formal and informative notice or (2) where the form of the notice and the manner of transmitting it substantially complied with the prescribed procedure.

Conversely, local law may dispense altogether with the requirement of formal service of process, as is done for example in connection with jurisdiction over plaintiffs for counterclaims. Moreover, a person may waive service of process.

D. CONTRACTUAL WAIVER OF PROTECTIONS

Surprisingly enough, a person may waive in advance all these procedural protections. However, the waiver of the due process rights must be voluntary, intelligent, and knowing.

Example: As part of a business deal, a corporation for consideration and on advice of counsel signed a "cognovit note" or confession of judgment, a device whereby a debtor consents that upon default its creditor may obtain a judgment without notice or hearing. An Ohio court entered judgment on the cognovit note. Under Ohio law, the court did have discretionary power to open the judgment later if there were a showing of a valid defense. (Result: entry of judgment comports with due process.) *D.H. Overmyer Co. v. Frick Co.,* 405 U.S. 174, 92 S.Ct. 775 (1972) (noting possibility of different result in consumer setting, and noting that cognovit notes are in many situations prohibited or restricted by statute).

XI

Procedural Incidents of Forum–Authority Doctrines

■ ANALYSIS

A. **Procedure for Raising**
1. Subject–Matter Jurisdiction
2. Territorial Authority to Adjudicate and Notice

B. **Consequences of Raising**
1. Subject–Matter Jurisdiction
2. Territorial Authority to Adjudicate and Notice

C. **Consequences of Not Raising**
1. Litigated Action
2. Complete Default

A. PROCEDURE FOR RAISING

The procedural treatment of subject-matter jurisdiction significantly differs from that of territorial authority to adjudicate and of notice.

1. SUBJECT–MATTER JURISDICTION

This requirement is considered so fundamental that its satisfaction is open to question throughout the ordinary course of the initial action. Being courts of limited jurisdiction, the federal courts apply this requirement somewhat more strictly than do most state courts. See generally Wright's Hornbook §§ 7, 69; Judgments Second § 11 cmt. d.

a. Pleading

The party invoking federal jurisdiction must affirmatively allege the grounds upon which subject-matter jurisdiction depends. See Federal Rule 8(a)(1) (complaint); 28 U.S.C.A. § 1446(a) (notice of removal). If challenged, that party bears the burden of showing that such jurisdiction exists.

b. Challenging

Any party may challenge federal jurisdiction at any time in the ordinary course of the initial action, and the trial or appellate court should on its own motion dismiss for lack of subject-matter jurisdiction whenever perceived. See Federal Rule 12(h)(3). Thus, even the party who invoked jurisdiction may, on his appeal from a judgment against him, challenge such jurisdiction.

2. TERRITORIAL AUTHORITY TO ADJUDICATE AND NOTICE

In the initial action the key for defendant is to raise these personal defenses in a way that avoids waiving them.

a. Special Appearance

This is the basic technique by which defendant raises these threshold defenses.

1) Availability

There are four significant judicial approaches to the availability of a special appearance.

a) Appearance Treated as Waiver

According to old case law, a state can constitutionally treat *any* appearance as waiving these threshold defenses. Thus, defendant would have to choose between (1) appearing in order to defend on the merits and (2) defaulting in order to preserve the important threshold defenses as grounds for relief from judgment. However, today all states have removed this wrenching dilemma by permitting some manner of special appearance.

b) Defense on Merits Treated as Waiver

Although allowing a special appearance, a few states rule that if the trial judge rejects such challenge, defendant must then choose between (1) defending on the merits and (2) appealing only on the basis of those threshold defenses. In other words, these states treat a defense on the merits as a waiver of any right to pursue further those threshold defenses.

c) Interlocutory Appeal Allowed

Some states mitigate this latter dilemma by permitting defendant to appeal an unsuccessful special appearance before defending on the merits.

d) Defense on Merits and Final Appeal Allowed

Most states, *and the federal courts*, permit in effect a special appearance. If that fails, defendant may proceed to defend on the merits. If that too fails, defendant may appeal both on those threshold defenses and on the merits. See *Harkness v. Hyde*, 98 U.S. 476 (1879) (federal approach).

2) Procedure

Defendant must be very careful to follow precisely the procedural steps of a special appearance, making immediately clear that she is appearing specially to challenge territorial authority to adjudicate or notice, or both, and that she is not appearing generally. The correct steps vary from state to state. See generally Judgments Second § 10 cmt. b. In federal court the "special appearance" is less formalistic, instead coming in the form of a Federal Rule 12(b) defense:

(1) Rule 12(b)(2) covers the defense of lack of territorial jurisdiction;

(2) Rule 12(b)(3) covers improper venue;

(3) Rule 12(b)(4) covers defects in the form of the summons; and

(4) Rule 12(b)(5) covers defects in the manner of transmitting notice.

Defendant must raise any such available defenses at the very outset, either in a Rule 12(b) motion or in her answer, whichever comes first. With some risk, defendant may first engage in certain preliminary procedural maneuvers, such as moving for an extension of time to respond. But if defendant first does anything more substantive, she waives those threshold defenses. See Rule 12(h)(1). Indeed, even after properly asserting such defenses, defendant may waive them by inconsistent activity, such as by asserting a permissive counterclaim.

b. Limited Appearance

To be sharply distinguished from a special appearance is the technique by which someone restricts his appearance in an action so as not to confer jurisdiction over his person for additional claims. The most frequently discussed example is the "limited appearance," whereby a defendant may limit her appearance to defending a nonpersonal proceeding on the merits without submitting to personal jurisdiction. Note that given the existence of proper nonpersonal jurisdiction but the absence of the limited-appearance option, defendant would have to choose between (1) losing her property or other such interests by default and (2) making a general appearance.

Example: In order to recover for personal injuries from a traffic accident in Japan, a New York plaintiff sues in New York for $60,000 by attaching the French defendant's land in New York worth $30,000. Defendant wishes to defend her property by contesting negligence, but without submitting to personal jurisdiction. (Result: fairness counsels that defendant should be able to make a limited appearance.)

Although there is disagreement, the better view is that adjudication pursuant to such a limited appearance should have *no res judicata effects* other than determining interests in the property. (See Part Six below.)

1) Availability

Confusion shrouds the availability of the limited appearance. The answer lies in scattered case law.

a) General Rule

The best view is that a limited appearance should be available if it is constitutionally unreasonable for the forum to exercise personal jurisdiction with respect to the additional claim concurrently with hearing the nonpersonal action.

> *Example:*   In order to foreclose a mortgage on a French defendant's land in New York, a New York plaintiff sues in New York by attaching the land. Defendant wishes to defend on the merits without submitting to personal jurisdiction for any excess amount owing on the underlying debt. (Result: efficiency counsels that defendant should not be able to make a limited appearance, because a New York forum may reasonably exercise personal jurisdiction with respect to the associated claim for debt against the appearing defendant.)

b) Effect of *Shaffer*

Since *Shaffer v. Heitner*, 433 U.S. 186, 97 S.Ct. 2569 (1977), prohibited unreasonable nonpersonal jurisdiction, there are few occasions to permit a limited appearance. If the nonpersonal jurisdiction is reasonable, then most likely the requisite personal jurisdiction will be reasonable too, making a limited appearance unavailable. But there may be situations where liability limited to the property is reasonable but unlimited personal liability would be unreasonable, as in certain instances of jurisdiction by necessity.

c) Effect of *Erie*

It is unclear whether state law on limited appearances ever applies in federal court under the *Erie* doctrine. The marginally better view is that this matter, just like the other procedural incidents, is governed by federal law in federal court.

2) Procedure

Defendant must make clear at the very outset her intention to limit her appearance. Note that defendant might also make a special appearance to challenge the court's jurisdiction over the property, as for example to dispute the situs of an intangible. Note also that defendant may choose to make a general appearance, which permits a personal judgment on any additional asserted claim.

B. CONSEQUENCES OF RAISING

If any of these forum-authority defenses is raised in the ordinary course of the initial action, the judge without jury (1) may, on the application of any party, hear and determine the defense in a pretrial proceeding or (2) may choose to defer the issue until trial. See, e.g., Federal Rule 12(i). In the post-trial period, a defense of lack of subject-matter jurisdiction will be determined whenever raised. After determination of a forum-authority defense, there may arise the question of its *res judicata* effects. The normal rules of res judicata apply. But there is the important additional question of the effect that a determination rejecting such a defense has on an attack on the resultant judgment, not in the ordinary course of review in the trial and appellate courts but in subsequent litigation. There the principle of finality generally outweighs the concern for validity, giving the determination preclusive effect and thus generating a special variety of res judicata labeled "jurisdiction to determine jurisdiction."

1. SUBJECT–MATTER JURISDICTION

A finding of the existence of subject-matter jurisdiction precludes the parties from attacking the resultant judgment on that ground in subsequent litiga-tion, except in special circumstances such as where (1) the court plainly lacked subject-matter jurisdiction or (2) the judgment substantially infringes on the authority of another court or agency. See generally Judgments Second § 12 cmts. c, e.

2. TERRITORIAL AUTHORITY TO ADJUDICATE AND NOTICE

A finding of the existence of territorial authority to adjudicate or adequate notice precludes the appearing parties from attacking the resultant judgment on either ground in subsequent litigation. See generally id. § 10 cmt. d.

C. CONSEQUENCES OF NOT RAISING

Consider finally the question of what happens if any of these forum-authority defenses is not raised at all in the ordinary course of the initial action. Here there is a basic distinction between litigated actions and complete defaults.

1. LITIGATED ACTION

a. Subject–Matter Jurisdiction

Because unraised subject-matter jurisdiction is supposedly always im-plicitly determined to exist in any action litigated to judgment, such determination has the *res judicata* consequences of an actually litigated determination of the existence of subject-matter jurisdiction insofar as foreclosing attack on the judgment. However, the court in subsequent litigation may here be more likely to find applicable an exception to res judicata. See generally id. § 12 cmt. d.

b. Territorial Authority to Adjudicate and Notice

By failing properly to raise any such threshold defense, an appearing defendant *waives* it. See, e.g., Federal Rule 12(h)(1). This precludes the appearing parties from attacking the resultant judgment on that ground in subsequent litigation.

2. COMPLETE DEFAULT

a. Subject–Matter Jurisdiction

There being no res judicata on this point in this situation, a party may later obtain *relief from judgment* on the ground of lack of subject-matter jurisdiction, provided that he has not induced another person's substantial reliance on the default judgment. See generally Judgments Second §§ 65–66.

b. Territorial Authority to Adjudicate and Notice

There being no res judicata or waiver on this point in this situation, an aggrieved party may later obtain *relief from judgment* on the ground of a constitutional defect in territorial authority to adjudicate or notice, provided that she has not induced another person's substantial reliance on the default judgment. The law of the court that rendered the judgment normally will treat as additional grounds for relief from a default judgment any violations of the nonconstitutional requirements of territorial jurisdiction and the important nonconstitutional requirements of notice, although the list of available grounds might contract as the mode, place, and time of the attack on the judgment become more distant from the initial action. See generally id. Under a radical view of some commentators, most or all of territorial authority to adjudicate (and even subject-matter jurisdiction too) should be simply removed from the list of available grounds for relief from judgment in subsequent litigation. All this raises squarely the problems of relief from judgment, which is covered more fully in Chapter XVII–C below.

Example: P sues D in the United States District Court for the District of Maine. Personal jurisdiction over D is questionable. What may D do? (Result: *either* D may suffer a default foreclosing the merits but then later attack the judgment on the jurisdictional ground as when P attempts to enforce it *or* D may appear in Maine's federal court to litigate fully the jurisdictional point and the merits, *but not both appear now and attack later.*)

REVIEW QUESTIONS

Questions (1)–(4): D, a large department-store chain, fired P for being late. But P believes that she was fired because she is female. There is no diversity of citizenship between P and D.

1. **T or F**   If P brings against D a gender discrimination action under the federal civil rights laws in federal court, the district judge should dismiss because there is no diversity jurisdiction.

2. **T or F**   P may join a state claim against D for breach of employment contract in the federal court.

3. **T or F**   If P instead brings her state contract claim in a state court, and if D's defense is based on federal law, D cannot remove to federal court.

4. **T or F**   If instead P brings her gender discrimination action in a state court, the state judge should dismiss because the Constitution prohibits state courts from hearing actions arising under federal law.

Questions (5)–(7): Dinc, an Ohio corporation with offices and operations solely in that state, manufactures chain saws. Dinc sells some to Dan, a Michigan citizen and hardware retailer. Dan sells one to Pat, a ballet dancer and Michigan citizen. While using the saw, Pat suffers an injury to her leg. She wishes to sue in federal district court on a state claim for $76,000 in damages.

5. **T or F**   If she sues Dinc and Dan, the court will have subject-matter jurisdiction because the constitutional requirement of partial diversity is satisfied.

6. **T or F**   If she sues only Dinc, and if the judge believes a recovery over $75,000 is highly unlikely, the judge should dismiss.

7. **T or F**   If Pat is young enough to have a guardian ad litem, if her guardian ad litem is from New York and sues only Dan on her behalf, and if there is no jurisdictional amount problem, the court will have subject-matter jurisdiction.

Questions (8)–(12): D of Massachusetts agrees to purchase a painting from P of New Jersey. In return for the painting, D draws a check on his New York bank to the order of P for $170,000. When P deposits the check, it bounces. So P sues D to recover the painting.

8. **T or F**   If P sues in a New York state court with the asserted basis of personal jurisdiction being D's consent to suit in a previous New York action against him on a different contract, there will be proper territorial jurisdiction.

9. **T or F**   If the New York state court has territorial jurisdiction but does not meet the venue requirement of 28 U.S.C.A. § 1391, the action will not be dismissed for that reason.

10. **T or F**   If the New York state court has territorial jurisdiction, the judge may nevertheless dismiss the action under the doctrine of forum non conveniens.

11. **T or F**   If P sues instead in a New York federal court, there will be proper territorial jurisdiction because D has minimum contacts with the United States.

12. **T or F**   If the action is improperly commenced in a New York federal court, and if it is then transferred to the Massachusetts federal court, the latter court will apply the law that the former court would have applied.

Questions (13)–(16): Peg sues Duke, a citizen of Ohio, in the Connecticut federal court.

13. **T or F**   Assume that Duke specially appears and unsuccessfully challenges the court's territorial jurisdiction, that he then litigates the merits and loses, and that he does not appeal. If Peg brings an action in Ohio state court to enforce the judgment, Duke cannot relitigate the rendering court's territorial jurisdiction.

14. **T or F**   If subject-matter jurisdiction was not litigated before or at trial in the initial action, Duke could not raise it after the trial.

15. **T or F**   Assume instead that Duke does not appear in the Connecticut action. If Peg brings an action in Ohio state court to enforce the default judgment, Duke may challenge the rendering court's jurisdiction as well as raise his defenses on the merits.

16. **T or F**   If in the initial action Peg did not actually serve Duke with copies of summons and complaint, but instead served Duke's authorized agent in Connecticut, notice was proper.

17. A, a citizen of New York, agrees to sell his cow to B. Which of the following best represents what the parties may fairly agree to?

   a. To have the law of New York govern their contract.

   b. To confer subject-matter jurisdiction for any contractual dispute on the United States District Court for the Northern District of New York.

   c. To confer exclusive territorial authority to adjudicate any contractual dispute on the state and federal courts in New York.

   d. Both (a) and (c).

   e. Both (b) and (c).

   f. All of (a), (b), and (c).

18. In which of the following situations is federal venue proper in the Southern District of New York for a federal civil rights action by P against D?

   a. P is from New Jersey, D is from Connecticut, and the claim arose in Delaware.

   b. P is from New Jersey, D is from Connecticut, and the claim arose in Ontario.

   c. P is from New York City, D is from Connecticut, and the claim arose in Delaware.

   d. P is from New Jersey, D is from Buffalo, and the claim arose in Delaware.

   e. None of the above.

19. Prepare an essay in response to this question:

Two years ago, in San Francisco, California, P's physician, at her request, inserted into her an intrauterine device manufactured and supplied by Drug Co., a huge Virginia corporation with its principal place of business in Richmond, Virginia, and with no officer or agent in Illinois. P moved to Chicago, Illinois, on July 1 of last year and has maintained her domicile there until the present.

In the following October, P developed an infection and resultant tubal abscess that required a surgical procedure known as a left salpingectomy (removal of the left fallopian tube) on October 28 at Cook County Hospital in Chicago. Recently, she underwent further exploratory surgery there on her right fallopian tube.

P has come to the Chicago law firm for which you work as an associate. A partner has rough-drafted a complaint that contains three counts against Drug Co. sounding under state law in negligence, strict liability, and breach of warranty, and seeking compensatory and punitive damages in excess of a million dollars.

The partner now comes to you, the firm's federal practice expert. He relates the above facts and asks you whether he can bring the action in the United States District Court for the Northern District of Illinois, taking into account requirements of (1) subject-matter jurisdiction, (2) venue, and (3) manner and circumstances of service. You look dazed, so he tells you to convey your opinion in a memorandum to him. He says that if you need more information, you should indicate what information is needed and how it would affect your answer.

PART FOUR

Complex Litigation

■ ANALYSIS

*

XII

Preliminary Considerations

■ ANALYSIS

A. HISTORICAL NOTE

The subject here is the restrictions regarding which claims and parties the litigants must or may join in their lawsuit. Historically, there has been a general movement in our legal systems toward more broadly requiring joinder of multiple claims and parties and toward permitting even more extensive joinder. And complex lawsuits have recently become much more common in practice.

1. COMMON LAW

The common law required and permitted joinder in very limited circumstances. For example, although plaintiff did not have to, he could join claims against defendant if the claims fell in the same form of action (such as different acts of trespass), but he could join little else. Compulsory and permissive joinder of parties was also strictly limited under a highly conceptual approach.

2. EQUITY

Equity took a broader and more instrumental approach to joinder, with the emphasis on effectuating the ideal remedies for the natural rights involved. Here lie the roots of the modern approach.

3. CODE APPROACH

The codes, as interpreted, followed a wooden approach between the legal and equitable traditions of joinder. Accordingly, joinder provisions in states still adhering today to the code approach are relatively narrow in scope.

4. MODERN APPROACH

The widely followed modern pragmatic approach, typified by the Federal Rules, requires and permits the broadest joinder consistent with efficiency and fairness.

B. FEDERAL FOCUS

In this Part Four, the primary focus will be on federal practice, as representative of the modern approach. There will be occasional references to contrasting state practice, where appropriate.

1. GOVERNING LAW

In any federal action, including diversity actions, the governing law on joinder is federal. Contrary state joinder provisions, as opposed to laws establishing the underlying substantive rights, do not apply under *Erie.*

2. FEDERAL JOINDER RULES

The critical provisions are found in Federal Rules 13–14, 17–24, and 42.

3. JURISDICTION AND VENUE

Each claim against a particular party must satisfy the federal requirements of subject-matter jurisdiction, territorial jurisdiction, and venue. Especially relevant here, however, are the ameliorating doctrines of supplemental jurisdiction and ancillary venue. (See Part Three above.)

C. ABUSES

The rationale behind the modern approach to joinder is the efficiency and even the fairness in disposing of much in one shot. Hence, there must be techniques to compel joinder. On the other hand, as things get too complex, fairness notions and even efficiency concerns begin to cut the other way. When the balance swings, there must be cures in the form of simplifying measures.

1. DEFENSES OF NONJOINDER AND MISJOINDER

A party can raise the opposing pleader's violation of the joinder rules in a variety of ways.

a. Nonjoinder

If a claim is unasserted in violation of the minimal rules of compulsory joinder, the defending party on that claim may raise a defense in the nature of res judicata when that claim is asserted in a later action. (See Part Six below.) If a person is not joined in violation of compulsory joinder rules, there is a defense immediately available under Federal Rule 12(b)(7) and (h)(2), or the court may raise the nonjoinder itself.

b. Misjoinder

If assertion of a claim exceeds the very liberal bounds on permissive joinder, a motion to strike or dismiss lies implicitly in the Federal Rules. If a party is joined in violation of permissive joinder rules, a motion to drop the party lies under Rule 21. The Rules are not too systematic on misjoinder and exhibit considerable overlap, so that more specific relief lies in some of the Rules embodying special joinder provisions. See, e.g., Rule 14(a)(4) (striking a third-party claim).

2. JUDICIAL POWER TO COMBINE AND DIVIDE

Even where the pleaders have initially formulated a proper case in that wide area between the limits of compulsory and permissive joinder, the court can reshape the litigation for efficient and fair disposition, upon motion or sua sponte. Thus, under modern joinder rules, the procedural emphasis has shifted from regulating the pleading stage to facilitating the pretrial and trial stages, with judicial discretion becoming the essential mechanism.

a. Expanding the Case

The court may order a *joint trial*, in whole or in part, of separate actions pending before it and involving "a common question of law or fact"; or the court may take the further step of *consolidation*, whereby such actions are treated together for most purposes. Federal Rule 42(a). Furthermore, when actions "involving one or more common questions of fact" are pending in different districts, the judicial panel on multidistrict litigation may transfer them temporarily to any single district for coordinated or consolidated pretrial proceedings. 28 U.S.C.A. § 1407.

b. Contracting the Case

The court may order a *separate trial* of any separate issue or any claim. Federal Rule 42(b). Or the court may take the further step of *severance*, whereby individual claims against particular parties are cut off to stand as separate cases. Rule 21. Again, more specific relief lies in some of the special Rules. See, e.g., Rule 14(a)(4) (court may order separate trial or severance of a third-party claim, or in its discretion may simply strike that claim).

XIII

Multiclaim Litigation

■ ANALYSIS

A. COMPULSORY JOINDER

The subject here is the adjudication of additional claims between the parties. More specifically, the immediate concern is the minimum aspect of initial joinder: What claims *must* be joined in the pleadings? Such joinder requirements are quite limited.

1. CLAIM PRECLUSION

Res judicata does not require a party (e.g., plaintiff) to join separate claims against his opponent, but it generally does in effect require him to put any asserted claim entirely before the court. The eventual judgment will extinguish that whole claim, precluding matters within the claim that were or could have been litigated in the action. (See Part Six below.)

a. Transactional View

The modern approach views "claim" for this purpose as including all rights of plaintiff to remedies against defendant with respect to the transaction from which the action arose.

b. Pleading

For technical pleading purposes, a party need not be concerned with the precise boundaries of his claims, as long as he puts fully before the court any grievances of which he complains. Federal Rule 8(d)(2) allows the party to "set forth two or more statements of a claim or defense alternatively or hypothetically, either in a single count or defense or in separate ones." See also Rules 18(a) and 10(b).

2. COMPULSORY COUNTERCLAIMS

Analogously, Federal Rule 13(a) generally requires a pleader (e.g., defendant) to put forward any claim that the pleader has against any opposing party, if it "arises out of the transaction or occurrence that is the subject matter of the opposing party's claim." Failure to assert such a counterclaim will preclude bringing a subsequent action thereon. See generally Wright's Hornbook § 79.

a. Same Transaction or Occurrence

"Transaction" is more inclusive than "occurrence," the latter word serving primarily to clarify that the former is not limited to a business sense. A counterclaim arises from the same transaction when it bears a "logical relationship" to the main claim, according to *Moore v. N.Y. Cotton Exchange*, 270 U.S. 593, 46 S.Ct. 367 (1926). Subsequent cases have employed this vaguely inclusive test to delimit compulsory counterclaims in a functional way, taking account of the Rule's purpose of efficiency and also considering the particular circumstances in which the question arises.

Example: P brings a diversity action against D, alleging D slandered him by saying that P had sold D worthless securities and thereby caused big damages. D counterclaims to recover the $5000 paid for those securities. P moves to dismiss the counterclaim for lack of subject-matter jurisdiction. (Result: the counterclaim is compulsory and so comes within the doctrine of supplemental jurisdiction. See *Albright v. Gates*, 362 F.2d 928 (9th Cir.1966). However, the counterclaim might have been deemed to have been noncompulsory under Rule 13(a)(1)'s transactional test if the issue had arisen instead in a subsequent state action and the issue's resolution would determine whether D was now precluded from asserting her omitted counterclaim.)

b. Exceptions

There are some exceptions whereby defendant is not obligated to assert a counterclaim arising from the same transaction or occurrence. See 6 Wright, Miller & Kane §§ 1411–1413. Rule 13(a) itself suggests five such exceptions.

1) No Pleading

Because Rule 13(a)(1) requires only inclusion of counterclaims in a "pleading," a defendant who wins a dismissal of the main claim by motion without filing an answer need not assert any counterclaim. See also Rule 7.

2) Unavailable Counterclaim

Because Rule 13(a)(1) applies only to counterclaims that the pleader has at the time of serving the pleading, a defendant need not assert any counterclaim later matured or acquired. See also Rule 13(e).

3) Additional Party

Rule 13(h) expressly authorizes bringing in additional parties to counterclaims. But Rule 13(a) provides that a defendant need not assert any counterclaim involving a necessary party (see Chapter XIV–A below) over whom the court cannot acquire personal jurisdiction.

4) **Another Pending Action**

Rule 13(a)(2)(A) provides that a defendant need not assert any counterclaim that "was the subject of another pending action" when the present action was commenced. Thus, plaintiff cannot force the defendant's counterclaim into a court of the plaintiff's choosing, if that counterclaim is already pending elsewhere.

5) **Nonpersonal Action**

Rule 13(a)(2)(B) provides that a defendant need not assert any counterclaim in an action commenced other than on personal jurisdiction. If she chooses to assert any of her counterclaims, however, the compulsory counterclaim Rule comes back into normal operation.

c. Pleading

The opposing party responds to any counterclaim in the ordinary fashion by motion and/or answer, the latter seemingly subject to Rule 13 regarding inclusion of further counterclaims.

d. State Practice

Some states have considerably more narrow counterclaim provisions. Indeed, some have no compulsory counterclaim statute or rule at all. But there is always the small category of common-law compulsory counterclaims (see Chapter XVIII–C below).

B. PERMISSIVE JOINDER

The concern here shifts to the maximum aspect of initial joinder of additional claims between the parties: What claims *may* be joined in the pleadings? The permissiveness of such joinder is almost unbounded, at least in federal court.

1. PARALLEL CLAIMS

Federal Rule 18(a) says that any party "asserting a claim, counterclaim, crossclaim, or third-party claim may join, as independent or alternative claims, as many claims as it has against an opposing party." There is no relatedness requirement. Permissive joinder of parallel claims is thus unbounded, except by usual requirements such as jurisdiction and venue. See generally Wright's Hornbook § 78.

2. PERMISSIVE COUNTERCLAIMS

Analogously, Federal Rule 13(b) permits a pleader to put forward any counterclaim that she has "against an opposing party." See generally id. § 79.

3. CROSSCLAIMS

Federal Rule 13(g) permits, but does not compel, a party to assert certain related claims for relief "against a coparty." Coparties for the purposes of such a crossclaim seemingly are parties who are not yet in opposing posture, which would justify a counterclaim instead. See generally id. § 80.

Example: P sues M and S for S's negligence. M is S's employer. M wishes to assert against S a contingent claim under applicable substantive law for indemnity. (Result: a crossclaim is proper.)

a. Required Relationship

To prevent undue complication by addition of crossclaims in which the main claimant has utterly no interest, a crossclaim must arise "out of the transaction or occurrence that is the subject matter of the original action or of a counterclaim" (a limitation that embodies a transactional test interpreted roughly the same as Rule 13(a)) *or* must relate "to any property that is the subject matter of the original action" (a limitation that permits, for example, crossclaims concerning the stake in an interpleader suit).

b. Judicial Construction

Some courts have held, probably incorrectly, that the purpose of the transactional requirement in Rule 13(g) is only to permit a party (whether defendant or plaintiff) to assert against a coparty a crossclaim growing out of the transaction or occurrence that is the subject matter of a claim (claim or counterclaim or crossclaim) *against that party.* Under that restrictive view, a coplaintiff in accident litigation could not crossclaim in the absence of some claim, such as a counterclaim, against him.

c. Pleading

Rule 13(g) states no time limit for asserting crossclaims, leaving this matter to judicial discretion.

*

XIV

Multiparty Litigation

■ ANALYSIS

A. GENERAL JOINDER PROVISIONS

The subject here is the adjudication of claims that involve multiple or additional parties. See generally Wright's Hornbook §§ 70–71.

1. COMPULSORY JOINDER

The immediate concern is the minimum aspect of initial joinder: What persons *must* be joined when any party (e.g., plaintiff) pleads a claim? Except for class actions, Federal Rule 19 is the governing provision, applying through Rule 13(h) even when the party is asserting a counterclaim or crossclaim.

a. Necessary Parties

Certain persons are so closely connected to an action that they not only could properly be joined but must be joined, unless joinder is not feasible under the requirements of jurisdiction and venue. Rule 19(a) rather broadly defines this group of "necessary parties" to include anyone:

(1) whose absence would prevent according complete relief among those already parties; *or*

(2) who claims an interest relating to the subject of the action, if proceeding in that person's absence might either impair that interest practically or subject any of those already parties to a substantial risk of double liability.

Example: P sues D for specific performance on a contract, but leaves out P's joint obligee. (Result: the absentee is a necessary party.)

b. Indispensable Parties

If a necessary party cannot be joined because of the restrictions of jurisdiction and venue, the court must decide between dispensing imperfect justice and not acting at all. Rule 19(b) formulates this problem of "equity and good conscience" in pragmatic terms, listing factors to be considered in the context of the particular case. These factors translate to include the interests of (1) the absentee in being included, (2) the defendant in not going forward without a complete cast, (3) the plaintiff in having a forum, and (4) the public in efficiently administering justice;

the court should also consider the availability of measures by these persons or the court to protect these interests. Note that upon a judicial decision not to proceed, "necessary parties" are termed "indispensable parties"; but these terms are merely conclusory labels and so do not play a part in the reasoning process. See *Provident Tradesmens Bank & Trust Co. v. Patterson*, 390 U.S. 102, 88 S.Ct. 733 (1968), validating Rule 19 as amended and rejecting the abstract approach of *Shields v. Barrow*, 58 U.S. 130 (1855).

c. Procedure

Normally, all persons joined pursuant to Rule 19 are brought in as defendants, including persons who should have been plaintiffs but who refused to join voluntarily.

1) Realignment

For the purpose of determining the existence of diversity jurisdiction, joined parties will be realigned according to the ultimate interest of each.

2) Involuntary Plaintiff

In *very narrow* circumstances, Rule 19(a)(2) allows the absentee to be made an "involuntary plaintiff" in order to circumvent the requirement of service of process that normally applies when a new party is brought into an action. A "proper case" for so doing is one in which the recalcitrant absentee is not subject to service, but equitable considerations require him to accept the burdens of permitting the use of his name as a plaintiff. Beware that in actual practice, however, *courts approve this procedure only in the factual setting where an exclusive licensee of a patent or copyright sues for infringement and seeks to join the recalcitrant owner of the patent or copyright as a coplaintiff.*

2. PERMISSIVE JOINDER

The concern here shifts to the maximum aspect of initial joinder of multiple or additional parties: What persons *may* be joined when any party (e.g., plaintiff) pleads a claim? This question is answered as part of the broader subject of who are "proper parties" to a lawsuit, a subject that entails three relevant limitations.

a.   Rule 20

Federal Rule 20(a)(1) permits multiple plaintiffs to join together if:

(1)   each asserts any right to relief "arising out of the same transaction, occurrence, or series of transactions or occurrences"; *and*

(2)   "any question of law or fact common to all plaintiffs will arise in the action."

Rule 20(a)(2) permits plaintiff to join multiple defendants if both these tests are analogously met. Of course, usual requirements of jurisdiction and venue still apply.

Example: P sues two joint tortfeasors, who are jointly and severally liable. (Result: such joinder is proper, although not compulsory.)

b.   Real Party in Interest

Federal Rule 17(a) changed the common-law practice by requiring every claim to be prosecuted only in the name of "real parties in interest," who are the persons entitled under applicable substantive law to enforce the right sued upon. Thus, assignees and subrogees must now sue in their own names. However, today the poorly drafted Rule 17(a) does create considerable confusion; some suggest that if it were abrogated, all that is correct in Rule 17(a) would still follow from the rest of modern procedural and substantive law.

1)   Representative Parties

Rule 17(a) specifies by way of illustration that certain representatives, including administrators and trustees, are usually the real party in interest. Thus, the real party in interest is not necessarily the beneficiary of the action; instead, the real party in interest is the person entitled under applicable substantive law to enforce the right sued upon.

2)   Procedure

Defendant has interests in being sued by the right person, including an interest in obtaining benefits of res judicata. So defendant may seasonably assert a defense based on Rule 17(a), which would be similar to the defense available under Rule 12(b)(6). If the Rule 17(a) defense succeeds, the defect may be corrected within a reasonable time, as by substitution of the real party in interest. In a case of honest mistake, such substitution relates back to the date of the action's commencement.

c. Capacity

Federal Rule 17(b) and (c) puts a further and separate limitation on who is a proper party. "Capacity" to sue or be sued is a fairly narrow concept comprising the personal qualifications legally needed by a person to litigate, and it is usually determined without reference to the person's particular claim or defense. For example, an infant or a mental incompetent lacks capacity to sue, and so must litigate through a representative.

1) Governing Law

Rule 17(b) and (c) lays down a few federal capacity rules, and also tells which state's law the federal court will adopt for the bulk of its capacity rules. For example, the capacity of a corporation is determined by the law under which it was incorporated.

2) Procedure

Rule 9(a)(2) requires that any party desiring to challenge capacity must raise the issue by "specific denial." If it is not so raised during the pleading stage, it is waived.

B. SPECIAL JOINDER DEVICES

There are five major devices that expand the scope of permissive joinder beyond Federal Rule 20 by providing specially for multiparty litigation. See generally Robert H. Klonoff, Class Actions and Other Multi–Party Litigation in a Nutshell (3d ed. 2007).

1. IMPLEADER

Impleader, or "third-party practice," allows but does not compel a defending party to assert a claim against a nonparty who is or may contingently be liable to that party for all or part of a claim already made against that party. Rule 14.

Example: P sues M for S's negligence. M is S's employer. Under applicable substantive law, S is liable over to M for any such recovery by P. (Result: M, as third-party plaintiff, may implead S, as third-party defendant.)

Impleader's advantage for the third-party plaintiff is to get the third-party defendant right into the case as an additional party, thus avoiding the waste of a separate suit against the third-party defendant and ensuring that the third-party defendant is bound under the judgment in the initial suit. Impleader claims are not uncommon. But beware that *impleader may be used only to assert the third-party defendant's obligation to cover the third-party plaintiff's liability to the original plaintiff, not to assert any liability that the third-party defendant might have directly to the original plaintiff.* See generally Wright's Hornbook § 76.

a. Third–Party Plaintiffs

The original defendant is usually the third-party plaintiff, but any defending party can implead. Rule 14(b) specifically authorizes a plaintiff defending against a counterclaim to bring in a third-party defendant. Moreover, Rule 14(a)(5) authorizes the third-party defendant to bring in a "fourth-party defendant," and so on.

b. Third–Party Defendants

The third-party defendant must be a nonparty. If the person liable over is already a coparty, the proper procedure for the defending party to follow is to assert a crossclaim under the second sentence of Rule 13(g).

c. Pleading

Even in the simple situation of plaintiff (P) suing defendant (D) who impleads a nonparty (T), pleading becomes very complex.

1) Pleading by Third–Party Plaintiff

D institutes impleader as if she were originally bringing an action, serving summons and complaint on T. However, if D files that complaint more than 10 days after serving her original answer, she must obtain leave of court to make service on T.

2) Pleading by Third–Party Defendant

T responds to the third-party complaint in the usual manner prescribed by Rules 12 and 13, with the central focus being the existence of his alleged duty to cover D's liability to P. In his third-party answer, T may also assert against P any nonpersonal defenses that D has to P's claim, and so may protect himself against any failure by D to defend vigorously. Moreover, Rule 14(a)(2)(D) permits T to assert against P any claim "arising out of the transaction or occurrence" that is the subject matter of P's claim against D; often this special kind of claim is considered to be technically neither a counterclaim nor a crossclaim, but under the better view it is considered a kind of crossclaim against a coparty.

3) Pleading by Original Plaintiff

P responds to any claim under Rule 14(a)(2)(D) in the usual manner prescribed by Rules 12 and 13, which response may or even must include counterclaims. In the absence of such a claim by T, Rule 14(a)(3) analogously permits P to assert against T any claim "arising out of the transaction or occurrence" that is the subject matter of P's claim against D; P may assert such a claim at any reasonable time by amending his complaint or by serving a new pleading.

d. Vouching In

Instead of impleading, a defending party can "vouch in" someone obliged to cover that party's liability on a claim already made against that party. Under this still-available common-law device, the defending party gives the vouchee simple notice of the action and offers control of the defense; whether or not the vouchee accepts control, the vouchee normally will be bound by the judgment on the questions of the voucher's liability, although the vouchee normally remains free later to contest the vouchee's obligation to cover that established liability. This device is especially useful where the restrictions of territorial jurisdiction prevent the use of impleader.

2. INTERPLEADER

Interpleader allows a person to avoid the risk of *multiple liability* by requiring two or more persons with actual or prospective claims against him to assert their respective *adverse* claims in a single action. See generally id. § 74.

Example: Bank A risks double liability by holding a deposit to which B and C have potential, conflicting claims. (Result: Bank A, as stakeholder, may bring interpleader against B and C, as claimants.)

a. Procedure

The stakeholder can commence interpleader as an original action; or if a claimant has already asserted a claim, the stakeholder can institute interpleader by counterclaim. The stakeholder need not be a "disinterested" party who admits full liability to someone, but can claim even the whole stake by contending that he owes nothing to every claimant.

1) First Stage

The "first stage" of interpleader embraces the steps involved in properly invoking interpleader. If the stakeholder is disinterested and if he deposits the stake into the court's registry or posts bond, the court will discharge him from the interpleader action.

2) Second Stage

The "second stage" involves the determination of the parties' interests in the stake. It may also include adjudication of additional claims, counterclaims, and crossclaims asserted between the parties within the bounds of joinder, jurisdiction, and venue rules.

b. Kinds of Interpleader

There are two kinds of federal interpleader: rule interpleader and statutory interpleader.

1) Rule Interpleader

Rule 22(a) descends directly from the old equitable origins of interpleader. The normal restrictions of subject-matter jurisdiction, territorial jurisdiction, and venue apply to such "rule interpleader." In particular, if such interpleader rests on diversity jurisdiction, then (1) there must be complete diversity of citizenship between the stakeholder on one side and the adverse claimants on the other and (2) the stake must exceed $75,000. Unless the stake is some tangible thing, there must be personal jurisdiction over the claimants under Rule 4. Venue is also governed by the usual provisions.

2) Statutory Interpleader

To provide a remedy in cases formerly beyond federal and state judicial power, statutory reform introduced an important alternative route, now found scattered in 28 U.S.C.A. § 1335 (subject-matter jurisdiction), § 2361 (service of process), and § 1397 (venue). If and only if (1) the parties laying conflicting claims to the stake (an interested stakeholder should be considered to be such a party) include both a state citizen and someone of different citizenship and (2) the stake is $500 or more, subject-matter jurisdiction for "statutory interpleader" exists. Personal jurisdiction over the claimants can then be obtained by effective service of process in any district of the United States, but claimants can be personally brought into the action only by such service and not by service abroad. Venue for such an interpleader action initiated by the stakeholder lies in, and only in, any district wherein resides any party claiming the stake. See *State Farm Fire & Cas. Co. v. Tashire*, 386 U.S. 523, 87 S.Ct. 1199

(1967). Unlike Rule 22(a), § 1335(a)(2) expressly requires the stakeholder to deposit the stake into the court's registry or to post bond and § 2361 expressly authorizes the court to enjoin the claimants from otherwise judicially pursuing their claims.

3. CLASS ACTION

A class action allows one or more members of a class of similarly situated persons to sue, or be sued, as representative parties litigating on behalf of the other class members without actually bringing them into court. Rule 23.

Example: Numerous purchasers of securities have been defrauded by false statements in a stock prospectus. A typical purchaser wishes to bring suit as the representative of the class of purchasers against the issuer. (Result: a class action lies, if all the requirements described below are met.)

A class action avoids the risk of inconsistent results and the often prohibitive cost of separate actions, while affording some hope of a manageable format for joinder. Such efficiency and substantive goals can generally be pursued consistently with the fairness notion of having one's day in court, as long as the *essential due process requirement of adequate representation* is met. But the obvious dangers of overwhelming the court and the parties and of disadvantaging the absent class members demand some other limits and protections. Even within those bounds and regulations, a class action may pose major problems; but on balance the device is a salutary one, with room for incremental improvement. See generally Herbert B. Newberg & Alba Conte, Newberg on Class Actions (4th ed. 2002); Wright's Hornbook § 72.

a. Requirements

Rule 23 and the relevant case law generally attempt to create a pragmatic screening device, which would let through all the cases appropriate for class-action treatment, but only those.

1) Rule 23(a)

    Plaintiff in the complaint must propose class-action treatment. To obtain such treatment, there are four initial requirements that must all be met:

    (1) the class must be "so numerous that joinder of all members is impracticable" (this test is not simply numerical, but classes usually involve far more than 25 members);

(2) there must be "questions of law or fact common to the class" (this requirement will be met if the below-described Rule 23(b) is met);

(3) the claims or defenses of the representatives must be "typical" of the class (this is largely ensured by the required commonality and adequacy of representation); *and*

(4) "the representative parties will fairly and adequately protect the interests of the class" (this is a key requirement, involving an inquiry into whether the particular representatives will vigorously champion class objectives through qualified counsel).

The first and fourth requirements are the most important, with the first trying to ensure that class-action treatment will yield benefits and the fourth trying to ensure that such treatment will impose only acceptable costs.

2) Rule 23(b)

The proposed class action must also fall into one of three situations, a requirement of linkage between class members, which tries further to ensure favorable costs and benefits from class-action treatment:

(1) the situation under Rule 23(b)(1) where bringing separate actions would create a risk of establishing incompatible standards of conduct for the class opponent (e.g., taxpayers' suit against a town to declare a bond issue invalid) or of substantially impairing the other class members' interests as a practical matter (e.g., suit involving numerous persons claiming against a fund insufficient to satisfy all those claims);

(2) the situation where defendant has allegedly based her conduct on the characteristics of the plaintiff class, thereby making appropriate class-wide final injunctive relief or equivalent declaratory relief, as opposed to relief consisting predominantly of money damages (Rule 23(b)(2) would thus include a desegregation case brought by a plaintiff class, but probably has no application to defendant-class actions); *or*

(3) the situation where the potential class action does not fall into category (1) or (2), but where "the questions of law or fact common to class members predominate over any questions

affecting only individual members" and also "a class action is superior to other available methods for fairly and efficiently adjudicating the controversy," with this issue of the desirability of class-action treatment entailing such factors as manageability (Rule 23(b)(3) could thus include an action by purchasers of securities, but less likely include actions arising from a mass tort).

The third category, embodied in Rule 23(b)(3), has presented most of the problems and controversy associated with the complex class-action device.

3) Defendant–Class Actions

Most class actions involve a class of plaintiffs, but defendant-class actions are possible. In appropriate cases, plaintiff would sue adequate representatives of the defendant class, which could for example comprise the members of a labor union. Rule 23 expressly authorizes such defendant-class actions, but it fails to think them all the way through. So Rule 23 must here be applied with particular sensitivity to the dangers of unfairness to the involuntary representatives and to the absent class members.

4) Actions Relating to Unincorporated Associations

Unincorporated associations, such as labor unions, sometimes may sue or be sued through representatives instead of as an entity. This class-action procedure is especially useful in avoiding the restrictions of diversity jurisdiction and capacity and in easing the requirements of service and venue. Because of these special reasons for utilizing the class-action device here, Rule 23.2 deals separately with such actions.

5) Jurisdiction and Venue

Important additional limitations on the availability of the class-action device lie in the rules of jurisdiction and venue.

a) General Approach

In applying the federal provisions regarding diversity of citizenship, service of process, and venue, only the named parties (not all the class members) are considered.

b) Jurisdictional Amount

However, in *Snyder v. Harris*, 394 U.S. 332, 89 S.Ct. 1053 (1969), the Supreme Court unfortunately ruled that every separate and distinct claim across the whole class must satisfy any federal jurisdictional amount requirement. This serious impediment to class actions based on diversity has been lessened by 28 U.S.C.A. § 1367.

c) CAFA

Another way around jurisdictional limitations came in the Class Action Fairness Act of 2005, which covered interstate class actions and had the expressed intent of defeating plaintiff lawyers' manipulation of state courts by funneling more class actions away from the state courts and into the federal courts. In new 28 U.S.C.A. § 1332(d), Congress bestowed original jurisdiction on the federal district courts for sizable multistate class actions, generally if there is minimal diversity between any plaintiff member of the class and any defendant and if the plaintiff class contains at least 100 members and their claims aggregated together exceed $5 million. In new 28 U.S.C.A. § 1453, Congress further provided that any defendant can remove such a class action from state court to the local federal district court—and the removing defendant can be a local citizen and need not seek the consent of the other defendants.

d) Territorial Jurisdiction

By an opinion with unclear implications, *Phillips Petroleum Co. v. Shutts*, 472 U.S. 797, 105 S.Ct. 2965 (1985), the Supreme Court held that in a state plaintiff-class action for money damages, personal jurisdiction over absent members need not otherwise exist, if they received notice and had a right to participate and a right to opt out. But if with respect to an absent class member the constitutional power and reasonableness tests are met without any such resorting to implied consent, as normally would be true in federal court, neither territorial jurisdiction nor this *Phillips* holding should in the author's view be of further concern with respect to that member.

b. Mechanics

Class actions pose major management problems for the courts.

1) Certification

Rule 23(c)(1) provides that soon after commencement of a proposed class action, the court must determine whether the above requirements are met and then enter an order either granting or denying certification as a class action.

a) Statute of Limitations

American Pipe & Constr. Co. v. Utah, 414 U.S. 538, 94 S.Ct. 756 (1974), established roughly the rule that commencement of a federal plaintiff-class action tolls for all members of the proposed class the applicable statute of limitations until denial of class treatment during the class action.

b) Limited Class Treatment

Rule 23(c)(4) and (5) provides that the court may limit class treatment to certain issues or divide the proposed class into independently treated subclasses.

c) Appealability

By the recent addition of Rule 23(f), the court of appeals in its discretion may permit an immediate appeal from an order granting or denying class certification.

2) Special Provisions for 23(b)(3) Actions

Rule 23(c)(2)(B) contains special provisions applicable only to actions under Rule 23(b)(3), not to the naturally more cohesive or desirable classes falling within Rule 23(b)(1) or (2).

a) Notice of Class Action

Procedural due process conceivably requires notice to absent class members only in the relatively rare circumstances where such notice is necessary to provide a fair assurance of adequate representation. Apparently going way beyond that standard, however, the Rule requires giving (b)(3) class members "the best notice that is practicable under the circumstances, including individual notice to all members who can be identified through reasonable effort." In *Eisen v. Carlisle & Jacquelin*, 417 U.S. 156, 94 S.Ct. 2140 (1974), the Court held that (1) this Rule actually does require individual notice to all class members identifiable with reasonable effort, even though the cost of individual notice is prohibitive, and (2) the named plaintiffs must initially bear all costs of such notice. *Eisen* thus erects another ill-designed barrier to the use of the class-action device.

b) Appearance Through Counsel

The (b)(3) class member has the right to enter an appearance through counsel, which would ensure his being kept currently informed about the case. This right is in addition to the possibility in any class action of a class member's intervening under Rule 24, which would allow much greater participation in the conduct of the case.

c) Opting-out

The (b)(3) class member also has the right to withdraw from the class, and thus escape the burdens (and lose the benefits) of the eventual judgment. He can do this by simply informing the court, in response to the notice, of his desire to opt out.

3) Orders in Conduct of Actions

Rule 23(d) authorizes a variety of appropriate "management" orders, thus confirming the court's authority to take an active role in running the case. In particular, Rule 23(d)(1)(B) authorizes the court in any class action discretionarily to order notice to class members advising them of any step in the action or any right they may have. See also Rule 23(g)–(h).

c. Termination

Most class actions are settled, but settlement may mark just the beginning of the procedural struggles.

1) Dismissal or Compromise

Rule 23(e) regulates the settlement stage of a certified class action in an attempt to protect the interests of the class members, whom the named parties or the class counsel may be abandoning in favor of self-interest.

a) Notice

Notice of the proposed settlement must be given to all class members who would be bound.

b) Approval

The court must pass on the fairness, reasonableness, and adequacy of the proposed settlement under Rule 23(e). This process involves a hearing where disgruntled class members may speak and where a very big issue is attorney's fees.

2) Judgment

Rule 23(c)(3) specifies that any class-action judgment, whether favorable or unfavorable to the class, must describe all class members, excluding those who opted out. Administering the judgment may be a heavy task. The propriety of "fluid recovery," which involves indirectly distributing the residue of a money judgment as by the defendant's lowering its future prices in a total amount equal to any unclaimed recovery, has sometimes been questioned.

3) Attacking the Judgment

Normally, any class-action judgment will bind those described therein. However, when the judgment is later invoked, it is subject to attack on the usual limited grounds. (See Chapter XVII–C below.) In addition, an absent class member should be able to attack its binding effect on him by raising the due process question of inadequate representation of his interests.

d. State Practice

States have their own class-action provisions, of lesser or greater scope and detail. See generally Thomas A. Dickerson, Class Actions: The Law of 50 States (1988); Mary Kay Kane, Civil Procedure in a Nutshell § 8–2 (6th ed. 2007). These may offer the opportunity to avoid some of the barriers to and protections of the federal device, but may be subject to their own peculiar limitations as well as possible judicial hostility.

4. SHAREHOLDERS' DERIVATIVE ACTION

A derivative action allows one or more persons to sue for the benefit of similarly situated persons on a claim that their common fiduciary refuses to assert. Rule 23.1 deals specifically with derivative actions by shareholders of a corporation *or* by members of an unincorporated association. See generally Wright's Hornbook § 73.

Example: A minority shareholder believes that his corporation should be asserting a claim against a third person (either an outsider or a wrongdoing corporate official). However, the corporation refuses to sue. (Result: the shareholder may institute a shareholders' derivative action upon the corporation's claim.)

a. Procedure

Plaintiff must file a *verified* complaint alleging, among other things, (1) that he was a shareholder or member at the *time of the transaction* sued upon (or that he later became such by a nonconsensual transfer), as well as at the *time of suit*, and (2) that he made an unsuccessful demand on the *directors* to sue, unless such a demand would have been futile, as well as on the *shareholders or members* if so required by applicable law.

1)   Corporation or Association as Defendant

The corporation or association must be named as a defendant along with the alleged wrongdoer, even though the relief sought is a judgment running in its favor.

2)   Analogy to Class Action

A shareholders' derivative action is basically similar to a class action. Thus, plaintiff must appear to be a fair and adequate representative of those similarly situated. Also, termination procedure is similar to that for a class action.

b.   **Jurisdiction and Venue**

The usual rules generally apply to a shareholders' derivative action. But in particular for diversity jurisdiction, the defendant corporation is rarely realigned as plaintiff, although the jurisdictional amount requirement is applied to the whole claim of the corporation. For territorial jurisdiction and venue, 28 U.S.C.A. §§ 1695 and 1401 respectively provide an additional service provision and additional places for suit.

5.   **INTERVENTION**

Intervention allows a person not named as a party to enter an existing lawsuit, coming in on the appropriate side of the litigation. Rule 24.

Example: A member of a class, feeling inadequately represented by the named parties, wishes to intervene in a class action. (Result: such a person normally may intervene.)

There are two kinds of intervention: by right and by leave of court. See generally Wright's Hornbook § 75.

a.   **Intervention of Right**

Either of two circumstances bestows the right to intervene.

1)   Statutory Right

Rule 24(a)(1) notes that a federal statute may confer this right. The most significant of the few such existing statutes is 28 U.S.C.A. § 2403, which gives the United States or a state the right to intervene in a federal action wherein the constitutionality of one of its statutes is questioned.

2) Rule 24(a)(2)

More importantly, a person has the right to intervene if she claims an interest relating to the subject of the action and if the action might practically impair her interest, unless her interest is adequately represented by existing parties. Cf. Rule 19(a)(1)(B)(i).

a) Required Interest

The courts have not yet succeeded in defining the requisite "interest," but probably should approach this term flexibly in light of the functions of intervention and in conjunction with the impairment requirement.

b) Practical Impairment

The cases have applied this requirement rather leniently and, for example, would allow intervention of right by an unrepresented person concerned with only the stare decisis effect on a very direct economic interest.

c) Adequate Representation

It is unclear who has the burden of proof on this point, but it appears that this test is not too high a hurdle. The would-be intervenor need at most show only that her interest *may* be inadequately represented. Better viewed, it is up to her opponent to show clearly that her interest *is* adequately represented.

b. **Permissive Intervention**

Either of two circumstances may prompt a court discretionarily to permit intervention, after taking into account the burdens that intervention would impose on those already parties.

1) Permission Related to Statute

Rule 24(b)(1)(A) notes that a federal statute may confer "a conditional right to intervene." Relatedly, Rule 24(b) itself goes on to provide that if a party relies for claim or defense upon any statute, order, or regulation administered by a federal or state officer or agency, then the officer or agency may be permitted to intervene.

2) Rule 24(b)(1)(B)

More importantly, anyone may be permitted to intervene if she has "a claim or defense that shares with the main action a common question of law or fact."

c.   Procedure

Rule 24(c) prescribes the procedure for intervention.

1)   Application

Any person seeking to intervene must make timely application, with the timeliness standard being left to judicial discretion and thus making all of intervention to some degree discretionary. The application consists of a motion stating the grounds for intervention, which must be accompanied by a pleading setting forth the applicant's claim or defense and must be served upon the parties like an ordinary motion.

2)   Participation

The intervenor comes in as a full party, being able freely to participate seemingly even to the extent of asserting additional claims—unless the court imposes restrictive conditions on its granting of the application to intervene, either when it grants that application or later. The court has undoubted power to impose conditions in the case of permissive intervention, but seems to have at most only limited power to do so for intervention of right.

d.   Relationship of Federal Joinder Rules

The following diagram suggests the relationship of Rules 19, 20, and 24. The connection of the extra party to the litigation diminishes with distance from the center of the diagram:

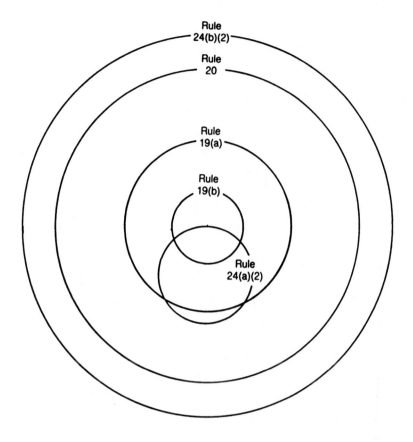

REVIEW QUESTIONS

Questions (1)–(3): Several hundred passengers, including P, were injured when D's airplane crashed while taxiing.

1. **T or F** If several passengers join together to sue D in a federal district court, the trial judge may order the issue of liability to be tried separately from the other issues in the case.

2. **T or F** If several such federal suits are filed around the country, D can move to transfer them to one court for pretrial proceedings.

3. **T or F** Assume that P sues in federal district court in New York for his broken arm and wins, and that he then sues for his crushed leg. D should now win with a defense based on P's failure to join this claim with his earlier suit.

Questions (4)–(6): Pete, an authorized dealer of Dodge cars, made numerous fraudulent requests for refunds on warranty repairs. As a result, Dodge terminated his dealership. So Pete brought suit in federal district court for unlawful termination of the dealership, suing Dodge and Donna, who is Dodge's president.

4. **T or F** If in this lawsuit Donna asserts a claim against Dodge for back-pay, that claim should be dismissed upon motion.

5. **T or F** If defendants answer Pete's complaint and try the case to judgment against Pete, Dodge can then sue to recover amounts paid Pete on his fraudulent refund requests.

6. **T or F** If, during that trial of Pete's action, Pete presents another fraudulent refund request that Dodge pays, Dodge will be precluded from suing to recover that payment in a subsequent action.

Questions (7)–(11): Ink, a New York corporation with its principal place of business in Ohio, purchased unusable supplies through D & D, a partnership of several New Yorkers dwelling in Manhattan. The $80,000 sale was induced by E, a citizen of Ohio employed by D & D, through means prohibited by applicable state fraud laws. After proper demands to sue, P, a citizen of New Hampshire and a shareholder of Ink, brings a derivative action in the United States District Court for the Southern District of New York against D & D.

7. **T or F** Ink can be joined as an involuntary plaintiff.

8. **T or F** If instead Ink is joined as a defendant but the court realigns it as a plaintiff, the suit should be dismissed.

9. **T or F** If Ink is treated as a defendant, its capacity to be sued will be determined by New York law.

10. **T or F** If under applicable substantive law E is liable over to D & D for any recovery in P's action, D & D can seek to implead E.

11. **T or F** If under applicable substantive law E is liable over to D & D for any recovery, but E is beyond the personal jurisdiction of the court, then P's action should be dismissed.

Questions (12)–(14): D'autocars introduces a new, high performance car that sells for $130,000. Ninety are sold. After 2500 miles, like clockwork, the engines fall out. Several of the purchasers file a class action on behalf of all purchasers against the manufacturer and its distributor in federal district court, alleging state contract claims.

12. Assuming any jurisdictional amount requirement is satisfied, which of the following confers subject-matter jurisdiction on the court?

   a. The class representatives and the defendants are of diverse citizenship.

   b. Suit is brought where the defendants can be served.

   c. Suit is brought in a district where the defendants reside.

   d. A majority of all purchasers are of citizenship diverse from the defendants'.

   e. Suit is brought in a district where all the class representatives reside.

13. Which of the following surely satisfies the jurisdictional amount requirement?

   a. The claims of all class members total $3,000,000.

   b. Each class member's claim equals $75,000.

   c. Each class representative's claim exceeds $75,000.

   d. Each class member's claim is $85,000.

e. All of the above except (b).

14. If the district judge preliminarily determines that the class action is likely to succeed, which of the following is true?

    a. The class representatives must initially pay for notice to the absent class members.

    b. Notice need not be given to the absent class members.

    c. Notice need be given only to those absent class members who are likely to appear through counsel or to opt out.

    d. Notice by publication suffices.

    e. Defendants must initially pay for notice to the absent class members.

15. P, a citizen of Rhode Island, rented out storage space in her warehouse behind her home. One day, the warehouse burned. Fortunately, the only item then stored in the warehouse was a piano. But the fire destroyed that piano and all of P's records. Another Rhode Island citizen, B, claims ownership of the piano and demands $600 for its destruction. A Florida citizen, C, claims ownership of the same piano and also demands $600 for its destruction. Which of the following is true?

    a. P may file an interpleader action in the United States District Court for the District of Rhode Island.

    b. Bringing interpleader in any federal court outside Florida forces P to proceed on nonpersonal jurisdiction with respect to C.

    c. If P makes no claim to the stake, federal venue for interpleader is proper in the District of Columbia.

    d. For federal interpleader, the stake must exceed $75,000.

16. Prepare an essay in response to this question:

Alf's Eats, Inc. ("Alf"), is a New York corporation with its principal place of business in Alabama. It has a branch restaurant called Alf's in Coatopa, Alabama, hard on the banks of the Sucarnoochee Creek.

On October 25th of last year, Bert, a traveling salesman with his domicile in Biloxi, Mississippi, and an office in Boligee, Alabama, was eating his birthday dinner at Alf's in Coatopa. Unhappily, the waitress, a dim local named Cis, had filled the saltcellar with sugar. Still more unhappily, Bert loved salt and hated sugar. In fact, sugar depressed him mightily and prompted him to violence. So Bert inadvertently and liberally "salted" his burger with sugar, and then went on a rampage that reduced Alf's to a shambles, which in the case of Alf's did not represent too great an effort. A witness to all this was Dale, a patron from Daleville, Mississippi, which as one should remember from geography lessons is just across the state border from Boligee.

Alf sued Bert in the United States District Court for the Northern District of Alabama, which district encompasses Coatopa and Boligee. Alf claimed $100,000 for destruction of property during Bert's rampage. Bert answered, setting up the "Twinkie defense," which attributes depressive and violent behavior to overdoses of sugar. Bert also counterclaimed for $85,000 in personal injuries caused by reaction to the sugar and incurred in the course of the rampage.

Alf then answered Bert and immediately impleaded Cis of Coatopa, asserting that she was liable to Alf for Bert's counterclaim. Next, in this same action, Bert asserted his $85,000 personal-injury claim directly against Cis and also another claim against Cis for $5000, alleging in connection with the latter claim that (1) she had slandered him by falsely telling people that Bert had wrecked Alf's in a drunken rage and (2) she had thus caused Bert to lose business customers. With those two claims Bert joined a claim against Dale, alleging similarly that Dale had slandered him back in Mississippi so as to inflict an additional $6000 in damages. A process server served Dale with process in-hand during the dessert course of a later lunch in the sumptuously rebuilt Alf's in Coatopa.

Dale is less than thrilled by this chain of events and lets you—her Alabama lawyer—know so. You want to get Dale completely out of this morass of a lawsuit before the merits are reached. Which procedural tactic can you employ toward that end with the greatest expectation of success?

*

PART FIVE

Governing Law

■ **ANALYSIS**

*

XV

Choice of Law

■ ANALYSIS

A. TECHNIQUES

A pervasive problem in litigation that involves nonlocal elements is choosing which sovereign's law to apply. Generally, it is the forum court's task to choose the governing law under some technique for choice of law.

1. EVOLUTION OF CHOICE OF LAW

The technique for choice of law followed in any particular jurisdiction has typically evolved from (1) a traditional set of wooden and crude rules that pointed with relative certainty to the law of a particular place where some particular event occurred (e.g., the rule of lex loci delicti, or the rule of the law of the place of the wrong, controlled the choice for substantive issues in tort cases; but the lex fori, or the law of the forum, applied on all issues that the forum court characterized as procedural) to (2) a very flexible and sensitive but quite uncertain approach of comparing as to each issue the interests of the involved sovereigns in having their own law applied (so-called interest analysis).

2. COMPETING METHODOLOGIES

Nevertheless, this is a subject dominated today by competing subtheories that elaborate or alter interest analysis, and these subtheories conflict sharply at least on the verbal level. Many of these modern differences of opinion have arisen as theorists have worked to reinject some degree of practical certainty into the theoretical precision of interest analysis. For example, one might use interest analysis to create a new series of general rules to cover common situations. Such matters are the subject of study in the upperclass course of Conflict of Laws.

B. CONSTITUTIONAL LIMITS

The Supreme Court has interpreted the Federal Constitution in a way that gives American courts a very free hand in choosing the governing law and, in particular, in choosing to apply their own law. The constitutional restriction was summarized in *Allstate Ins. Co. v. Hague*, 449 U.S. 302, 308, 101 S.Ct. 633, 637–38 (1981) (plurality opinion) (citations and footnotes omitted):

> In deciding constitutional choice-of-law questions, whether under the Due Process Clause or the Full Faith and Credit Clause, this Court has traditionally examined the contacts of the State, whose law was applied, with the parties and with the occurrence or transaction giving rise to the litigation. In order to ensure that the choice of law is neither arbitrary nor fundamen-

tally unfair, the Court has invalidated the choice of law of a State which has had no significant contact or significant aggregation of contacts, creating state interests, with the parties and the occurrence or transaction.

*

XVI

Choice Between State and Federal Law

■ **ANALYSIS**

A. STATE LAW IN FEDERAL COURT: *ERIE*

The subject here is extraordinarily important. It concerns the special choice-of-law problem ubiquitously encountered in our federal system: the choice between state and federal law. More specifically, the immediate concern here is the solution of that problem in actions brought in federal court. This situation involves a "choice of law" in the sense that the federal authority is deciding whether federal law should be generated to apply to a given issue or state law should be left to govern. The decision on this "vertical" choice of law is often reached by a process similar to that employed for the "horizontal" choice of law examined in Chapter XV above.

1. CONSTITUTIONAL LIMITS

The Federal Constitution can dictate a choice in favor of federal law, and of course this is binding. An example is the Seventh Amendment's guarantee of trial by jury. But most often the Constitution does not so dictate. In many such circumstances Congress can validly make a choice by statute in favor of federal law, and that choice will bind the federal courts. In the absence of such a congressional directive, the federal courts can sometimes validly choose to apply federal law. This recurrent stress on "validly" raises a difficult threshold question: To what extent does the Constitution limit the powers of the federal government—either the federal courts or Congress—to choose to apply federal law in federal court? In other words, when does the Constitution dictate a choice in favor of state law?

a. Leading Cases

The Supreme Court has gone from a constitutional interpretation giving the federal government wide powers to choose federal law to a slightly more restrictive view.

1) *Swift*

In *Swift v. Tyson*, 41 U.S. 1 (1842) (Story, J.), the Court ruled that in a diversity contract case, federal law effectively governed the issue of whether satisfaction of a pre-existing debt constituted valid consideration. The Court explained that only state statutes (and state judicial construction thereof) and local usages (such as state decisional law on real estate and other immovable and intraterritorial matters) were binding "laws of the several states" within the Rules of Decision Act of 1789—now with slight changes 28 U.S.C.A. § 1652 [hereinafter RDA], which in its present form reads:

The laws of the several states, except where the Constitution or treaties of the United States or Acts of Congress otherwise require or provide, shall be regarded as rules of decision in civil actions in the courts of the United States, in cases where they apply.

The Court further explained that the federal courts, in the absence of any applicable congressional directive, were free to depart from the general common law declared by the state courts and should make their own rulings thereon. So in the *Swift* case itself a federal view of the common law governed the point of commercial law in issue.

2) *Erie*

Coming at the problem with a changed jurisprudential view and with a recognition of the serious defects in the administration of justice caused by the persisting gap between state and federal precedents, the Court overruled *Swift* in *Erie R.R. v. Tompkins*, 304 U.S. 64, 58 S.Ct. 817 (1938) (Brandeis, J.). However, the actual basis for overruling was a fairly narrow constitutional one. The *Erie* Court held that the broad power to make general common law that the federal court system had appropriated under the *Swift* doctrine occasionally took those courts into areas constitutionally prohibited or, more properly phrased, took those courts beyond the powers constitutionally bestowed on the federal courts. It is true that the federal courts have significant lawmaking power under the Constitution. But there is a boundary beyond which the federal courts' lawmaking power cannot extend consistently with the Constitution. Because *Swift* would permit occasional extension beyond that boundary, *Swift* had to fall.

b. Constitutional Limit on Federal Courts

Article III's reference to the "judicial power" extending to cases within federal jurisdiction signifies the federal courts' power to create some law in the limited areas of high federal interest (e.g., admiralty). But the federal courts would unconstitutionally exceed their power by lawmaking in areas of very high state interest (e.g., immunity of charities from tort liability), whether the state interest finds expression in state statutory law or state decisional law. As already suggested, it is helpful to envisage this scheme as a boundary, albeit inevitably ill-defined, beyond which lie matters that the federal courts' lawmaking power cannot constitutionally reach. Equivalently, this boundary represents the ultimate limit on the federal courts' power to choose on their own to apply federal law, because whenever they so choose they are extending and hence making federal law.

c. Constitutional Limit on Congress

The *Erie* case concerned only the power appropriated by the federal court system in the realm of general common law. *Erie* did not directly address the scope of the *power of Congress* to mandate federal law *applicable in federal court*. Nevertheless, it is clear that under Articles I and III and the Necessary and Proper Clause, Congress has broad power so to legislate (e.g., Federal Rules of Evidence). But Congress would presumably exceed its constitutional power by so legislating in areas of extremely high state interest (e.g., title to real estate). That is to say, Congress cannot unreasonably affect those primary decisions concerning human conduct that the Constitution did not subject to federal legislation and so reserved to the states. This boundary demarking the lawmaking power represents the limit on the congressional power to choose to apply federal law in federal court.

d. *Erie*'s Constitutional Limits in General

Beware of overemphasizing the constitutional aspects of the *Erie* doctrine.

1) Comparison of Judicial and Congressional Limits

Both limits permit significant lawmaking activity by the federal government. However, it would seem that the boundary demarking constitutionally permissible matters for the federal courts might be more restrictive than the boundary applicable to Congress. The idea is that the lawmaking function of Congress is more expansive, permitting greater intrusion into matters of state interest; the constitutional structure of separation of powers thus limits the federal courts' power to lawmake on their own.

2) Specific Constitutional Restrictions

Specific constitutional provisions, most importantly the Due Process Clause of the Fifth Amendment with its equal protection ingredient, might further limit slightly the powers of the federal courts and Congress to choose to apply a distinctive federal law solely in federal court.

3) Role of Constitutional Limits in *Erie* Doctrine

The *Erie* case used the Constitution to overturn *Swift*. *Erie* did not use the Constitution to solve the actual choice-of-law problem before the Court. That is, *Erie* did not suggest that henceforth in practice the line between federal and state law applied in federal court should lie at the outer constitutional limits. Indeed, *Erie* suggested that the line would lie inside those boundaries outlining the permissibility of choosing federal law, and later cases confirm that the line lies far inside those boundaries. Thus, in federal court today state law will apply in many situations where such application is not constitutionally compelled, the federal government so deferring to state law and declining to exercise the full extent of its constitutional powers. Consider in particular the range of cases in which the federal courts must make the choice of law:

(1) *Easy Cases.* Whenever an issue entails such high state interest as to raise a question of the federal courts' constitutional power to choose federal law, state law will almost invariably apply on that issue as a matter of federal deference or comity. There is no practical difference whether state law governs the issue by constitutional compulsion or it governs as a result of federal deference. Therefore, such an issue presents an easy case with respect to choice of law.

(2) *Hard Cases.* A hard case arises when the issue falls farther inside the constitutional boundary applicable to the federal courts, because of either lower state interest or heightened federal interest. An example would be a procedural issue in a diversity case. It then becomes critical to locate the line that marks the choice, as a matter of deference, between federal and state law; it is this line that has great practical significance. For such an issue that falls close to this line, the Constitution is a distant consideration and does not directly affect the decisional process.

In this sense, it can be concluded that the Constitution does not enter into solving the usual choice-of-law problem under the Erie *doctrine.*

2. LEGISLATIVE LIMITS

The next question is to what extent Congress, either directly or through an authorized administrative delegate, can limit the power of the federal courts to choose the applicable law in federal court.

a. Choice of Law

As already suggested, within constitutional limits Congress can expressly or impliedly make the choice between state and federal law, and its choice will bind the federal courts. If Congress chooses the applicable law, the only choice-of-law question remaining is whether that choice was constitutionally valid, because the Constitution imposes the only bounds on the congressional power.

b. Content of the Chosen Law

If Congress chooses federal law, it can specify the content of that federal law, although it sometimes delegates to the federal courts the task of generating part or all of that federal law.

c. Rules of Decision Act

Conceivably, the above-quoted RDA broadly made a choice in favor of state law. However, neither the development of the *Erie* doctrine nor its current condition is consistent with a view that the RDA actively affects the choice-of-law process. That is, the judicial interpretation of the RDA has significantly softened the impact of its words. The question is how the courts have done this.

1) "Laws of the Several States"

It is possible to argue that these words retain a narrow meaning. *Swift* read them to mean local laws, that is, state statutes and local usages but not general common law. *Swift* went on to claim for the federal courts a broad lawmaking power with respect to general common law. The *Erie* case stated its view that as a matter of statutory construction this narrow reading of "laws of the several states" had been erroneous, but under the dictates of stare decisis it arguably left that construction intact. *Erie* then addressed the federal courts' power outside the statute and invoked the Constitution to overturn *Swift* just on that point. *Erie* observed that *the RDA was merely declarative of the rule that would exist in its absence.* Therefore, the inherent restrictions on the federal courts' power in the realm of general common law would henceforth be equivalent to the statutory restrictions on their power in the realm of local laws covered by the RDA. Hence, any narrowness possibly implicit in the term "laws of the several states" is without practical significance in reading the RDA.

2) **"In Cases Where They Apply"**

This language is not significant either. It seems merely to make the obvious point that state law should apply only where relevant. Thus, for example, state tort law would apply only in tort cases.

3) **The "Except" Clause**

This is the RDA's key exception, allowing the federal courts to apply federal law where the Constitution or federal statutes "otherwise require or provide." There are various ways this exception could be read. However, the federal courts now seem to read it sensibly as not only accommodating express federal constitutional and statutory directives but also preserving a judicial choice-of-law power otherwise required or provided by the whole federal constitutional and statutory scheme. Thus, the RDA provides that state law presumptively applies in federal court—except where the Constitution, a statute, or the judicially developed choice-of-law technique displaces it.

In this sense, the RDA declares the obvious (or rather the natural) and incorporates the Erie *jurisprudence by reference.*

3. CHOICE–OF–LAW TECHNIQUE

The remaining basic question is how a federal court should choose between state and federal law for application to a particular issue in a case before it, in circumstances where the federal courts are free under the Constitution and federal statutes to go either way. That is, when neither the Constitution nor Congress determined the law applicable to a particular situation, how should a federal court exercise its choice-of-law power and hence its potential lawmaking power?

a. Competing Methodologies

Since 1938 the Supreme Court, with the lower federal courts in tow, has progressed through a sequence of choice-of-law techniques for judicially handling the Erie *problem. But the Court has not yet arrived at any truly clear or optimal solution.*

1) *Erie*

On its facts, *Erie* ruled that in a diversity tort case, state law governed the issue of the plaintiff's status as trespasser or licensee. The Court made clear that nothing turned on whether the state law was statutory law or decisional law. But *Erie* did not explain its technique for choosing between state and federal law. Apparently, the Court saw the choice as a relatively easy one. So all it offered on the problem was an exposition on the undesirability of applying federal law in federal court to issues of state concern like the issue before it: differences in applicable law between federal and state courts (1) fostered forum-shopping between the two court systems, (2) put the person who had a choice between the two systems in an unfairly favored position, and (3) infringed on the states' authority. The only guidance, then, was that these considerations would be relevant in resolving future state-federal conflicts. Thus, the *Erie* case was surely a fountainhead, but not an especially eloquent one.

2) **Substance/Procedure Test**

Despite the marked absence of any formula in *Erie*'s majority opinion, the federal courts in the late 1930's and early 1940's seized upon a substance/procedure dichotomy as the test for choosing between state and federal law. Seeking refuge from the difficulties of the choice-of-law problem posed by *Erie*, the courts succumbed to the attractions of apparent certainty in the crude and mechanical method of adjudication suggested by this familiar but deceptive dichotomy. If the issue was one of substantive law, then state law applied; if procedural, then federal law governed. Although the deficiencies of such a test did not go completely unnoticed at the time, this simplistic technique came to be accepted by the lower courts and, quite possibly, by the Supreme Court in *Cities Serv. Oil Co. v. Dunlap*, 308 U.S. 208, 60 S.Ct. 201 (1939) (state law governs burden of proof on matter governed by state law in diversity case).

3) **Outcome–determinative Test**

In *Guaranty Trust Co. v. York*, 326 U.S. 99, 65 S.Ct. 1464 (1945) (Frankfurter, J.) (state statute of limitations applies to state-created claim), the Court rejected the substance/procedure test, argued for a more policy-oriented approach, and stressed the goal that "the outcome of the litigation in the federal court should be substantially the same, so far as legal rules determine the outcome of a litigation, as it would be if tried in a State court." In later cases, this new approach sank back into oversimplification. The seeming certainty of a mechanical and crude test that dictated the choice of state law whenever federal law would affect the outcome provided a tempting alternative to the dreary task of examining each issue, identifying the interests involved, and weighing them in some ill-defined manner. The Supreme Court itself yielded to the temptation of the outcome-determinative test in *Ragan v. Merchants Transfer & Warehouse Co.*, 337 U.S. 530, 69 S.Ct. 1233 (1949) (state statute governs when action is deemed commenced for statute-of-limitations purposes), *Woods v. Interstate Realty Co.*, 337 U.S. 535, 69 S.Ct. 1235 (1949) (state statute closing courthouse doors to nonqualifying foreign corporations applies), and *Cohen v. Beneficial Indus. Loan Corp.*, 337 U.S. 541, 69 S.Ct. 1221 (1949) (state security-for-suit statute applies), and again later in *Bernhardt v. Polygraphic Co. of Am.*, 350 U.S. 198, 76 S.Ct. 273 (1956) (state law on enforceability of agreements to arbitrate applies). All were diversity cases.

4) Interest Analysis

In *Byrd v. Blue Ridge Rural Elec. Co-op.*, 356 U.S. 525, 78 S.Ct. 893 (1958) (Brennan, J.), the Court in a diversity case faced a choice of law on whether a certain fact-based element of a state-created defense should be decided by a judge, in accordance with South Carolina law, or by a jury, in accordance with federal practice. Bypassing a possible route along Seventh Amendment lines, the Court elaborated a more general threefold analysis. *First*, the Court looked at the interests of the state, in light of all legitimate policies reflected by the content of its law, in having its legal rule applied in federal court on this particular issue. Here in this case those interests were weak, as the state rule appeared to be primarily the result of historical accident. *Second*, the Court examined the federal interests in having federal law govern, calling these interests "affirmative countervailing considerations." Here those interests were considerable, there being a federal interest in uniformly controlling the judge-jury relationship in the federal courts and also a federal policy favoring jury decisions on disputed fact questions. *Third*, the Court acknowledged an offsetting federal interest in uniform enforcement of state-created rights and duties. Here the outcome-determinative effect of granting a jury trial as opposed to a bench trial was not too weighty, however, as the likelihood of a different result seemed not great. Finally, using this complex approach—(1) the state's interests balanced against the difference of (2) affirmative countervailing considerations less (3) outcome-determinative effect—the Court concluded that the federal jury practice should apply. This sensitive and flexible approach rejected simplistic tests and represented a hearty embrace of the goals implicit in *Erie*, but it seemed unpredictable and imposed on the courts the heavy practical burden of carefully discerning and delicately weighing all competing state and federal interests involved in the particular issue. The lower courts after *Byrd* did their struggling best to apply the new approach.

5) *Hanna*

In *Hanna v. Plumer*, 380 U.S. 460, 85 S.Ct. 1136 (1965) (Warren, C.J.), the Court attempted to afford a degree of relief by reinjecting some certainty.

a) *Hanna-Sibbach* Rule

The *Hanna* Court held that whenever a valid Federal Rule of Civil Procedure is in point, as the service-of-process Rule supposedly was in that case, the Rule applies. The Rule need only be valid under the Constitution, as very broadly read in *Hanna*, and under the Rules Enabling Act, as very permissively interpreted in *Sibbach v. Wilson & Co.*, 312 U.S. 1, 61 S.Ct. 422 (1941). This "*Hanna-Sibbach*" test effectively insulates the Federal Rules of Civil Procedure from attack.

b) *Hanna-Erie* Test

In extended dicta, the *Hanna* Court considered the application of *Erie* when no Federal Rule is in point. There is some play in how the Court's position here should be read. On the surface, however, the Court formulated a *refined* version of the outcome-determinative test. Under this "*Hanna-Erie*" test, the federal courts should not look to mere differences in outcome, but only look to differences in law that would undermine "the twin aims of the *Erie* rule: discouragement of forum-shopping and avoidance of inequitable administration of the laws." When necessary to avoid differences that are significant in such ways, the federal courts should apply state law.

c) Criticism

The courts tried to follow *Hanna*. But in gross terms, *Hanna-Sibbach* ignored relevant state interests, and *Hanna-Erie* ignored relevant federal interests. Furthermore, the *Hanna* opinion failed to reject definitely the more precise *Byrd* approach. Consequently, some lower courts launched significant rebellions against both *Hanna-Sibbach* and *Hanna-Erie*, with the rebels resorting to ad hoc balancing in cases where those simplistic formulations yielded results that seemed to conflict with the broader aim of *Erie* and *Byrd* to reconcile state and federal interests. See, e.g., *Szantay v. Beech Aircraft Corp.*, 349 F.2d 60 (4th Cir.1965) (declining to apply a state door-closing statute that was based on forum non conveniens notions). All this left the *Erie* doctrine in some confusion.

6) *Hanna-Byrd* Approach

Increasingly the lower courts perceived the need for some *compromise* between sophisticated but uncertain interest analysis and the somewhat more certain but simplistic tests. A desirable and popular compromise was to create a series of fairly general rules that soundly made the choice between state and federal law for all the common situations. For example, federal law governs when a Federal Rule of Civil Procedure is in point. A practical way to create these general rules, and a way that had support in actual practice, was *initially* to apply a sophisticated interest-analysis approach to resolve the choice-of-law problem for a broad area or "pocket" of the law, and *then* to rely on a tough stare decisis approach to prevent the resultant general rule from later being eaten up by exceptions in appealing cases. The long-term effect would be an extensive series of fairly workable and predictable general rules that, when laid end-to-end, approximate the line between state and federal law ideally mandated by the goals of *Erie*. This compromise thus would obtain considerable accuracy as well as certainty. It might be thought of as either "gross balancing" or "sensitive rulemaking," and it might be dubbed the *"Hanna-Byrd"* approach.

a) Establishing the Rules

The court should resolve an *Erie* question of first impression by deduction from a general rule. But the court should initially create that general rule by balancing the interests involved across a broad pocket of the law, a process involving two steps:

(1) *Defining the Pocket.* The initial difficulty obviously is to define the pocket. The solution for the court is to extend out from the instant case as far as the relevant state and federal interests remain substantially constant; if the proper bounds of the pocket are not evident, as is likely, the court should resort to certain canons: (1) the court should opt for a pocket that can be described in a communicable form

(this fosters the application of stare decisis); and, if still in doubt, (2) the court should lean toward defining the pocket broadly, even sweeping up narrow situations with aberrational state and federal interests (this fosters certainty in the application of the *Erie* doctrine). An example of a broad, communicable pocket is the *Hanna-Sibbach* pocket comprising the Federal Rules; however, that pocket may be too broad, there being some doubt whether the relevant state and federal interests remain substantially constant throughout the pocket.

(2) *Balancing the Interests.* Next the court should establish the general rule that state law governs in the pocket, unless the state interests are overcome by the federal interests involved across the whole pocket. More precisely, the court should functionally weigh (1) the interests of the states generally in having state law applied in federal court to this particular pocket against the net federal interests, which are (2) the federal interests in having federal law govern in the pocket less (3) the federal interests in avoiding differences in the laws applied in the federal court and the forum state court that would incur the systemic costs of forum-shopping between federal and state courts or would cause the unfairness of treating similarly situated individuals differently given that certain classes of people have a choice of court systems. This formula—*(1) states' interests balanced against the difference of (2) affirmative countervailing considerations less (3) the forum-shopping and inequality ingredients of the outcome-determinative effect*—is basically the *Byrd* formula with its outcome-determinative element replaced by *Hanna-Erie*'s quite proper refinement of that factor.

b) Applying the Rules

Once one of these general rules has been formulated, as many have been, it should normally be binding under stare decisis in the same court and lower courts. That general rule would resolve all future cases within its scope, even when a narrow and aberrational case involves state and federal interests that support a contrary resolution. The later court could not create an explicit exception to the general rule, as that is inconsistent with the proposed approach. Moreover, the later court should be very hesitant to escape the general rule by narrowly redefining the established pocket, because that in effect creates an exception and leads back down the road to ad hoc balancing. Only rarely, when the later court perceives such a stark imbalance of the relevant state and federal interests as almost to demand the contrary rule, should that court entertain the possibility of narrowly redefining the established pocket in order to treat the case before it as a new *Erie* question or entertain the less promising possibility of rebalancing with respect to the established pocket. In sum, resolving most *Erie* questions will entail only identifying the predefined pocket that embraces the particular issue and then applying the established choice-of-law rule for that pocket.

c) Behavior of Federal Courts

This *Hanna-Byrd* approach surely sounds bizarre. However, it offers an intellectually defensible means to reconcile and preserve as "good law" all the cases thus far cited. Moreover, it seems to explicate and rationalize what the federal courts have been doing and also why casual commentators tend to discuss *Erie* in terms of rules for various areas of the law. In creative retrospect, then, a generous selection of general rules has already evolved, most of which rules are sound and all of which rules act to remove much of the uncertainty from the *Erie* doctrine. For example, state law governs countless clearly "substantive" pockets and also:

(1) statutes of limitations on state-created claims;

(2) territorial jurisdiction on state-created claims, a result now codified in Federal Rule 4;

(3) door-closing statutes of the *Woods*-type, but not the *Szantay*-type, on state-created claims;

(4) horizontal choice of law on matters governed by state law under *Erie*; and

(5) burden of proof on matters governed by state law under *Erie*.

But, for example, federal law governs countless clearly "substantive" pockets of federal concern as well as countless "procedural" pockets in connection with federal question cases, and federal law also governs even in diversity cases such pockets as:

(1) judge-jury relations, probably including sufficiency of the evidence;

(2) order of trial;

(3) the pocket of law occupied by the Federal Rules of Civil and Appellate Procedure;

(4) venue and forum selection; and

(5) joinder of claims and parties.

Intervening Supreme Court decisions were consistent with the *Hanna-Byrd* approach. In particular, two dealt with methodological difficulties, while also exhibiting a strong affection for stare decisis:

(1) *Exceptions to Rules.* There have been predictable instances of lower courts undermining general rules by creating exceptions. Perhaps even too zealously, the Supreme Court slapped down such an attempt on appealing facts to create an exception to the state-law rule for the horizontal-choice-of-law pocket. *Day & Zimmermann, Inc. v. Challoner*, 423 U.S. 3, 96 S.Ct. 167 (1975).

(2) *Scope of Pockets.* Difficulties in determining the scope of the pockets are also predictably inevitable. The Supreme Court accordingly stepped in to settle that the issue of when an action is deemed commenced for statute-of-limitations purposes is indeed still in the statute-of-limitations pocket rather than the Federal Rules pocket, at least for state-created claims. *Walker v. Armco Steel Corp.*, 446 U.S. 740, 100 S.Ct. 1978 (1980).

d) Role of Congress

As already explained, Congress is the senior partner in the cooperative venture of drawing the line between state and federal law in federal court. Ideally, Congress would use a similar technique when it legislates a choice between state and federal law. It too would define a pocket and, after considering state and federal interests, dictate the applicable law. That congressional choice would thenceforth bind the federal courts. See, e.g., Federal Rule of Evidence 302 (presumptions). However, *Congress may properly opt for federal law more often than the federal courts would*, because under our constitutional structure Congress should be the more active articulator of federal interests.

7) *Gasperini*

In *Gasperini v. Center for Humanities, Inc.*, 518 U.S. 415, 116 S.Ct. 2211 (1996), the Court uttered its most recent major words on *Erie*, but failed miserably to make them clear ones. The case held in a diversity case, first, that New York's tort-reform interests called for applying its intrusive new trial standard for setting aside a jury verdict in the federal district court, but, second, that the federal interests prevailed to call for applying the deferential federal standard of appellate review in the federal court of appeals. *Gasperini* seemed to embrace modern interest analysis as the appropriate *Erie* methodology outside the realm of the Federal Rules: (1) the state's interests balanced against the difference of (2) affirmative countervailing considerations less (3) the forum-shopping and inequality ingredients of the outcome-determinative effect. However, its holding required a crabbed reading of Federal Rule 59, to the effect that the Rule does not cover the standard for judicial review of jury decisionmaking; this implies that *Hanna-Sibbach* will henceforth be applied narrowly. Moreover, the case undercut *Hanna-Byrd* by imposing an ad hoc approach to balancing; as the different results on the two *Erie* issues in *Gasperini* proved, the courts must balance interests issue-by-issue, and they must now weigh the very specific state and federal interests at stake; thus, federal judge-jury law prevails over South Carolina's weak interests in *Byrd*, but falls to New York's strong interests in *Gasperini*.

8) Summary

a) The *Erie* Problem

In clearly "substantive" areas of great state concern, state law rather surely governs in federal court, sometimes even by constitutional necessity. As one moves into more "procedural" areas of some state concern, the hard *Erie* cases arise and so do disputes over the proper methodology. Finally, as one moves into areas of strong federal concern, such as clearly "substantive" areas of great federal interest, federal law surely applies, sometimes even by constitutional command. The following diagram suggests this scheme. The relative intensity of state interests in having state law applied in federal court increases with distance from the center of the diagram:

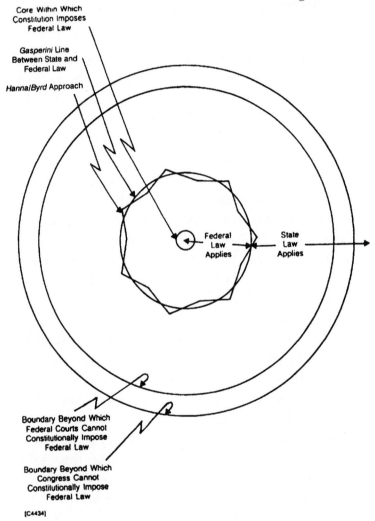

b)   The *Erie* Line

The following diagram depicts and evaluates the history of judicial choice-of-law techniques that tried to answer the *Erie* problem (not the cases' specific results), with the passage of time progressing down the page.

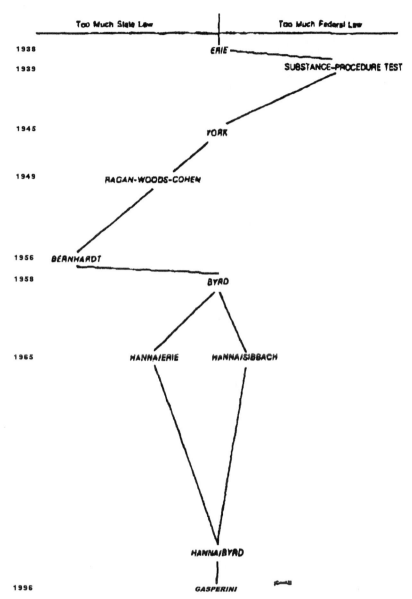

c) The *Erie* Pendulum

A classic theme in law is the clash between the demand for rule-based certainty and the desire for individualized precision. Looking back over the history of the attempts to draw the *Erie* line between state and federal law, one can see that the courts have been regularly oscillating from some certain but inaccurate fixed test to a sophisticated but uncertain ad hoc balancing approach, back to a certain but inaccurate test, and so on. The jurisprudential task is to still this pendulum by compromise, but at the right line of division between state and federal law. Perhaps before *Gasperini* the lower courts were in the process of doing so. *Gasperini*, however, seems to have reactivated the pendulum, as the Court embraced anew individualized precision in marking the *Erie* line.

b. *Erie* Precepts

Regardless of the choice-of-law technique adopted, certain precepts are observed by the federal courts.

1) ### What Is the Role of the Type of Jurisdiction?

   The type of subject-matter jurisdiction, such as diversity of citizenship or federal question, is not determinative on the *Erie* problem. The choice-of-law technique applies issue-by-issue in each case. So, in a diversity case, certain issues will be governed by federal law. And although heightened federal interests will call for federal law on most issues in a federal question case, some issues of great state concern may be governed by state law, as for example an issue of mortgage law arising in bankruptcy proceedings.

2) ### Which State Supplies the Governing Law?

   This was yet another one of those points left open by the *Erie* case. The Supreme Court has since decided that in connection with matters governed by state law under *Erie*, the forum state's law governs the pocket of law comprising interstate (and international) choice of law. *Klaxon Co. v. Stentor Elec. Mfg. Co.*, 313 U.S. 487, 61 S.Ct. 1020 (1941). The *Klaxon* rule is perhaps questionable in wisdom, but is clearly established. So, to find the potentially applicable state law for any matter in the case, one looks to the forum state's choice-of-law doctrine. That doctrine will tell which state's law would govern that matter if state law is to be applied.

3) ### How Is the Content of State Law Determined?

   Sometimes there is no clear state law on a particular issue to be governed under *Erie* by state law. In such case, the federal trial or appellate court should fabricate state law as if it were then sitting as the forum state's highest court, taking into account all the precedent and other data that court would. Alternatively, the federal court may use the potentially burdensome and troublesome procedure of certifying an unsettled question concerning a state's law directly to that state's highest court, if that state has made provision for responding to such certified questions.

c. Federal Law in Federal Court

Obviously, federal law very often applies in federal question cases and often even in diversity cases, as a consequence either of a constitutional or congressional choice or of a judicial choice-of-law decision. Oftentimes when federal law governs by nonjudicial choice, the Constitution or Congress formulates the content of the applicable federal law, which of course is then binding on the federal courts. In all other situations when federal law governs, the Constitution and Congress do not formulate the applicable federal law, which means that the federal courts must step in by formulating *federal common law*. This is occasionally termed "specialized federal common law," to distinguish it from the general common law that the federal courts formerly created under *Swift*. For a prime example of modern federal common law, see *Clearfield Trust Co. v. United States*, 318 U.S. 363, 63 S.Ct. 573 (1943) (perhaps questionably, Court chooses and creates federal law to govern rights and duties of the United States on its commercial paper).

1) **Realm of Federal Common Law**

The federal courts might have to formulate federal common law pursuant to a congressional delegation of power. Or, as in *Clearfield*, the federal courts might on their own choose federal law. This latter, or *Clearfield*, problem is little more than a facet of the *Erie* problem. If the judicial choice-of-law technique ends up pointing to federal law rather than state law, then the federal courts must formulate the chosen federal law.

2) **Adopting State Law as Federal Common Law**

In formulating the content of federal common law, federal courts sometimes purely create common law and sometimes simply extend some closely related or analogous federal statutory provision. But often federal courts opt to adopt the appropriate state's law concerning the point in issue, which law is already formulated although it may vary from state to state. This is a simple route to take, tends to reduce the federal courts' involvement in lawmaking, and might also serve to accommodate any state interests that may be involved. Indeed, whenever unformulated federal law governs by virtue of the *Clearfield* balance, there is a rebuttable presumption in favor of adopting state law as the federal common law. That is, federal courts should so adopt state law, unless there is a relatively significant federal interest in uniformity of the federal law throughout the nation or there are relatively important federal interests calling for a particular content to the federal law or for particular limits on the content. See, e.g., *Owens v. Okure*, 488 U.S. 235, 109 S.Ct. 573 (1989) (in absence of federal statute of limitations for federally created claim, federal courts ordinarily should apply the basic aspects of the forum state's statute of limitations for the most closely analogous general type of state cause of action). Such adoption of state law as the federal law is distinguishable from the binding application of state law in federal court under *Erie*. Consequently, federal courts adopting the appropriate state's law as the federal law can alter or ignore part or all of the relevant state law if it actually impinges on federal interests in the particular case at bar. See, e.g., *Holmberg v. Armbrecht*, 327 U.S. 392, 66 S.Ct. 582 (1946) (federal tolling notion read into state statute of limitations for particular federal suit on federal claim).

B.   FEDERAL LAW IN STATE COURT: REVERSE–*ERIE*

If the Constitution or Congress (the latter acting within constitutional limits) expressly or impliedly makes federal law applicable in state court, that choice to preempt state law is binding on the state courts under the Supremacy Clause. In the absence of such a constitutional or congressional directive, the state courts and ultimately the U.S. Supreme Court must decide whether federal law applies in state court by employing a federally mandated choice-of-law technique similar to the Erie *technique, and any choice in favor of federal law is binding on the state courts under the Supremacy Clause.*

1.   CONSTITUTIONAL LIMITS

Not unlike the *Erie* scheme, there are constitutional limits on the powers of Congress and the Supreme Court to choose the applicable law. The limits on imposing federal law on the state courts are quite significant here. The federal government cannot extend beyond the relevant boundary demarking the matters constitutionally reserved to the states.

2.   LEGISLATIVE LIMITS

Just as for *Erie*, within constitutional limits Congress can make the choice between state and federal law, and its choice will bind the courts.

3.   CHOICE–OF–LAW TECHNIQUE

Analogously, the courts must use some technique for choosing between state and federal law when they may under the Constitution and federal statutes go either way.

a.   Competing Methodologies

There is no clearly developed choice-of-law technique here. However, the developments on the *Erie* front should shed some light. Generally, courts facing the reverse-*Erie* problem appear to balance state interests in having state law applied in state court against federal interests in having federal law displace the rule of this particular state, while trying to avoid difference in outcome. Note, however, that here the outcome-determinative effect now *adds* to the other federal interests in having federal law applied in state court.

b. Reverse–*Erie* Practice

In areas of strong state concern, such as clearly "substantive" areas of great state interest, state law naturally governs in state court, often by constitutional necessity. As one moves into questions of access to state court on federally created claims and other more "procedural" areas of federal concern, the hard reverse-*Erie* cases arise. Finally, as one moves into clearly "substantive" areas of great federal concern, federal law more surely applies, sometimes even by direct constitutional command. However, this scheme is not simply the mirror image of *Erie*. One major difference is that reverse-*Erie* seems to be the slightly more intrusive doctrine: state courts must apply federal law to federally created claims more extensively than federal courts must apply state law to state-created claims. The explanation is that the Supremacy Clause weights the scales in favor of federal law, by preempting any state law that conflicts with existing federal law.

Example: Plaintiff brought an FELA action in a Georgia state court. Defendant demurred. Contrary to federal practice, a Georgia rule would construe allegations most strongly against the pleader and so result in dismissal of the plaintiff's complaint with prejudice. (Result: the Georgia pleading rule bows to the more lenient federal practice.) *Brown v. Western Ry.*, 338 U.S. 294, 70 S.Ct. 105 (1949). See also *Dice v. Akron, C. & Y.R.R.*, 342 U.S. 359, 72 S.Ct. 312 (1952) (jury right).

C. SUMMARY

In areas of clear state "substantive" concern, state law governs in both state and federal courts. As one moves into "procedural" areas, state law *tends* to govern in state court and federal law *tends* to govern in federal court. Finally, as one moves into areas of clear federal "substantive" concern, federal law governs in both state and federal courts. So the interlocking *Erie* and reverse-*Erie* doctrines ultimately form a logical pattern. But there are profound complexities lurking here, which the complications of federalism itself necessarily impose.

REVIEW QUESTIONS

Questions (1)–(6): A New York citizen, P, was driving along the New Jersey Turnpike when D, a New Jersey citizen, crashed into her car. Two years later, P sues D in a New York state court, seeking $100,000 for personal injuries. D removes to the New York federal district court. The New Jersey statute of limitations for such a claim is one year. The New York period is three years.

1. **T or F** The decision whether to apply the New Jersey, the New York, or a federal limitations period is confided to the sound discretion of the district judge.

2. **T or F** Federal law would probably be applied by the district judge because statutes of limitations are procedural.

3. **T or F** The federal court cannot constitutionally apply the New York limitations period.

4. **T or F** If Congress had passed a statute of limitations for any federal action arising from an automobile accident on an interstate highway, that statute would displace any state time period.

5. **T or F** If under both New Jersey and New York law automobile accident cases were tried before judges without juries, P would not be entitled to a jury trial in her federal action.

6. **T or F** If the otherwise applicable state negligence law is judge-made rather than statutory, the federal court is not bound to apply that law in the absence of a congressional directive to do so.

Questions (7)–(8): Espire, a California domiciliary, left an unrestricted bequest of several hundred thousand dollars to the federal government. California law, however, prohibited such a bequest. There was no existing federal law on the point. The federal government sued in California state court to recover the bequest.

7. **T or F** The entitlement of the United States to the bequest was a question of state law.

8. **T or F** If the federal government had instead sued in a federal court, state law would have governed its entitlement to the bequest.

Questions (9)–(10): Dan deprives Pat of her civil rights, but wrongfully conceals this for three years. When Pat learns the facts, she sues Dan in federal court under the federal civil rights statutes. Those statutes specify no limitations period. The analogous state statute of limitations for general personal injury is two years, and that statute is not tolled by the defendant's concealment of his acts.

9. **T or F** The federal court will apply the state limitations period, but may toll the statute under federal law.

10. **T or F** If Pat instead sued under state tort law in a federal diversity action, the federal court would apply the state limitations period and could apply a federal tolling doctrine.

Questions (11)–(14): D invents and manufactures appliances. He sells P a food processor under a warranty. The processor explodes one week later, and P is injured. So P files a state-law breach-of-warranty action in federal court, and then serves D. Diversity jurisdiction exists.

11. The state statute of limitations is three years. P files suit within three years, but does not serve D until after the three-year period has expired. Which of the following is most accurate?

   a. The claim is not time-barred because P filed the action within three years.

   b. The claim is time-barred if state law requires service within the limitations period.

   c. The claim is time-barred if federal law requires filing within the limitations period.

   d. The claim is not time-barred because it was timely commenced under Federal Rules 3 and 4.

12. Under the particular state's practice, the defense of lack of territorial jurisdiction is waived unless raised in a pre-answer motion. D makes no motions, but includes that defense in his answer. Which of the following is most accurate?

   a. The defense is waived because applying a contrary federal rule would be outcome-determinative.

   b. The defense is not waived because state procedural law is inapplicable in federal court.

c. The defense is waived because state interests outweigh federal interests.

d. The defense is not waived because Federal Rule 12(h) preserves it.

13. The venue is improper under state law, although proper under federal law. So, by appropriate procedure, D raises the defense of improper venue. Which of the following is most accurate?

    a. The defense should succeed because *Erie* requires the application of state venue rules in diversity actions.

    b. The defense should fail because the federal courts have decided that federal venue rules displace state venue rules in diversity actions.

    c. The defense should succeed if the federal venue rules violate the Rules Enabling Act.

    d. The defense should fail because Congress has decided that federal venue rules displace state venue rules in diversity actions.

14. If P instead sued in state court under the federal warranty law, which of the following would be most accurate?

    a. The state court must apply federal procedural rules.

    b. The state court must apply federal substantive law.

    c. Federal law is more intrusive in this context than state law is in diversity actions.

15. Prepare an essay in response to this question:

On October 23, Pedro, a citizen of Mexico, fell from the second floor of a building in California owned by Don, a citizen of California. On October 25 of the following year, Pedro filed a diversity action for negligence in a California federal court, seeking to recover $100,000 for personal injuries and serving Don that same day.

California has a statute of limitations allowing one year to file such a claim. However, the normally final day for filing, October 23, fell on a Sunday; and both federal and state courthouses were closed. Monday, October 24, was a federal holiday (Veterans Day), but not a state holiday (California observed Veterans Day on November 11); and so the federal courthouse was closed, but the state courthouse was open. Federal Rule 6(a) seems to extend all deadlines falling on a weekend or legal holiday to the next day that is not a Saturday, Sunday, or legal holiday; California law extends any deadline falling on a weekend or state holiday to the next day that is not a Saturday, Sunday, or state holiday.

Don raises the statute-of-limitations defense in his answer, and then moves for summary judgment thereon. What result?

*

PART SIX

Former Adjudication

■ **ANALYSIS**

*

XVII

Preliminary Considerations

■ ANALYSIS

A. INTRODUCTION TO FORMER ADJUDICATION

The subject here is a previously rendered judgment's impact in subsequent civil litigation. The most important doctrine within this subject is res judicata or, as it used to be called, res adjudicata. Res judicata tends to be discussed only when a litigant goes wrong, but it has much greater significance. Because it specifies what has been adjudicated by a judgment, which is after all the primary objective of most adjudicative proceedings, res judicata doctrine is of universal importance in understanding and implementing procedure, both before and after judgment.

1. MODERN FOCUS

Res judicata is a classic common-law doctrine. Each jurisdiction generates its own distinctive body of rules, almost entirely judge-made. In this Part Six, the primary focus will be on the modern approach to res judicata, as exemplified by the federal doctrine or by the excellent and authoritative Restatement (Second) of Judgments (1982). There will be occasional references to contrasting older practice, where appropriate.

2. RULES

Authorities categorize and label the rules of res judicata in various ways. The modern approach is first to divide the doctrine into claim preclusion and issue preclusion, and then to subdivide and supplement this complex doctrine. See generally 18 Wright, Miller & Cooper § 4402.

a. Claim Preclusion

Outside the context of the initial action, a party *generally* may not relitigate a claim decided therein by a valid and final judgment. The judgment extinguishes the whole claim, precluding all matters within the claim that were or could have been litigated in that initial action. (See Chapter XVIII below for more detail.)

1) Merger

If the judgment in the initial action was in the *plaintiff's favor*, his claim is said to "merge" in the judgment. Plaintiff cannot bring a second action on the claim in the hope of winning a more favorable judgment. However, he can seek to enforce his judgment, and defendant cannot then avail herself of defenses that were or could have been interposed in that initial action.

2) Bar

If the judgment in the initial action was in the *defendant's favor*, plaintiff's claim is said to be "barred" by the judgment. Plaintiff cannot bring a second action on the claim in the hope of winning this time.

b. **Issue Preclusion**

Outside the context of the initial action, regardless of who won judgment, a party *generally* may not relitigate any issue of fact or law actually litigated and determined therein if the determination was essential to a valid and final judgment. (See Chapter XIX below for more detail.)

1) Direct Estoppel

If the second action is on the *same claim* as the initial action (the second action presumably falling within some exception to claim preclusion), then the applicable variety of issue preclusion is "direct estoppel."

2) Collateral Estoppel

Much more commonly, the second action is on a *different claim*. Then the applicable variety of issue preclusion is "collateral estoppel."

c. **Special Situations**

For the moment, consider only the subsequent effects of (1) a personal judgment rendered in an action seeking coercive relief in a civil court, (2) where the parties to the subsequent litigation are the same as those to the initial action, and (3) where the subsequent litigation is in the same court system as the initial action. Special situations will be covered later, when consideration will be given to (1) the effects of less ordinary kinds of judgment in Chapter XX below, (2) the effects on nonparties in Chapter XXI below, and (3) the effects of nondomestic judgments in Chapter XXII below.

3. **COMPARISONS AND CONTRASTS**

Distinguish res judicata from related doctrines. See generally Robert C. Casad & Kevin M. Clermont, Res Judicata: A Handbook on Its Theory, Doctrine, and Practice 13–27 (2001) (also distinguishing a former adjudication being used as evidence, judicial estoppel, other action pending, and double jeopardy).

a. **Stare Decisis**

Intended to give stability to the law, this doctrine provides that a court's holding on a legal question will normally be followed, by the same court and any lower courts in that judicial hierarchy, in future cases presenting undistinguishable facts. Contrasted with res judicata, stare decisis (1) permits courts to handle precedent much more flexibly, (2) applies only to issues of law, and (3) governs even in cases involving wholly new parties.

b. Law of the Case

Intended to foster judicial economy, this doctrine provides that a court, and any coordinate or lower courts as well, will normally adhere to a ruling it has declared in a particular action if a party later raises the point again in the same action. Contrasted with res judicata, law of the case (1) applies rather flexibly, (2) applies traditionally but not exclusively to issues of law, and (3) applies only in the one case at hand.

c. Former Recovery

Intended to prevent double recovery, this distinctive doctrine provides that an award by judgment will be diminished by the amount recovered on any earlier judgments for the same injury.

d. Estoppel

This doctrine, which includes most importantly the subdoctrine named "equitable estoppel," or "estoppel in pais," generally provides that a party may not take a position in litigation when that position is inconsistent with earlier conduct and the change would unfairly burden another party. Contrasted with res judicata, the flexible doctrine of estoppel looks to the party's earlier out-of-court or in-court conduct, rather than to a prior judgment. For an example of where this many-faceted doctrine might apply, consider the situation of a party having admitted a fact in some lawsuit and then in subsequent litigation unfairly trying to assert the contrary.

e. Election of Remedies

Also focusing on party-conduct, this doctrine provides that a party who ordinarily would have a choice among alternative remedies can disentitle himself to one or more of those remedies by engaging in conduct deemed inconsistent therewith. For example, alteration of a purchased chattel may foreclose rescission as a remedy for fraud, leaving damages as the only available remedy. For another example, which represents an increasingly outmoded view, mere commencement of an action seeking a particular remedy may foreclose other "inconsistent" remedies.

B. RATIONALE OF RES JUDICATA

The basic idea behind res judicata is that at some point the pursuit of truth must and should cease: justice demands that there be an end to litigation.

1. EFFICIENCY

Society has an interest in avoiding the expenditure of time and money in repetitive litigation. Society also has an interest in avoiding any increase of uncertainty or instability in the judicial branch of our legal system. Society has a similar interest in avoiding possibly inconsistent adjudications, which at the least would erode faith in our system of justice. An important efficiency consideration is the long-run deterrent effect of res judicata: a harsh result in the case at hand might encourage many future litigants to dispose of their disputes in a single lawsuit.

2. FAIRNESS

Fairness supports the use of res judicata to avoid the burdens of repetitive litigation on the party invoking the doctrine, to avoid infringing on reliance and equality interests, and also to avoid the possibility of the other party's profiting from sneaky or otherwise undesirable litigation tactics. A litigant is entitled to a day in court, but not to inflict a repetition of it.

3. EXCEPTIONS

Contrary considerations, especially those resting on fairness, support exceptions to this principle of finality. Indeed, the grand trend in the development of the modern doctrine of res judicata has been expanding the theoretical applicability of the principle while at the same time recognizing more and more exceptions of considerable scope and discretionary nature. On the one hand, even the many existing exceptions do not remove all the bite from the sometimes harsh doctrine of res judicata. On the other hand, as exceptions continue to multiply, the question arises whether a narrowing and increasingly discretionary doctrine of res judicata is really preferable to a bare but clear minimum of preclusion. It must be recognized that if instead the doctrine of res judicata is deemed worth preserving, it must be applied with some breadth and woodenness.

C. APPLICATION OF RES JUDICATA

1. RAISING THE DOCTRINE

Res judicata is not self-executing. The person wishing to rely on it must raise it.

a. Timing

Res judicata can be used only after judgment, and outside the context of that initial action (and any appeal). Thus, plaintiff in Action #2 might invoke res judicata to preclude defendant from defending on the underlying merits in an action upon a judgment rendered in Action #1, or to foreclose relitigation of certain issues decided in Action #1. Similarly, defendant in a subsequent action might invoke claim or issue preclusion as a defense. Accordingly, it is the court handling the subsequent action that decides the applicability of res judicata.

b. Procedure

1) Pleading

Plaintiff in a subsequent action usually would raise res judicata by pretrial motion, such as a summary judgment motion. Defendant in a subsequent action usually should plead res judicata as an affirmative defense. See, e.g., Federal Rule 8(c).

2) Burden

The burden of persuasion that res judicata applies is on the party raising it, but then the burden of proof that an exception to res judicata applies is on the other side.

3) Evidence

In deciding the applicability of res judicata, the court may consider extrinsic evidence regarding what the prior judgment actually decided.

2. CONDITIONS FOR APPLICATION: VALIDITY AND FINALITY

a. Validity

For a judgment to have res judicata effects, it must be "valid." To be treated as valid, the judgment must withstand any attack in the form of a request for "relief from judgment."

1) Avenues of Attack

Relief from judgment refers to procedural techniques, other than in the ordinary course of review in the trial and appellate courts, for avoiding the effects of the judgment. Relief from judgment encompasses three major techniques.

a) Motion

A party may attack a judgment in the rendering court by a motion for relief from judgment. This extraordinary motion is technically considered a continuation of the initial action. This is the preferred means of overturning a judgment, being the most direct and orderly technique. See, e.g., Federal Rule 60(b).

b) Independent Suit

If adequate relief from judgment is unavailable by motion because of any applicable limitations on use of such motion, a person may bring an independent suit against the judgment-holder to nullify or enjoin the enforcement of the judgment. This suit is preferably, but not necessarily, brought in the rendering court.

c) Defensive Attack

If someone in a subsequent action relies on a prior judgment as a basis for claim or defense, as in a subsequent action where plaintiff sues upon the judgment to enforce it or where defendant pleads res judicata, the opponent may in that subsequent action attack the judgment to prevent its use. The court will entertain this attack if adequate relief by another procedural technique is not available and more convenient. This is often termed a "collateral attack." Because invocation of res judicata tends to provoke collateral attack, the study of res judicata frequently involves problems of collateral attack.

2) Traditional Approach to Grounds for Attack

Motions and independent suits for relief from judgment have traditionally been limited to cases of extraordinary harm, such as judgments involving fraud or lack of jurisdiction. Defensive, or collateral, attacks have been even more limited. The traditional rule of thumb there has been that a defensive attack will succeed on the ground that the rendering court failed to satisfy the requirement of (1) subject-matter jurisdiction, (2) territorial jurisdiction, or (3) adequate notice; indeed, such an attack will succeed *only* on one of those three grounds and not on the ground of any other error, which should have been corrected on appeal or other direct attack.

3) **Fluid Approach to Grounds for Attack**

The ultramodern view is that courts should, and to some extent apparently do, approach relief from judgment as a discretionary balancing of equities. Various factors determine the availability of relief:

(1) the nature and importance of the judgment's alleged infirmity;

(2) the technique of relief from judgment employed, this being based on the view that such techniques form a spectrum and that the list of available grounds for relief should contract as the mode, place, and time of attack become more distant from the initial action;

(3) the impact of the relief requested; and

(4) the position of the parties, including diligence in seeking relief and reliance on the judgment.

Under this fluid approach, it can still be said that judgments usually are treated as valid for res judicata purposes if and only if they meet the requirements of subject-matter jurisdiction, territorial jurisdiction, and adequate notice. But there are exceptions. Sometimes and for some purposes judgments not meeting those three requirements have effect, and other judgments meeting those three requirements do not have effect when all the above factors are taken into account.

4) **Effect of Res Judicata on Attack**

Remember that on any such attack, res judicata may apply. In particular, the res judicata doctrine of jurisdiction to determine jurisdiction may foreclose relitigation of a prior determination of the existence of subject-matter jurisdiction, territorial jurisdiction, or adequate notice. (See Chapter XI above.)

b. **Finality**

For a judgment to have res judicata effects, it must be "final."

1) **Meaning of Finality**

This variable condition is discussed in Judgments Second §§ 13–14.

a) **Claim Preclusion**

For the purposes of claim preclusion, a judgment becomes final when the trial court has concluded all regular proceedings on the claim other than award of costs and enforcement of judgment. Thus, a judgment is final even though a motion for new trial or an appeal is pending. But a determination of liability is not final if the trial court still has to determine damages.

b) Issue Preclusion

For issue preclusion, an adjudication is sometimes treated as a final judgment at an earlier stage. According to some authorities, the court in the second action has discretion cautiously to treat a prior determination as final if after adequate hearing and full deliberation the initial court made a firm decision on the issue, even though in that initial action there is as yet no final judgment on the whole claim.

2) Effect of Appeal

If a judgment is modified by appeal (or otherwise), its preclusive effects will henceforth be in accordance with its modified terms. If in the meantime some other later judgment has been based on that earlier judgment before the appeal, then relief from the later judgment normally may be had by appropriate proceedings. See generally id. § 16.

3) Inconsistent Judgments

If by failure to invoke or apply res judicata two inconsistent judgments are rendered, then the judgment later rendered has the controlling preclusive effects. This somewhat arbitrary provision is called the last-in-time rule. See generally id. § 15.

*

XVIII

Claim Preclusion

■ ANALYSIS

A. REQUIREMENTS OF CLAIM PRECLUSION

Claim preclusion prohibits repetitive litigation of the same claim. The key requirement, then, is identity of claim. This necessitates definition of a "claim."

1. TRANSACTIONAL VIEW

The modern view is that a claim includes all rights of plaintiff to remedies against defendant with respect to the transaction from which the action arose.

Whether particular facts constitute a single "transaction" is a pragmatic question, turning on such factors "as whether the facts are related in time, space, origin, or motivation, whether they form a convenient trial unit, and whether their treatment as a unit conforms to the parties' expectations or business understanding or usage." Judgments Second § 24(2).

a. Rationale

The modern view rests on the idea that plaintiff *should* in a single lawsuit fully litigate his grievances arising from a transaction, just as modern rules of procedure *permit* him to do. This increases efficiency, with an acceptable burden on fairness.

b. Former View

The old view, to which some jurisdictions still adhere, defined "claim" more narrowly in terms of a single legal theory or a single right or remedy of plaintiff.

2. APPLICATION

Plaintiff must be careful to put any asserted claim entirely before the court, because judgment will not only preclude actual relitigation but also preclude later pursuit of the claim's unasserted portion. Under the transactional view, a claim is big enough to include:

(1) different harms;

(2) different evidence;

(3) different legal theories, whether cumulative, alternative, or even inconsistent;

(4) different remedies, whether legal or equitable; and

(5) a series of related events.

See generally id. § 25. Any plaintiff who asserts only a part of his claim is said to have "split" his claim.

Example: P sues D for personal injury resulting from an automobile accident. After valid and final judgment, P sues D for property damage in the same accident. D pleads res judicata. (Result: under the transactional view, the second action is precluded. See id. § 24 cmt. c, illus. 1–2.)

Even under the transactional view, however, the typical claim involves only a single plaintiff and a single defendant; and so multiple parties on either side typically mean multiple claims.

B. EXCEPTIONS TO CLAIM PRECLUSION

Predictably, this broad conception of claim preclusion has generated several significant exceptions.

So sometimes plaintiff is permitted to bring a second action on part, or all, of the same claim. See generally id. § 26.

1. JURISDICTIONAL OR PROCEDURAL LIMITATION

Whenever plaintiff is unable in his first action to present his entire claim because a jurisdictional or procedural limitation prohibits asserting a certain legal theory or demanding a certain remedy, he can bring a second action on that theory or for that remedy.

Example: P sues D for fraud in state court. After judgment, P sues D on the same transaction in federal court under the Federal Securities Exchange Act, an action within the exclusive federal jurisdiction. D pleads res judicata. (Result: no claim preclusion. See id. cmt. c, illus. 2.)

Important to note here is that this exception allows plaintiff only to preserve the part of his claim that would clearly not be entertained by the first court. Thus, if in the preceding example plaintiff had chosen first to sue in federal court, he would there have had to assert both federal and state grounds in order to avoid losing them to claim preclusion. Moreover, this exception allows plaintiff only to preserve the part of his claim that he could not have joined with the rest of his claim by selecting some other court in the same court system. Thus, if plaintiff voluntarily chooses to sue in a state court of limited jurisdiction and recovers the maximum amount that court can award, claim preclusion will prevent his suing for any unrecovered excess, for example in a state court of general jurisdiction.

2. PARTY AGREEMENT

The parties can agree that plaintiff may split his claim, or defendant might even inadvertently acquiesce in splitting.

Example: Simultaneously in the same court, P brings an action for personal injury and another action for property damage resulting from the same accident. D defends, without raising in either action the defense of "other action pending." One action goes to judgment, and D then raises res judicata in the other. (Result: no claim preclusion, because at least in these circumstances failure to object to claim-splitting is deemed acquiescence. See id. cmt. a, illus. 1.)

3. JUDICIAL PERMISSION

Unless prohibited by statute or rule, the court in the first action can specify that its judgment is "without prejudice" to bringing a second action on a portion or all of the same claim. The court will do so where special circumstances justify a second action, such as where only at the prior trial could the plaintiff's counsel finally perceive the breadth of the claim. The court in the second action will defer to a specification of this sort.

4. ADJUDICATION NOT ON THE MERITS

Formerly, claim preclusion operated only if the judgment was rendered "on the merits." Today that requirement has broken down to give preclusion wider application, but still certain threshold dismissals that are not based on evaluation of the substance of the action are treated as exceptions to claim preclusion. See generally id. § 20.

a. No Bar

Certain dismissals not on the merits do not constitute a bar, such as:

(1) most voluntary dismissals, as provided for example in Federal Rule 41(a);

(2) dismissals for lack of subject-matter jurisdiction or territorial jurisdiction, improper venue, inadequate notice, or nonjoinder or misjoinder of parties, as recognized for example in Federal Rule 41(b); and

(3) most dismissals for prematurity of suit or failure to satisfy a precondition to suit, this exception being established by case law (note that Federal Rule 41(b) is not read to be an exhaustive listing of such exceptions to the rule of bar).

Unless prohibited by statute or rule, the court in the first action can specify that its dismissal is not to act as a bar; and the court in the second action will defer to that specification.

b. Bar

Other dismissals, which are perhaps not in any real sense on the merits but which were preceded by an ample opportunity for plaintiff to litigate his claim, have of late come to operate as a bar, at least in the view of many courts and legislatures. Examples include:

(1) a dismissal for failure to prosecute or to obey a court order or rule;

(2) a dismissal for failure to state a claim; and

(3) a summary judgment, judgment on partial findings, or judgment as a matter of law.

If the court in the first action takes upon itself to specify that its dismissal is "with prejudice" to an action elsewhere, the court in the second action will ordinarily give that specification great weight in deciding whether bar applies.

c. Statute of Limitations

The courts have developed a special rule for dismissals on limitations grounds, which is applicable when plaintiff later recasts his action or brings a new action elsewhere in an attempt to circumvent the statute of limitations. See generally id. § 19 cmt. f. Such a dismissal acts as a bar in courts applying the same jurisdiction's statute of limitations, but for reasons difficult to fathom it does not act as a bar to suit elsewhere on the same claim. (Perhaps the way to explain this result is to resort to issue preclusion rather than claim preclusion. Although the first judgment may not have bar effect, it did determine the issue of the particular statute's application to that particular claim. The fact that the statutory period for that claim had expired was litigated and determined in the first suit, and relitigation of that broad issue but not the claim should be foreclosed by principles of direct estoppel. Nevertheless, courts persist in speaking in terms of bar or no bar.)

5. GENERALIZED EXCEPTION

In treating prior judgments, courts show a *limited* amount of flexibility in making case-by-case exceptions to claim preclusion, such as where reasons of constitutional, statutory, or other substantive policy counsel that plaintiff should be allowed to split his claim.

C. COUNTERCLAIMS

Claim preclusion also applies to claims asserted by defendant against plaintiff.

1. INTERPOSITION OF COUNTERCLAIM

Defendant who asserts a counterclaim is generally treated, with respect to that claim, as a plaintiff under the normal rules of claim preclusion. See generally id. §§ 21(1), 23. The rarely applicable exception centers on the rule that if defendant wins on her counterclaim but is unable to obtain an award for full recovery because of the court's jurisdictional or procedural limitations (e.g., a ceiling on damages in a court of limited jurisdiction from which defendant could not transfer the case to a court of general jurisdiction in the same court system), claim preclusion does not operate to preclude a subsequent action for the unrecovered excess. See generally id. § 21(2).

2. FAILURE TO INTERPOSE COUNTERCLAIM

Defendant who does not assert a counterclaim is generally unaffected by claim preclusion with respect to that claim. This majority rule is most difficult to justify when the facts forming the basis of the potential counterclaim also constitute the basis of a defense that defendant does assert. But the thought is that the majority rule is relatively workable and less of a trap for the unwary, that the defendant's interest in selecting the forum for bringing her claim outweighs the undesirability of possibly duplicative litigation, and that here as elsewhere issue preclusion will apply to retrieve in part the policies behind res judicata. See generally id. § 22(1). Nevertheless, there are two important areas where claim preclusion prevails. See generally id. § 22(2).

a. Compulsory Counterclaim Statute or Rule

A statute or rule might effectively provide that under certain circumstances, failure to assert an available counterclaim precludes bringing a subsequent action thereon. See, e.g., Federal Rule 13(a). However, some courts view this preclusion solely in terms of equitable estoppel or waiver, rather than in terms of the more rigid doctrine of res judicata.

b. Common–Law Compulsory Counterclaim

Even in the absence of a statute or rule, failure to assert an available counterclaim precludes bringing a subsequent action thereon if granting relief would *nullify* the judgment in the initial action. Note that this narrow principle applies only where the relief sought in the second action would inherently undo the first judgment.

Example: P sues D for contract damages, D defaults, and P executes on the valid and final judgment. D later sues to rescind the contract and obtain restitution of the amount recovered. (Result: claim preclusion. See Judgments Second § 22 cmt. f, illus. 9.)

*

XIX

Issue Preclusion

■ ANALYSIS

A. REQUIREMENTS OF ISSUE PRECLUSION

Where claim preclusion does not apply, issue preclusion acts to prevent relitigation of essential issues.

There are three requirements for application of issue preclusion. See generally Judgments Second § 27.

1. SAME ISSUE

Prohibiting relitigation of the same issue requires definition of an "issue."

a. Functional View

The modern view is that the scope of an issue should be measured in light of the efficiency-fairness rationale of res judicata. Whether a matter to be presented in a subsequent action constitutes the same issue as a matter presented in the initial action is a pragmatic question, turning on such factors as the degree of overlap between the evidence and legal argument advanced with respect to the matter in the initial action and that to be advanced with respect to the matter in the subsequent action.

b. Application

Consider two contrasting illustrations. In a litigated tort action that defendant won because of the plaintiff's failure to prove negligence, an issue was the broad matter of the defendant's negligence, thus precluding in a subsequent action between the parties the plaintiff's assertion of a different manner in which defendant may have been negligent in that incident. It was fair and efficient to require plaintiff to air all negligence grounds in the first action. However, in an installment contract action that plaintiff won, the sole litigated and determined issue was the narrow defensive matter of the contract's illegality, thereby leaving open the defense of the contract's nonexecution as a different issue in a subsequent action on a later installment.

2. ACTUALLY LITIGATED AND DETERMINED

For preclusive effect, the parties to be bound and benefited must have submitted the issue for determination, and the adjudicator must have determined the issue. Thus, issue preclusion does not result from a default, admission, or stipulation. The idea is that a rule of issue preclusion without the requirement of "actually litigated and determined" would unnecessarily and undesirably intensify litigation.

3. ESSENTIAL TO JUDGMENT

Under the majority view, issue preclusion applies only to a determination that was essential to judgment. Thus, a determination not necessary to reaching the court's ultimate result is not binding. The idea behind this requirement is that such a determination in the nature of dicta may not have been fully litigated and considered, and appeal on it may have been unavailable or unmotivated. Moreover, we want neither to stimulate the parties to fight further over such asides nor to encourage courts so to make unnecessary pronouncements.

B. EXCEPTIONS TO ISSUE PRECLUSION

Courts apply issue preclusion quite flexibly, invoking many exceptions.

Efficiency concerns might counsel exceptions, especially the policy against encouraging parties to over-litigate by fighting every conceivable issue to the death. Fairness concerns also might suggest exceptions, as where there has been no full and fair opportunity to litigate. Finally, independent substantive policies might overwhelm the policies behind res judicata. See generally id. § 28.

1. CERTAIN ISSUES OF LAW

Courts tend not to apply issue preclusion to a relatively *pure* issue of law arising in a claim substantially *unrelated* to the claim in which it was previously determined. More broadly, courts tend not to apply issue preclusion to any issue of law on which it would create *inequity*, such as where binding someone to a legal ruling outmoded by a later change in the decisional law would cause troublingly different legal treatment of similarly situated people. In cases such as these, we rely on the more flexible doctrine of stare decisis to guide the courts' handling of past legal rulings.

2. INFERIOR RENDERING COURT

Consider a subsequent action that is beyond the jurisdiction of the initial court. The court in the subsequent action will not carry over a determination by an inferior court having very much more informal procedures, such as a small claims court. Also, a court of special competence will not carry over a determination by a court of restricted jurisdiction if the jurisdictional scheme indicates a legislative intent against such issue preclusion.

3. DIFFERENT BURDEN OF PERSUASION

Courts will not preclude an issue if the burden of persuasion in the subsequent action would be more favorable to the side that initially lost on the issue than it was in that initial action.

4. INABILITY TO APPEAL

Courts generally will not bind a party on an issue if as a matter of law that party could not in the initial action have obtained appellate review on that issue.

5. UNFORESEEABILITY

In compelling circumstances, a court will not apply issue preclusion if such application was unforeseeable at the time of the initial action and such unforeseeability may have affected the effort therein by the party now sought to be precluded.

6. GENERALIZED EXCEPTION

In compelling circumstances, a court will not bind someone on an issue who for some reason lacked a full and fair opportunity to litigate it, and a court will not apply issue preclusion when substantive policies overwhelm res judicata.

C. MULTIPLE ISSUES

Some special applications of issue preclusion illuminate how it works.

1. CUMULATIVE DETERMINATIONS

If several issues in a case were litigated and determined, each is precluded provided that its determination was essential to judgment.

Example: P sues D for extensive property damage resulting from an automobile accident. D defends by denying both her own negligence and P's ownership of the car. After trial, there is a valid and final judgment for P. Pursuant to an agreement between P and D permitting claim-splitting, P then sues D for personal injury in the same accident and invokes issue preclusion on D's negligence denial, with ownership not being in issue as to personal injury. (Result: issue preclusion or, more precisely, direct estoppel applies.)

On the other hand, if the adjudicator in the initial action ruled that D had been negligent but that P's nonownership prevented recovery, there would be no issue preclusion in the subsequent action because the finding of negligence was not essential to judgment.

2. AMBIGUOUS DETERMINATIONS

If one cannot tell which of several possible issues was determined in a case, then none is precluded.

Example: Same as preceding example, except that in the initial action D wins by a jury's general verdict, and in the subsequent action D pleads issue preclusion to refute her negligence. (Result: no issue preclusion, because one cannot tell if the jury found non-negligence or nonownership.)

3. ALTERNATIVE DETERMINATIONS

Here is a special rule on a very close question: if the adjudicator determined several issues in a case and each of those determinations without the others sufficed to support the judgment, then none by itself is precluded under the "modern" view of Judgments Second § 27 cmt. i. Older authority held each to be precluded, and this might still be the preferable view and does seem to be regaining favor in the courts.

Example: Same as preceding example, except that in the initial action D wins by a jury's special verdict finding both nonnegligence and nonownership. In the subsequent action D pleads issue preclusion to refute her negligence. (Result: no issue preclusion, under the "modern" view. The idea is that any one of the alternative findings may not have been fully litigated and considered, and the loser may have been rightly discouraged from appealing by the strength of the other alternative finding.)

On the other hand, if there was an appeal, then any alternative determination that was affirmed is binding, even under the "modern" view. The idea is that the exercise of appellate review swings the balance of conflicting policies toward preclusion. Moreover, even without an appeal, if all the alternative "issues" arise in the subsequent action, issue preclusion will apply. The idea here is that the alternative rulings can then be viewed as merely alternative bases for an essential determination of a single issue more broadly defined.

*

XX

Nonordinary Judgments

■ ANALYSIS

A. NONPERSONAL JUDGMENTS

The question here is what effects of claim and issue preclusion a nonpersonal judgment has in a subsequent civil action, assuming it was a valid and final judgment.

1. PURE IN REM

A judgment in rem has only two sorts of such effects. It determines, conclusively with regard to all persons, the interests of all persons in the thing. Also, any actual litigant is subject to issue preclusion, under the normal rules of that doctrine. See generally Judgments Second § 30.

2. JURISDICTION OVER STATUS

Such a judgment determines, conclusively with regard to the parties and usually with regard to all other persons as well, the status in question. Also, any actual litigant is subject to issue preclusion. See generally id. § 31.

3. QUASI IN REM—SUBTYPE ONE

Such a judgment determines, conclusively with regard to the named parties, the interests of the named parties in the thing. Also, any party who actually litigated any issue is subject to issue preclusion. Note that a claim targeting the thing (e.g., a claim seeking to foreclose a mortgage) and any associated claim against the person (e.g., a claim seeking to recover the underlying debt) are treated as different claims.

4. QUASI IN REM—SUBTYPE TWO

Such a judgment determines, conclusively between the parties, the plaintiff's right to apply the particular thing to the satisfaction of the particular unrelated claim against defendant, but no more than that. Thus, plaintiff may freely sue again for the unsatisfied portion of that claim, suing either in personam or on attachment of other property belonging to defendant. And although there is disagreement, the better view is that determinations litigated on this shaky jurisdictional basis, pursuant to a limited appearance, should have no issue-preclusion effects.

B. NONCOERCIVE JUDGMENTS

A valid and final judgment in a suit solely for *declaratory relief* has two sorts of effects in a subsequent civil action. It is conclusive between opposing parties as to the matters declared, but it has no further claim-preclusion effects and so does not preclude a later action for damages or other coercive relief. Also, a litigant is subject to issue preclusion, under the normal rules of that doctrine. See generally id. § 33.

C. NONJUDICIAL OR NONCIVIL PROCEEDINGS

The question here is what effects of claim and issue preclusion a nonjudicial or noncivil decision has in a subsequent civil action, assuming that it was a valid and final decision.

1. ADMINISTRATIVE ADJUDICATION

An adjudication by an administrative tribunal is treated like a court judgment, unless the essential elements of judicial adjudication were not employed or unless legislative policies support relitigation. See generally id. § 83.

2. ARBITRATION AWARD

An award by arbitration is generally treated like a court judgment, usually having claim-preclusion effects, and also having issue-preclusion effects unless the essential elements of judicial adjudication were not employed or unless legislative policies or contractual provisions support relitigation. See generally id. § 84.

3. CRIMINAL JUDGMENT

Criminal judgments are now widely viewed as giving rise to normal issue preclusion in a subsequent civil action. Thus, a convicted defendant will generally be bound on essential issues actually litigated and determined, unless some exception applies as where the criminal offense was of such piddling importance as to deny the accused an adequate incentive to litigate. However, the government will almost never be bound by an acquittal, because an exception to issue preclusion (e.g., less favorable burden of persuasion) almost always applies. See generally id. § 85.

Example: The government by trial convicts D of arson involving a government building. The government later sues D civilly for damage to the building. (Result: D is subject to preclusion on the common issues.)

a. Plea of Guilty

Because a guilty plea means the issues were not "actually litigated and determined," the general view is that a conviction based thereon does not give rise to issue preclusion. However, the plea itself will normally be admissible in evidence as an admission, and it may also later equitably estop defendant from taking an inconsistent position in a subsequent civil action.

b.   Plea of Nolo Contendere

Such a plea and the resultant conviction have none of these preclusive or evidentiary effects in a subsequent civil action.

c.   Conviction as Evidence

If under applicable law a conviction does not have conclusive effect in a subsequent civil action, it should be noted that some jurisdictions have adopted a special exception to their hearsay rule. This exception makes a conviction for a serious offense, by trial or guilty plea, admissible evidence on any issue of fact that had been essential to the conviction. See, e.g., Federal Rule of Evidence 803(22).

XXI

Nonparty Effects

■ ANALYSIS

A. **Privies**
    1.   Nonparties Treated as Parties
    2.   Application of Res Judicata

B. **Strangers**
    1.   Parties Treated as Nonparties
    2.   Application of Res Judicata

A. PRIVIES

This conclusory label is used to describe people who were nonparties to an action but who in certain circumstances are nevertheless subjected to generally the same rules of res judicata as are the former parties, the basis for this treatment being some sort of representational relationship between former party and nonparty. The only safe thing to say here is that this subject is dominated by many complicated rules.

1. NONPARTIES TREATED AS PARTIES

There are two basic categories of privies for purposes of res judicata.

a. Procedural Privity

Privies include persons who were actually represented in the litigation by a party, thus including beneficiaries represented by a trustee or administrator but not including persons who merely share common interests with the party. See generally *Taylor v. Sturgell*, 128 S.Ct. 2161 (2008) (rejecting "virtual representation"); Judgments Second §§ 41–42. A similar idea makes privies of persons who assumed control of the prosecution or defense of an action, as well as persons who agreed to abide by an action between others. See generally id. §§ 39–40.

b. Substantive Privity

Privies also include persons who have or had any one of a wide variety of substantive legal relationships with a party, where that relationship in a sense created a representative role. For example, a successor in interest to property is a privy with respect to a judgment determining his predecessor's interest in that property. See generally id. §§ 43–44. For a different example, a member of a partnership is to a limited extent deemed a privy with respect to a judgment to which her partner was a party. See generally id. § 60.

2. APPLICATION OF RES JUDICATA

Generally, a privy is *bound* by and entitled to the *benefits* of claim and issue preclusion as though the privy stood in the shoes of the related party. Note, however, that as the intensity of the privity relationship tails off, as in the partnership example, exceptions and qualifications to the binding effects of the judgment start sprouting up. This is what makes this subject so complicated.

B. STRANGERS

A person who had nothing to do with a judgment might benefit from its res judicata effects, but the judgment cannot bind such a person who is neither party nor privy. Good policy entitles everyone to his day in court, personally or through his representative, before a judgment has any legally binding effect on that person.

1. PARTIES TREATED AS NONPARTIES

One marginal kind of "stranger" needs special mention. A party who litigated in one capacity is not treated like a former party when in a subsequent action she appears in another capacity. The two capacities are deemed two different persons. For example, someone who sued as a representative for others is not precluded in a later action that she brings as an individual. This rule supposedly ensures a full and fair opportunity to litigate, and it avoids potential conflicts of interest. See generally id. § 36.

2. APPLICATION OF RES JUDICATA

A stranger to a prior judgment cannot be *bound* by it. However, he can *benefit* from it. The most important example of such benefit is a stranger using the prior judgment for collateral estoppel against a former party.

a. Mutuality of Estoppel

This old doctrine held that a person may not benefit from a prior judgment if he would not have been bound by any outcome of that initial action. Because strangers were never bound, they could therefore never benefit. There came to exist, however, substantial exceptions to the mutuality doctrine, allowing strangers in some circumstances to benefit.

b. Modern View

Mutuality of estoppel was rejected wholesale in *Bernhard v. Bank of Am. Nat'l Trust & Sav. Ass'n,* 19 Cal.2d 807, 122 P.2d 892 (1942). Most jurisdictions have since come to agree in some significant part. The modern view is that a stranger may invoke collateral estoppel against a former party, unless the former party lacked a full and fair opportunity to litigate the issue in the initial action. See generally Judgments Second § 29.

1) Rationale

The idea is that the former party is entitled to only one opportunity to litigate an issue, regardless of any change in adversaries. But perhaps this view elevates simplistic notions of efficiency over real concerns of fairness.

2) Defensive Use

A *defendant in the subsequent action* can invoke collateral estoppel against a former party. Such "defensive use" by a stranger was authorized as part of the federal common law of res judicata by *Blonder–Tongue Labs., Inc. v. University of Ill. Found.*, 402 U.S. 313, 91 S.Ct. 1434 (1971) (alleged infringer as defendant can preclude patentee as plaintiff on issue of patent invalidity, using judgment in unsuccessful prior suit brought by patentee against another alleged infringer).

3) Offensive Use

Although some jurisdictions balk at going further, the modern view even permits a *plaintiff in the subsequent action* to invoke collateral estoppel against a former party. Such "offensive use" by a stranger was authorized as part of the federal common law of res judicata by *Parklane Hosiery Co. v. Shore*, 439 U.S. 322, 99 S.Ct. 645 (1979) (securities plaintiff can preclude defendants in damages action, using judgment in successful prior suit for injunction brought by SEC against same defendants).

4) Exceptions

In an attempt to avoid real threats to efficiency and fairness, courts apply the modern view with great flexibility. They apply all the usual exceptions to issue preclusion. Additionally, courts exercise discretion to deny preclusion when the former party lacked a full and fair opportunity to litigate in the initial action or when all the circumstances otherwise justify allowing her to relitigate the issue. Factors affecting that discretion include among many others:

(1) whether there is some reason to suspect the accuracy of the prior determination, such as where it is inconsistent with some other adjudication of the same issue (a factor that partially solves the "multiple-plaintiff anomaly," where a string of potential plaintiffs sue an alleged tortfeasor seriatim, until one wins and theoretically so triggers collateral estoppel for the future plaintiffs);

(2) whether the stranger could reasonably have been expected to join or intervene in the initial action; and

(3) whether the former party did not choose the forum for the initial action.

On the one hand, note that the absence of a jury right in the initial action is not such a factor, according to *Parklane*. On the other hand, note that the Supreme Court has simply declared nonmutual offensive collateral estoppel to be unavailable against the federal government, in *United States v. Mendoza,* 464 U.S. 154, 104 S.Ct. 568 (1984).

*

XXII

Nondomestic Judgments

■ ANALYSIS

A. GENERAL RULES

The problem here is what treatment a judgment should receive in a subsequent civil action in another judicial system.

1. RECOGNITION

A court will "recognize," or give effect under the doctrine of res judicata to, a nondomestic judgment that is valid and final.

a. Validity and Finality

When the second court faces the question of whether the prior judgment is valid and final, it applies the law of the judgment-rendering sovereign, which of course is subject to any applicable external restraints, such as due process and other federal provisions imposed on and becoming part of state law.

b. Res Judicata

When the second court faces a question of res judicata based on the prior judgment, it similarly applies the law that the rendering court would, including any applicable external restraints.

2. ENFORCEMENT

The second court will enforce a judgment entitled to recognition. However, with respect to the method of enforcement, the second court applies its own law, subject to the requirement that the method not be so complex or expensive as to burden unduly the enforcement of nondomestic judgments.

a. Action upon Judgment

The traditional method of enforcement is for plaintiff to bring in the second jurisdiction a new action upon the prior judgment and thus obtain a regularly enforceable domestic judgment.

b. Registration

Federal law provides for registration in any district court of another district court's judgment for recovery of money or property, thus automatically converting the registered judgment into a regularly enforceable local judgment. 28 U.S.C.A. § 1963. Some states have built on this idea to permit registration of federal or sister-state judgments, obviating the need for an action upon the judgment.

B. JUDGMENTS OF AMERICAN COURTS

The above rules for handling a nondomestic judgment are in large part obligatory on American courts when that judgment comes from another American court. These rules help us to realize the benefits of a unified nation.

1. STATE—STATE

When the prior judgment was rendered by a state court and the second action is brought in a court of another state, the *Full Faith and Credit Clause* of the Federal Constitution *and* its *implementing legislation* in 28 U.S.C.A. § 1738 require the second court to give the same effect to a valid and final judgment as the judgment would have in the courts of the rendering state. See generally Conflict of Laws Second §§ 93, 100.

a. Same Effect

The better view is that full faith and credit requires the second court to give neither more effect nor less effect than the rendering state would.

b. Exceptions

There are narrow exceptions where some or all of the dictates of full faith and credit do not apply, such as where recognition or enforcement would so grossly and improperly interfere with the second state's important interests as to create a national interest against such recognition or enforcement. Specific examples are rare: the rendering state has purported to transfer title to land in the second state or has enjoined litigation in the second state's courts. But even where full faith and credit does not compel recognition or enforcement, the second court, unless prohibited by federal statute, can still choose to give the same effect as the rendering state would. See generally id. §§ 102–103.

2. STATE—FEDERAL

When the second court is instead a federal court, then *28 U.S.C.A. § 1738* likewise compels the second court to give the same effect to a valid and final judgment as the judgment would have in the courts of the rendering state. However, in narrow circumstances grounded on strong federal substantive or procedural policies, federal law may provide against (or conceivably for) recognition or enforcement, such as where federal courts infrequently construe statutes bestowing exclusive federal jurisdiction so as to permit relitigation of certain issues. See generally Judgments Second § 86.

3. FEDERAL—STATE

When the prior judgment was rendered by a federal court and the second action is brought in a state court, the second court must similarly give the same effect to a valid and final judgment as the judgment would have in the rendering court. Usually, a uniform federal law of res judicata applies. This federal law includes the federal common law of res judicata, which comprises the modern rules described in this Part Six. Federal law controls in the second court by virtue of the *Supremacy Clause*. See generally id. § 87. However, when the basis of federal subject-matter jurisdiction in the first court was diversity, the second court adopts the first court's local state law of res judicata as the federal common law, except when that state law is incompatible with federal interests. See *Semtek Int'l Inc. v. Lockheed Martin Corp.*, 531 U.S. 497, 121 S.Ct. 1021 (2001).

4. FEDERAL—FEDERAL

When the second court is instead another federal court, still the same precept of looking to treatment in the rendering court prevails, because the two courts are *arms of the same sovereign*.

C. JUDGMENTS OF FOREIGN NATIONS

American courts treat judgments of foreign nations pretty much like American judgments, although their approach to such foreign judgments is more flexible because their respect generally flows from *comity* rather than from legal obligation. See generally Conflict of Laws Second § 98.

1. EXCEPTIONS

An American court will not recognize or enforce a foreign judgment that failed to meet our basic notions of due process. An American court might apply other limitations on comity, such as refusing recognition or enforcement if the original claim is directly contrary to strong local public policy.

2. GOVERNING LAW

In a diversity action, the federal court under *Erie* looks to state law on how to treat a foreign judgment. However, an argument could be made that in all federal cases, and even in all state cases as well, federal law should control because of the federal interest in foreign relations. At any rate, as already indicated, that state or federal law will most often refer to the foreign law for specifying the extent of recognition.

REVIEW QUESTIONS

Questions (1)–(3): P successfully sues D in a New York state court. Before rendition of judgment, however, D moved herself and all her assets to New State.

1. **T or F**   If D appeals on both legal and factual grounds, the doctrine of res judicata bars the relitigation of the trial judge's findings of fact.

2. **T or F**   If after prevailing on the appeal P brings an action in New State to enforce his judgment, and if D moves in that action to dismiss on the ground that P's claim is merged in his first judgment, the New State court should deny D's motion.

3. **T or F**   In a New State action on his original claim, P may introduce evidence in order to increase his recovery, but D may not introduce evidence supporting a new defense on the merits.

Questions (4)–(7): Peter and Phil, passengers on a small cruise ship, were injured when the ship sank. After an extensive trial, Peter prevailed against the ship owner-operator on a claim that defendant had negligently operated the ship. Phil then brings a similar action and seeks to use Peter's judgment to establish conclusively the defendant's negligence.

4. **T or F**   Defendant is bound by the prior judgment.

5. **T or F**   Defendant is precluded from maintaining that Phil was contributorily negligent.

6. **T or F**   Even if Phil failed to raise the res judicata issue, the court would raise it on its own.

7. **T or F**   If instead defendant had prevailed in Peter's action, it could use that judgment conclusively to establish against Phil the absence of negligence.

Questions (8)–(10): P sues D for stock fraud in state court. In defense, D maintains that she never sold the stock to P and, in the alternative, that the sale was not fraudulent. After an extensive bench trial, D prevails on the no-sale defense, with no ruling on the no-fraud defense. So P then sues in federal court under the federal securities law, alleging the same facts. Now D raises res judicata.

8. **T or F**   There is no claim preclusion.

9. **T or F** P can relitigate the sale issue.

10. **T or F** If instead the state trial judge found that there had been a sale but no fraud, and if the federal court reaches the sale issue, D could relitigate the sale issue in the federal action.

Questions (11)–(13): Delia sells two adjacent plots of land to Perry and Pierce, respectively. In a fraud action by Perry seeking damages, Delia admits that she did not own either piece of property. Perry prevails, recovering $3000 from Delia.

11. **T or F** In a later fraud action by Pierce, Delia is precluded on the issue of ownership.

12. **T or F** In a later criminal fraud prosecution, the state cannot offensively estop Delia.

13. **T or F** If Perry brought suit in a state court with a jurisdictional limit of $3000, he could now sue in a state court of general jurisdiction in order to increase his recovery.

14. Several thousand people have a consumer complaint against D Co. One of these people, P–1, brings a class action against D Co. on behalf of all such people within the state. The suit is filed in a state court that follows the Federal Rules model. The class including P–2 and P–3 among many others is properly certified and adequate notice is given, and then P–3 opts out. Ultimately, D Co. loses, and damages are awarded. So D Co. appeals. While the appeal is pending, P–2 and P–3 join together in an action against D Co. on the same grievance. Which of the following is most correct?

   a. Claim preclusion will prevent P–2 and P–3 from recovering.

   b. Claim preclusion does not apply because an appeal is pending.

   c. P–3 can offensively estop D Co.

   d. Claim preclusion will prevent P–2 from recovering.

15. A sues B in federal court for negligence; B defends by denying negligence; but after trial A wins. Then B sues A for her injuries from the same accident. Which of the following is most correct?

   a. B is precluded from bringing the second action.

   b. B is not precluded from bringing the second action, because her obtaining relief would not nullify A's judgment.

c. B will be estopped on the issue of her negligence.

d. B is not precluded from bringing the second action, if a reasonable amount of time has passed between the rendition of A's judgment and the institution of B's action.

16. Prepare an essay in response to this question:

P sues D in state court in State One on a contract, and D defends on the ground of lack of personal jurisdiction and also on the merits. After D loses on both grounds, judgment is entered for P.

P then sues D in state court in State Two upon that judgment, and D collaterally attacks on the ground of lack of personal jurisdiction in the first action. In response, P invokes full faith and credit and also res judicata, but is unsuccessful in convincing the court that these arguments should prevail or indeed that personal jurisdiction existed. So D wins, and P appeals the judgment unsuccessfully to the highest court of State Two. Next P petitions for certiorari, which is denied by the Supreme Court of the United States.

Still trying to enforce his State One judgment, P sues D in state court in State Three upon that judgment. Now D invokes the State Two judgment as res judicata. What result?

*

APPENDIX A

Answers to Review Questions

PART ONE: GENERAL CONSIDERATIONS

1. *False.* The American law of civil procedure is shaped by several sources: constitutions, legislatures, courts, and litigants. However, the discretion of trial judges is undoubtedly an important contributor.

2. *False.* Only a court of equity could grant specific performance, and only when the legal remedies were inadequate. Today, specific performance is still considered extraordinary relief.

3. *True.* Although there were exceptions to the requirement of a writ, the predominant use of writs gave birth to the writ system and hence the forms of action.

4. *False.* Under the mature common law, a party could not testify at all because he was viewed as an interested witness. Today, that blanket prohibition has disappeared.

5. *True.* The judge decided cases himself. However, he could refer disputed facts on an advisory basis to a common-law jury, a practice that was the model for today's advisory jury under Federal Rule 39(c).

6. *False.* The Field Code created a unitary civil action.

7. *False.* The Supreme Court must approve the proposed rules and report them to Congress, and at least seven months must pass without congressional rejection.

8. *False.* Although some commentators have argued for such an approach, *Sibbach v. Wilson & Co.*, supra, apparently rejected it. The REA authorized rulemaking throughout the realm of civil procedure.

9. *d.* Plaintiff would probably have had to sue at law, seeking damages that represented the benefit of his bargain and invoking the form of action called special assumpsit. He could have gone to any of the three superior courts of common law, and he would have been there entitled to a jury trial.

10. *e.* Sibbach **upheld Rule 35 in these circumstances. Answer (a) is wrong because, among other reasons, many personal-injury cases are brought under diversity jurisdiction; (b) is wrong because the Federal Rules apply over conflicting state law; (c) is wrong because the REA authorized rulemaking throughout the realm of civil procedure; and (d) is wrong because Rule 35 validly applies to any party.**

11. S's suit should probably be dismissed.

As a threshold matter, D.O. should not have moved to dismiss. Under New Jersey practice, he should have raised res judicata as an affirmative defense and then moved for summary judgment. [See Part Two of the outline.]

However, courts tend to entertain such sloppy motions to dismiss, elevating the policy of reaching the merits over procedural technicalities. [See Part One of the outline; 5 Wright & Miller § 1277, at 635 n.13; *Kelleher v. Lozzi*, 7 N.J. 17, 25, 80 A.2d 196, 200 (1951); cf. *O'Connor v. Altus*, 67 N.J. 106, 116, 335 A.2d 545, 550 (1975) (statute of limitations defense).]

So reaching the merits of the res judicata defense, the court faces the initial issue of what is the governing law. The New Jersey court must here apply federal law as to compulsory counterclaims in determining the effects of this federal diversity judgment. [See Part Five of the outline; 6 Wright, Miller & Kane § 1417, at 140–41.]

S failed to plead his claim as a counterclaim in the first action. In these circumstances, under federal law, S appears to be barred from now asserting his claim. [See Part Six of the outline.]

First, S's claim came within the scope of Federal Rule 13(a) on compulsory counterclaims when D.O. asserted against S his claim under Rule 14(a)(3). Those Federal Rules governed joinder in that first action, even though it was supposedly a diversity action. [See Part Four of the outline.]

Second, S is correct that there was no subject-matter jurisdiction for D.O.'s claim against S, because supplemental jurisdiction does not extend to such a claim under Rule 14(a)(3) and because their common citizenship meant there was no independent basis of jurisdiction. However, this defect should have been raised in the first action. In this second action, the doctrine of jurisdiction to determine jurisdiction forecloses this collateral attack. [See Part Three of the outline; *Owen Equip. & Erection Co. v. Kroger*, supra (no supplemental jurisdiction); *Des Moines Navigation & R.R. v. Iowa Homestead Co.*, 123 U.S. 552, 8 S.Ct. 217 (1887) (no collateral attack).]

PART TWO: LITIGATING STEP–BY–STEP

1. *True.* Federal law governs the mechanics of pleading in any federal action, including diversity actions.

2. *False.* Although federal pleading rules are quite liberal, a complaint must contain a jurisdictional allegation, a statement of the claim, and a demand for relief. The complaint in question adequately states the claim, see Federal Form 10, but it lacks a jurisdictional allegation and a demand for relief.

3. *False.* Under Federal Rule 12(h)(1)(A), an available jurisdictional defense under Rule 12(b)(2) is waived if omitted from D's initial pre-answer motion.

4. *True.* Under Rule 12(h)(3), subject-matter jurisdiction may be raised in any fashion.

5. *False.* Federal pleading usually stops with the answer. A plaintiff neither must nor may reply to defenses, unless the court specially orders him to reply under Rule 7(a)(7).

6. *True.* The amendment will relate back to the date of the original complaint, because the amendment concerned the same transaction and because Donna received timely notice of the misdirected lawsuit. Rule 15(c)(1)(C).

7. *False.* Paul can amend as a matter of course at any time before Donna serves her answer. Rule 15(a)(1)(A).

8. *False.* Under Rule 26(b)(1), inadmissibility by itself is not ground for objection.

9. *True.* Rule 35 requires Paul to show "good cause" and requires Donna's physical condition to be "in controversy." It is unlikely that Paul could meet these tests in this case. See *Schlagenhauf v. Holder*, 379 U.S. 104, 85 S.Ct. 234 (1964).

10. *True.* The question gives the federal standard for judgment as a matter of law under Rule 50(a). Note, however, that the judge can choose to deny the motion, even if the standard is met, in order to let the trial proceed toward completion.

11. *False.* Whenever one side rests, the other side may move for judgment as a matter of law. Rule 50(a).

12. *False.* The question gives the federal standard for a new trial under Rule 59(a)(1)(A).

13. *False.* Under Rule 50(b), a party can renew the motion only if he has unsuccessfully moved for judgment as a matter of law under Rule 50(a).

14. *d.* If plaintiff seeks only equitable relief, there is no jury right. If plaintiff seeks only legal relief, there is a jury right. If plaintiff seeks the two kinds of relief cumulatively, a federal court will allow both plaintiff and defendant a jury right on the legal and common issues. All this makes Answer (d) correct. Answer (e) is wrong because either Dave might demand a jury trial or the court might relieve Paula's waiver where there is a jury right, or the court might order a jury trial by consent.

15. *c.* Under Rule 69(a)(1), the usual tool for enforcing a money judgment is a writ of execution addressed to the marshal. Answer (a) is wrong because Paula would normally bring such an action upon the judgment only if she sought enforcement in another jurisdiction; (b) is wrong because Rule 69(a)(2) allows such discovery; and (d) is not quite right because eventually there can sometimes be supplementary proceedings leading to a court order enforceable by contempt.

16. *a.* Only the contempt sanction against a nonparty is treated as a final decision.

17. *b.* The court of appeals gives nondeferential review to questions of law. Answer (a) is wrong because Rule 52(a)(6) imposes a "clearly erroneous" test; (c) is wrong because appellate courts do not hear testimony, but instead remand to the trial court for further testimony; and (d) is wrong because there is no such thing as a directed verdict in a nonjury trial, and there never was.

18. Pip's two jury wishes should come true.

A. Jury Right

First, federal law governs the right to trial by jury in federal court, even in a diversity action and even where the state law grants a more expansive jury right. [See 9 Wright & Miller § 2303.]

Second, the Seventh Amendment to the Federal Constitution is expansively read to extend the federal jury right to this situation of alternative legal (damages) and equitable (specific performance) remedies. Actually, it is extraordinarily complicated to recreate the plaintiff's historical choice of remedies in today's merged procedural system. This problem has therefore created considerable scholarly dispute. Nevertheless, looking to the trend of Supreme Court precedent, the lower federal courts opt for the simplistic solution of giving plaintiff and defendant a jury right on the legal and common issues. [See id. § 2306.]

Hence, Pip should get a jury trial on the legal and common issues that are contested and factual.

B. Unanimity

First, federal law governs on this point too.

Second, such a provision by local rule for simple-majority verdict is probably violative of the Seventh Amendment, as it changes the substance and not merely the form of common-law trial by jury. However, the court need not reach the constitutional point because, since the 1991 amendments, Rule 48 requires unanimity, unless the parties otherwise stipulate. Thus, the local rule is inconsistent with a Federal Rule, and so invalid under Federal Rule 83.

Hence, if Pip raises this point, he should ultimately succeed in invalidating the local rule's nonunanimity provision and in thus requiring a unanimous verdict.

PART THREE: AUTHORITY TO ADJUDICATE

1. *False.* Federal question jurisdiction exists here under the general provision in 28 U.S.C.A. § 1331 and also under the special civil rights statute in 28 U.S.C.A. § 1343.

2. *True.* The doctrine of supplemental jurisdiction satisfies the requirement of subject-matter jurisdiction.

3. *True.* D could remove in these circumstances only if P's state action were within the district courts' original jurisdiction. This action is not removable because her contract claim by itself does not come within any statutory provision for federal jurisdiction. And the federal defense by D does not create federal jurisdiction. Contrast 28 U.S.C.A. § 1443.

4. *False.* Most cases within federal jurisdiction are within concurrent state jurisdiction. The Constitution does not make any federal original jurisdiction exclusive. To exclude state original jurisdiction, there must be a federal statute making federal jurisdiction exclusive. Here, the particular federal civil rights statute does not make this kind of action exclusively federal.

5. *False.* Although the Constitution requires only partial diversity, which exists here, the statutory provision in 28 U.S.C.A. § 1332(a) requires complete diversity. This does not exist, because citizens of Michigan are on opposing sides of the action. Because this diversity statute must be satisfied, there will be no federal subject-matter jurisdiction.

6. *False.* Although the matter in controversy must exceed $75,000 under § 1332(a), any allegation in excess of $75,000 survives challenge unless there is legal certainty that damages will not exceed $75,000. Where a ballet dancer sues for a leg injury by a chain saw, there seems to be no such legal certainty, even if a big recovery is highly unlikely. The judge should not dismiss.

7. *False.* Courts ignore the citizenship of any legal representative of an infant, such as a guardian ad litem. 28 U.S.C.A. § 1332(c)(2). Treating the case as Pat versus Dan, there is no diversity of citizenship.

8. *False.* Although consent is a basis of personal jurisdiction, the extent of that basis is defined by the terms of the consent. Unless D's consent was broad enough to include this later action by P or there is some other basis not revealed by the question, there will be no territorial jurisdiction.

9. *True.* The federal venue provision applies only in federal court.

10. *True.* Like most states, New York has adopted the doctrine of forum non conveniens. N.Y.C.P.L.R. 327. Thus, the judge may discretionarily decline existing jurisdiction if the judge "finds that in the interest of substantial justice the action should be heard in another forum."

11. *False.* Although part of the constitutional test requires minimum contacts with the United States, there are other constitutional and nonconstitutional restrictions on territorial authority to adjudicate. Significantly, the service provision in Federal Rule 4 must be and apparently cannot be met.

12. *False.* This transfer would be under 28 U.S.C.A. § 1406(a). The transferee court then will not apply transferor law, although it would after transfer under 28 U.S.C.A. § 1404(a).

13. *True.* A finding of the existence of territorial jurisdiction is res judicata, precluding Duke from attacking the resultant judgment on that ground in subsequent litigation. He could have pursued that point on appeal, but not on collateral attack.

14. *False.* Subject-matter jurisdiction was open to challenge throughout the ordinary course of the initial action—even on appeal, but probably not on collateral attack. Rule 12(h)(3).

15. *False.* Although Duke may challenge the rendering court's jurisdiction, he may not now litigate the merits. A valid default judgment cuts off defenses on the merits.

16. *True.* Such service satisfies constitutional and nonconstitutional requirements of notice. Rule 4(e)(2)(C).

17. *d.* The parties cannot confer subject-matter jurisdiction by consent, but the other matters are subject to agreement.

18. *e.* Under 28 U.S.C.A. § 1391(b), venue lies in the district where D resides or where a substantial part of the claim arose. In none of the answers does D reside or did the claim partly arise in the Southern District of New York.

19. The only real difficulty involves the circumstances of service or, equivalently, personal or territorial jurisdiction.

As for *subject-matter jurisdiction*, diversity jurisdiction clearly exists under 28 U.S.C.A. § 1332(a).

As for *venue*, 28 U.S.C.A. § 1391(a) permits suit at the defendant's residence, which under § 1391(c) includes any district in which the corporate defendant is subject to personal jurisdiction. So, we need not face any other mysteries of the venue statute.

As for *manner of service*, one possibility is Federal Rule 4(h)(1)(B), which includes the typical provision for out-of-state personal delivery of process to an officer or agent of the corporation—if personal jurisdiction exists. Such service would of course satisfy the constitutional requirement of notice. So, if we arrange to serve a copy of the summons and the complaint (in accordance with Federal Rule 4(a)–(d), (*l*), and (m)) by personal delivery to an officer or agent of Drug Co. in Virginia, then the only remaining issue is personal jurisdiction.

As for this critical issue of *circumstances of service*, Rule 4(k)(1)(A) specifies that the federal court can reach only as far as an Illinois state court could reach under the state's long-arm statute and the Fourteenth Amendment.

The Illinois long-arm statute authorizes personal jurisdiction to the extent constitutionally permitted. Ill.Comp.Stat. ch. 735, § 5/2–209(c).

Turning to those constitutional limits, we must ask whether Illinois can constitutionally exercise personal jurisdiction. Although such jurisdiction does not appear unreasonable, there is a serious question of power over defendant. See *Asahi Metal Indus. Co. v. Superior Court*, supra; *World-Wide Volkswagen Corp. v. Woodson*, supra.

To answer this last question, we must learn more about the defendant's level of activity with respect to Illinois, which at least relates to this lawsuit. For example, how many of its products are sold in Illinois? Did it actively serve the market for IUDs there, even though this action does not arise from an Illinois sale? We can then determine whether the quality and nature of the defendant's state-directed activity are such that it is fair to require Drug Co. to defend this action in Illinois.

I suspect that the huge Drug Co. may have enough state-directed activity to subject itself to the power of Illinois for this action. If and only if Drug Co.'s state-directed activity turns out to be sufficient, this action can be brought in the United States District Court for the Northern District of Illinois. [See id. (dicta concerning car's German manufacturer and American importer); *Duignan v. A.H. Robins Co.*, 98 Idaho 134, 559 P.2d 750 (1977).]

PART FOUR: COMPLEX LITIGATION

1. *True.* The judge may pursue efficiency by ordering separate trial of a separate issue under Federal Rule 42(b).

2. *True.* Under 28 U.S.C.A. § 1407, D can file a motion with the judicial panel on multidistrict litigation to transfer dispersed federal actions "involving one or more common questions of fact" to any single district for coordinated or consolidated pretrial proceedings.

3. *True.* P has split his claim. His whole claim, which is transactionally defined, was extinguished by the initial judgment. His claim for injuries to his leg merged in that initial judgment, and the doctrine of claim preclusion forecloses his second suit.

4. *True.* This is an attempted cross-claim under Rule 13(g). A defendant's cross-claim must be transactionally related to the main claim. Donna's claim is not so related, and thus should be dismissed upon motion.

5. *False.* Under Rule 13(a), Dodge's claim was a compulsory counterclaim in the initial action, because both Pete's and Dodge's claims arose out of the same transaction or occurrence. See *Semmes Motors, Inc. v. Ford Motor Co.*, 429 F.2d 1197, 1202 (2d Cir.1970). Failure to assert a compulsory counterclaim precludes bringing a subsequent action thereon.

6. *False.* Under Rule 13(a)(1), a defendant's counterclaim is compulsory only if it was available at the time of serving the answer. Because this claim accrued later, Dodge can assert it in a subsequent action.

7. *False.* Joining a party as an involuntary plaintiff under Rule 19(a)(2) is a very narrowly available procedural tactic. Here it is clearly unavailable, because among other reasons Ink is subject to service of process.

8. *True.* Realignment would destroy complete diversity under 28 U.S.C.A. § 1332 and thus require dismissal for lack of subject-matter jurisdiction. Note, however, that in derivative actions courts seldom realign the defendant corporation as a plaintiff, because it is acting contrary to the interests of the plaintiff shareholder. See Wright's Hornbook § 73, at 532.

9. *True.* Rule 17(b) says that the capacity of a corporation is determined by the law under which it was incorporated.

10. *True.* Rule 14(a) authorizes impleader here, if E can be effectively served with process.

11. *False.* Impleader requires territorial jurisdiction, so it is not permissible here. However, E is neither a necessary nor an indispensable party under Rule 19, so P's action can proceed without E. In that situation, D & D might consider vouching in E.

12. *a*. In determining diversity of citizenship for a non-CAFA class action, only the named parties are considered. Answer (d) is wrong because the citizenship of absent class members is irrelevant, and the given fact does not ensure that all the class representatives' citizenships will be different from D'autocars'; (b) is wrong because it concerns territorial jurisdiction; (c) is wrong because it concerns venue; and (e) is simply irrelevant.

13. *d*. To be sure in this case, every class member's claim must exceed $75,000 to come within 28 U.S.C.A. § 1332. This restrictive rule was established by the Supreme Court in *Snyder v. Harris*, supra. Moreover, supplemental jurisdiction under 28 U.S.C.A. § 1367 does not apply to state-law claims against multiple defendants. Answer (d) alone satisfies the restrictive rule.

14. *a*. This class action falls under Rule 23(b)(3). Thus, Rule 23(c)(2)(B) requires individual notice to all absent class members identifiable with reasonable effort, according to *Eisen v. Carlisle & Jacquelin*, supra. Moreover, Rule 23(c)(2)(B), as read by the *Eisen* Court, requires the class representatives to bear initially all costs of such notice. The district court's leanings on the merits do not affect this Rule. All this means that Answer (a) is alone correct.

15. *a*. Statutory interpleader is possible in the Rhode Island federal court, because B and C are of diverse citizenship and the stake is $500 or more, because nationwide service of process is available, and because venue lies where any party claiming the stake resides. Rule interpleader is not possible because of a lack of subject-matter jurisdiction. Answer (b) is wrong because nationwide service of process is available for statutory interpleader; (c) is wrong because nobody involved resides in the District of Columbia; and (d) is wrong because $500 suffices for statutory interpleader.

16. Working through all the applicable joinder rules reveals one effective solution: I can move to dismiss under Rule 12(b)(1) for lack of subject-matter jurisdiction.

Every claim in federal court must satisfy the federal requirements of subject-matter jurisdiction. For the claim by Bert against Dale, both parties appear to be citizens of Mississippi, and the claim is for only $6000. The requirements of 28 U.S.C.A. § 1332 are therefore unsatisfied. Furthermore, recent cases indicate that supplemental jurisdiction cannot be used here to avoid the requirements of that diversity statute. See *Owen Equip. & Erection*

Co. v. Kroger, supra. Now, 28 U.S.C.A. § 1367(b) codifies that case's indications. There is no other basis for federal subject-matter jurisdiction.

Because I shall prevail under Rule 12(b)(1), I need not reach my weaker arguments concerning improper joinder under Rule 20 and the desirability of a separate trial or severance.

PART FIVE: GOVERNING LAW

1. *False.* Under the *Erie* doctrine, the district judge must apply state law. Under the *Klaxon* rule, the district judge must look to the forum state's choice-of-law rules to see which state's statute of limitations applies. Here N.Y.C.P.L.R. § 202 provides that the New York limitations period applies.

2. *False.* The Supreme Court rejected the substance/procedure test in 1945 and called for state law in these circumstances. *Guaranty Trust Co. v. York*, supra.

3. *False.* If the federal court looks to the New York limitations period under *Klaxon*, the only question is whether New York could constitutionally apply its own law. New York could do so under *Allstate Ins. Co. v. Hague*, supra, because it has significant contact with the litigation in that plaintiff is a New York citizen.

4. *True.* Under its power over interstate commerce and over federal procedure, Congress probably would have the constitutional power so to legislate. Its choice of federal law, and its specification of the content of that law, would oblige the federal courts to ignore otherwise applicable state law.

5. *False.* The Seventh Amendment to the Federal Constitution applies to all federal civil actions, and it provides a jury right in these circumstances.

6. *False.* In the *Erie* case, the Supreme Court rejected such old notions, making clear that nothing turned on whether the state law was statutory law or decisional law.

7. *True.* In the absence of a constitutional or congressional directive, state law will govern in state court unless the state interests involved are outweighed by federal interests in having federal law govern. That the federal interests were too weak in these circumstances was decided in *United States v. Burnison*, 339 U.S. 87, 70 S.Ct. 503 (1950).

8. *True.* On a "substantive" issue like this, changing to a federal forum should not alter the applicable law.

9. *True.* In the absence of a federal statute of limitations for a federally created claim, the federal court should ordinarily adopt as federal common law the forum state's limitations period for the most closely analogous general type of state cause of action. However, the federal court can alter or ignore part or all of such adopted state law if it actually impinges on federal interests. Thus, the federal court here can and probably will apply a federal tolling notion based on the defendant's concealment.

10. *False.* Here there is a binding application of state law in federal court under *Erie* and its progeny. The state statute of limitations, along with its integral parts such as the state tolling rules, applies.

11. *b.* In a diversity action, state law governs as to when an action is deemed commenced for statute-of-limitations purposes. *Ragan v. Merchants Transfer & Warehouse Co.*, supra; *Walker v. Armco Steel Corp.*, supra. Thus, this claim is time-barred if state law requires service within the limitations period, as opposed to mere filing within the period. Answers (a) and (c) are obviously wrong; and (d) is wrong because Rule 3 has been read not to address commencement for state statute-of-limitations purposes, but rather commencement for other procedural purposes, and because Rule 4 requires prompt service, but in addition to any statute-of-limitations requirements.

12. *d.* Rule 12(h)(1) preserves this defense in these circumstances, and it is valid. Under *Hanna-Sibbach*, it applies even in a diversity case. Answer (a) is wrong because the outcome-determinative test is not relevant to the Federal Rules and because applying this Rule is not outcome-determinative in the refined modern sense anyway; (b) is inaccurate because the substance/procedure test has been rejected and also because some state "procedural" law does apply in federal court when no Federal Rule is in point; and (c) is wrong because the relevant state interests do not outweigh the relevant federal interests anyway.

13. *d.* Congress in enacting 28 U.S.C.A. § 1391(a) constitutionally chose federal law as applicable in this action. Answers (a) and (b) are wrong because the *Erie* choice-of-law technique is thus inapplicable; and (c) is wrong because the venue law was not enacted pursuant to the REA.

14. *c.* Reverse-*Erie* is a more intrusive doctrine than is *Erie*. Answer (a) is wrong because most federal "procedural" rules do not apply in state court; and (b) is slightly inaccurate because the substance/procedure line is not the strictly proper way to formulate either the *Erie* or the reverse-*Erie* doctrine.

15. Don's motion should be denied, because Pedro timely commenced his federal action by filing on October 25.

Federal law made the final day for filing October 25, but state law made it October 24. Happily for Pedro, federal law governs in the form of Rule 6(a).

That Federal Rule of Civil Procedure is best read as directly addressing this issue of timeliness. [See 4B Wright & Miller § 1163.] That Rule is valid under the Constitution and the REA, and so that Rule applies under *Hanna-Sibbach*. [See id. § 1164.] This case is distinguishable from *Ragan v. Merchants Transfer & Warehouse Co.*, supra, and *Walker v. Armco Steel Corp.*, supra, because those cases did not involve a Federal Rule that directly addressed the issue there in question.

Even if Rule 6(a) does not address extension of time for statute-of-limitations purposes and if the relevant choice-of-law technique were the extreme *Hanna-Erie* test, federal law would still apply because it would neither encourage forum-shopping nor cause unfairness by favoring certain classes of citizens with a choice of court systems. An extra calendar day in this bizarre setting is not the kind of thing that a plaintiff takes into account in planning to sue in federal court; and it is not unfair to give federal litigants what state litigants already have, namely, one extra day when the courthouse is open. So again *Ragan* and *Walker* are distinguishable. In formulating that federal common law, the federal court would pursue the federal interests in uniformity, simplicity, and fairness by making law equivalent to the words of Rule 6(a).

The same result follows under the competing choice-of-law techniques:

(1) Under the *Hanna-Byrd* approach, this issue falls within the Federal Rules pocket, not the statute-of-limitations pocket, and so is governed by federal law.

(2) Under *Gasperini*'s interest-analysis approach, weak state interests are overcome by the difference of strong federal interests less a weak outcome-determinative effect, thus resulting in the application of federal law. The state interests in the repose and other benefits of its statute of limitations are not significantly affected by applying this federal law rather than the state extension provision; the federal interests in applying its own uniform, intact rules of procedure and in deciding cases on the merits are heavy; and, as already explained, the outcome-determinative effect is slight.

Therefore, under federal law Pedro timely commenced his action. [The sole fly in the ointment is that the only modern case in point, *Alonzo v. ACF Prop. Mgmt., Inc.*, 643 F.2d 578 (9th Cir.1981), calls for the application of state law. However, that case appears incorrectly decided, being based on a misreading of *Ragan, Hanna,* and *Walker.*]

PART SIX: FORMER ADJUDICATION

1. *False.* Res judicata applies only outside the context of the initial action and any appeal. Appellate courts exhibit deference to the trial judge's findings of facts, but that has nothing to do with res judicata.

2. *True.* Merger prevents the successful plaintiff from bringing a second action on the claim in the hope of winning a more favorable judgment, but does not prevent him from seeking to enforce his judgment. Thus, P can bring an action upon his judgment.

3. *False.* Under the dictates of full faith and credit, merger can be invoked under New York law to prevent P from suing again on his claim or trying to increase his recovery, as well as to prevent D in any action from interposing a defense on the merits.

4. *True.* Under the modern view, a stranger may offensively use collateral estoppel to bind defendant. However, some exception not suggested by the facts might apply.

5. *False.* On the bare facts as stated, Phil's contributory negligence could not have been an essential issue in the first action. For this among other reasons, there could be no collateral estoppel thereon.

6. *False.* The interested party must raise res judicata. The policies behind the doctrine are not strong enough to require the court to raise it on its own.

7. *False.* Good policy dictates that a former party can never bind a person who was neither party nor privy.

8. *True.* Such a federal action is within the exclusive federal jurisdiction. Because P could not assert this federal ground in the state action, P can now sue in federal court.

9. *False.* Even though there is no claim preclusion, issue preclusion does apply if invoked in these circumstances. So if sale vel non is the same issue under state and federal law, then P is precluded on the sale issue.

10. *True.* Issue preclusion applies only if the determination was essential to judgment. Here the finding on the sale was unnecessary to rendering judgment for D in state court.

11. *False.* The issue of ownership was not actually litigated and determined in the first action. For this among other reasons, there can be no collateral estoppel thereon.

12. *True.* Because of the much higher degree of persuasion required in a criminal case, among other reasons, the state cannot use collateral estoppel.

13. *False.* Assuming Perry voluntarily chose to sue in a state court of limited jurisdiction and recovered the maximum amount that court could award, a defense of claim preclusion would prevent his suing for any unrecovered excess otherwise available in a state court of general jurisdiction.

14. *d.* A class member, such as P–2, is treated like a party for preclusion purposes. Hence, P–2 is subject to claim preclusion, assuming no exception applies and the judgment is valid. Answer (a) is wrong because someone who opts out of a class action escapes the burdens of the eventual judgment; (c) is wrong because opting-out also sacrifices the benefits of the judgment; and (b) is wrong because a pending appeal does not affect finality.

15. *a.* B's claim was a compulsory counterclaim under Federal Rule 13(a), and so the failure to assert it in A's action precludes bringing a subsequent action thereon. Answer (b) is wrong because it is irrelevant that this was not a common-law compulsory counterclaim; (d) is wrong because the passage of time is also irrelevant; and (c) is inaccurate because issue preclusion is not reached if claim preclusion applies.

16. The result is unclear and unsettled under current law.

Ordinarily, the Full Faith and Credit Clause and statute would require the third court to apply the last-in-time rule, looking to the second judgment and the res judicata law of State Two. Presumably, State Two would treat its judgment as prevailing over the first judgment. Accordingly, D should win, with the State Two judgment so barring P's action.

However, it is odd that the Full Faith and Credit Clause and statute should demand respect for a judgment that was based on a irremediable rejection of full faith and credit. Under the constitutional clause and its implementing statute, State Two should have given res judicata effect to State One's jurisdictional determination, as State One would presumably have done; P tried fully to correct this error, but was rebuffed by the Supreme Court. Perhaps in this narrow setting there should be an exception to the last-in-time rule, because here the impartial arbiter's refusal to review undermines the rather arbitrary rationale of the last-in-time rule. Accordingly, P should win, with State Three reconsidering State Two's full-faith-and-credit decision and consequently upholding State One's judgment.

It is an open question whether the court here would follow woodenly the general rule or create this policy-based exception. The better view perhaps favors the latter course. [See Judgments Second § 15 cmt. e; Conflict of Laws Second § 114 cmt. b; Ruth B. Ginsburg, Judgments in Search of Full Faith and Credit: The Last-in-Time Rule for Conflicting Judgments, 82 Harv.L.Rev. 798, 803–06, 831–32 (1969).]

APPENDIX B

Practice Examination

This examination consists of six questions, all of which should be completed in three hours. You may refer to a copy of a Federal Rules pamphlet.

QUESTION I *(Suggested time: 40 minutes)*

J.R. Industries, Inc., a Delaware corporation, and Chrissy Industries, Inc., a California corporation, signed a merger agreement in March of last year. Unhappily, a dispute soon arose. Indeed, all the following dates fell in that same year.

On May 18, Chrissy brought an action under the federal securities laws against J.R. in the United States District Court for the District of Delaware ("Delaware action"). On September 4, J.R. filed an answer that included a counterclaim; because of various previous motions, this filing was timely. On September 24, Chrissy replied to J.R.'s counterclaim, denying its substance.

On September 14, J.R. brought a diversity action under state contract law against Chrissy in the United States District Court for the Central District of California ("California action"). Although the California and Delaware actions had arisen from the same transaction, J.R. had not asserted the California action's claim for relief in its counterclaim in the Delaware action. After a timely answer consisting only of denials, Chrissy moved in the California district court to transfer the California action to the District of Delaware pursuant to 28 U.S.C.A. § 1404(a), making that motion on December 3.

In the absence of Chrissy's Delaware action, J.R. could not have originally instituted the California action in Delaware, because Chrissy was not subject to service there. However, the California action's claim for relief could have been included in the Delaware action's counterclaim.

How should the motion to transfer be decided? Explain.

QUESTION II *(Suggested time: 20 minutes)*

Consider the following recently proposed amendment to our federal appellate system:

> Section 1292(b) of title 28, United States Code, is amended by deleting ":
> *Provided, however,* That application" and inserting in lieu thereof a period and
> the following: "The Court of Appeals may permit an appeal from a decision
> of a district court, not otherwise appealable under this section, after a refusal
> by a district court judge to make such a statement in writing, if the Court of
> Appeals determines in its discretion that an appeal is required in the interests
> of justice and because of the extraordinary importance of the case. Applica-
> tion".

Write a position paper in support of or in opposition to that proposal.

QUESTION III *(Suggested time: 30 minutes)*

You are the attorney for an author. He is a citizen of New York State and a resident of Ithaca, which is in the Northern District of New York. His publisher is a New York corporation with its principal place of business in Minnesota; its New York home office is in the Eastern District of New York, and it does business in New

York State only there. Your client and his publisher have just been sued together for $85,000 each in a contract action brought in the Southern District of New York by a Maine plaintiff; this is a diversity action, and the claim arose solely in Massachusetts.

You are unhappy about the venue and wish to attack it via Rule 12(b)(3). Construct the best legal argument you can that venue is improper as to your client. (Alternatively, if you can see no such argument, explain precisely why venue is proper.)

QUESTION IV *(Suggested time: 30 minutes)*

Assume that a bank of State X has been sued in the federal district court in State X by B of State Y to recover a deposit of $85,000, which had been made by A of State Y with provision that it could be withdrawn by B upon satisfactory completion of a transaction involving a car in State Y. Doubt exists as to whether there has been such satisfactory completion. How should the bank defend? Explain.

QUESTION V *(Suggested time: 40 minutes)*

You work for a law firm representing a New York plaintiff who has pending a big medical malpractice action in the United States District Court for the Eastern District of Pennsylvania against a Philadelphia doctor, who crippled the plaintiff in an operation performed last year in Pennsylvania.

The defendant seeks dismissal without prejudice on the basis of a Pennsylvania statute providing that a medical malpractice plaintiff may not have his claim heard on the merits by a Pennsylvania state court until (1) arbitration proceedings before one of Pennsylvania's Arbitration Panels for Health Care have first been completed and (2) an appeal has then been filed for trial de novo in the state trial court in accordance with the state rules regarding appeals from compulsory civil arbitration and with the Pennsylvania Rules of Civil Procedure. Essentially, then, the Pennsylvania Health Care Services Malpractice Act requires the state plaintiff to go first to an arbitration panel, which functions much like a court. If one is unhappy with the panel's decision, one can then appeal to a normal trial court, which starts the case over from scratch. However, the statute provides that the panel's findings are evidence in that de novo appeal. The statute also provides that filing a complaint with the arbitration panel tolls the statute of limitations.

Your plaintiff has good reason for wanting to avoid this state statute, and thus to go directly to federal court. Pennsylvania's arbitration system for medical malpractice claims has been judicially described as a "resounding flop." Of 2466 medical malpractice claims lodged since the statute's enactment, only nine have reached the arbitration hearing stage and only two of these have made it into the court system. The plaintiff deems it essential to circumvent this logjam.

So the partner from your firm who is working on the case calls you in. He describes the case and says that he has a narrowly defined project for you. He asks you to construct the best argument or arguments you can that this state arbitration requirement does not apply in the federal district court and then to comment on how you think your argument or arguments will fare in that court. Do so.

QUESTION VI *(Suggested time: 20 minutes)*

The doctrine of claim preclusion is subject to exceptions. Likewise, exceptions to the doctrine of issue preclusion exist. To which doctrine should the courts be more ready to find exceptions? Why?

APPENDIX C

Glossary

See generally Black's Law Dictionary (Bryan A. Garner ed., 8th ed. 2004)

A

Additur A procedure whereby a judge can grant, on the ground of inadequate damages, a new trial that defendant can avoid by agreeing to pay increased damages. Although some states allow additur, the federal courts do not. See *Remittitur*.

Adversary System A procedural system that involves active and unhindered parties combatively formulating and propelling the case.

Advisory Jury A jury that a judge uses to assist in trying an issue and that delivers a nonbinding verdict. Federal Rule 39(c).

Appealable Decision A decision that can receive immediate appellate review. See *Reviewable Issue*.

Attachment Legal process directing seizure of the defendant's property that is in the hands of defendant. This term usually describes a provisional remedy. See *Garnishment*.

B

Bench Trial A nonjury trial.

Bill The complaint in equitable procedure.

Burden of Allegation The obligation of a certain party to plead a matter in order to insert it into the lawsuit.

Burden of Persuasion The obligation of a certain party to persuade the fact-finder of the truth of an element in order to avoid suffering an adverse determination on that element.

Burden of Production The obligation of a party, at a given time during proceedings, to produce evidence on an element in order to avoid suffering the judge's adverse determination on that element; also termed the "burden of going forward."

Burden of Proof A sometimes confusing term encompassing both burden of production and burden of persuasion.

C

Capacity Legal qualification or competency. In particular, capacity to sue or be sued comprises the personal qualifications legally needed by a person to litigate. For example, an infant lacks capacity to sue, and so must litigate through a representative. Federal Rule 17(b)–(c).

Cause of Action A predecessor term for "claim." However, "cause of action" was often restricted in scope, so that each legal theory by which plaintiff sought relief against defendant might have constituted a separate cause of action. See *Claim*.

Certiorari A writ issued by a court to a lower court requiring it to produce a certified record of a case to be reviewed. The usual route of review by the Supreme Court of the federal courts of appeals is a writ of certiorari. 28 U.S.C.A. § 1254(1).

Chancellor Originally, the king's chief secretarial officer. Later, the judge of a court of equity.

Choice of Law The process of determining which sovereign's law to apply in a case that involves nonlocal elements. See *Conflict of Laws*.

Civil Procedure The societal process for handling disputes of a noncriminal sort.

Claim A fuzzy and chameleonic term, frequently taken to mean all rights of plaintiff to remedies against defendant with respect to the transaction from which the action arose. See *Cause of Action*.

Clean-up Doctrine An equitable doctrine whereby, at the plaintiff's request, the equity court had discretion to retain jurisdiction in order to pass on additional or sometimes even alternative legal relief.

Code The Field Code or one of its variants. See *Field Code*.

Coercive Relief Active judicial relief, be it of the legal type such as damages or the equitable type such as an injunction, that the government will enforce. See *Declaratory Judgment*.

Comity The respect that one sovereign gives to the governmental acts of another sovereign, not out of obligation but out of deference.

Common Law Decisional law, as opposed to constitutional, statutory, and administrative law. William L. Reynolds, Judicial Process in a Nutshell (3d ed. 2003). Or the Anglo–American legal system, as opposed to other systems such as the civil law that prevails in Europe and elsewhere. Or the law common to all of old England, as opposed to local custom. Also, an old system of courts, procedure, remedies, and substantive law in England; the common-law courts offered trial by jury, but gave relief only in the form of money damages or recovery of possession pursuant to a rigid regime of substantive law. See *Equity*.

Common-Law Compulsory Counterclaim Rule A res judicata principle providing that even in the absence of a statute or rule, failure to assert an available counterclaim precludes bringing a subsequent action thereon if granting relief would nullify the judgment in the initial action.

Conflict of Laws The body of law dealing with the problems arising when a case involves nonlocal elements and thus creates a conflict of sovereign authority. It covers most notably choice of law, but also territorial authority to adjudicate as well as the treatment of foreign judgments. David D. Siegel & Patrick J. Borchers, Conflicts in a Nutshell (3d ed. 2005). See *Choice of Law*.

Constructive Service An act deemed to fulfill the requirement of service of process, such as publication, where it is not possible to serve in a way fairly intended to give actual notice. More generally, service by a method not fairly intended to give actual notice.

Contempt Disobedience to or disrespect of a court or legislative body. A contemptuous act may lead to civil contempt proceedings, which compensate or compel, or to criminal contempt proceedings, which punish, or to both. John F. Dobbyn, Injunctions in a Nutshell 216–32 (1974).

Costs A monetary award, as part of a judgment, that is made to the prevailing party to cover certain litigation fees and expenses and that is enforceable against the losing party. Federal Rule 54(d); 28 U.S.C.A. § 1920.

Count A separate statement of grievance in a pleading. For example, a complaint may contain one count or several counts, each of which alone constitutes ground for suit according to

plaintiff. Note, however, that a count and a claim are not the same concept, a count being simply a formal pleading matter. Thus, several counts may state the same claim, or several claims may be stated in a single count. See *Claim*.

Counterclaim Any claim a defending party has against any opposing party. Federal Rule 13. See *Cross-claim*.

Crossclaim Any of certain related claims that a party asserts against another party who is not yet in an opposing posture. Federal Rule 13(g). See *Counterclaim*.

D

Declaration The complaint in common-law procedure.

Declaratory Judgment A judgment that declares the rights and other legal relations of the parties. 28 U.S.C.A. §§ 2201–2202; Federal Rule 57. See *Coercive Relief*.

Demurrer Under common-law and code systems, the defense of failure to state a claim upon which relief can be granted. Delmar Karlen, Procedure Before Trial in a Nutshell 103–20 (1972).

Directed Verdict A verdict entered upon the order of the trial judge, who thereby short-circuits the trial by taking the case away from the jury because a reasonable jury could not decide the case in any other way. Federal Rule 50(a), which now calls this a judgment as a matter of law.

Disclosure A pretrial system whereby each party must reveal as a matter of course certain core information about the case. See *Discovery*.

Discovery A pretrial system whereby each party may request others to reveal considerable information about the case. See *Disclosure*.

E

Equity A system of courts, procedure, remedies, and substantive law in old England. Equity arose to overcome the evolving inadequacies of the common law. Equity courts did not conduct jury trials, but did give relief in the form of an order to do or not to do something pursuant to a rather dynamic substantive law. See *Common Law*.

***Erie* Doctrine** A doctrine that derives its name from *Erie R.R. v. Tompkins*, 304 U.S. 64, 58 S.Ct. 817 (1938), and that deals with the choice between state and federal law.

Estoppel A doctrine generally providing that a party may not take a position in litigation when that position is inconsistent with earlier conduct and the change would unfairly burden another party. Also, a shorthand term for direct or collateral estoppel, which are branches of the doctrine of res judicata and which are technically distinct from the doctrine of estoppel. See *Res Judicata*.

Execution Legal process directing seizure of the losing party's property to satisfy the prevailing party's judgment. This is the usual tool for enforcing a legal-type judgment. See *Supplementary Proceedings*.

Expedient Service Service of process in such manner as the court directs when no service technique has been specified by statute or rule or when no usual technique can be employed.

F

Fact Pleading A procedural system under which the pleadings must detail the relevant facts. For example, a complaint would have to state the facts constituting a cause of action. This is the code approach. See *Issue Pleading; Notice Pleading*.

Federal Common Law The law formulated by the federal courts for use whenever federal law governs and neither the Constitution nor Congress has formulated the applicable federal law.

Field Code The New York Code of Procedure of 1848, which was the first comprehensive Anglo–American code of civil procedure and later a model for the Federal Rules of Civil Procedure.

Final Decision A judgment in a case fully treated by the court, except for award of costs and enforcement of judgment. A final decision of a federal district court is appealable under 28 U.S.C.A. § 1291. See *Interlocutory Decision*.

Form of Action The distinctive procedural and substantive law that evolved under each original writ at common law, such as the forms of action named "trespass" and "trover." See *Writ System*.

Forum Non Conveniens A doctrine by which a court may discretionarily decline existing territorial jurisdiction if the court is a seriously inappropriate forum and if a substantially more appropriate forum is available to plaintiff. This doctrine has been largely preempted in the federal courts by transfer of venue. See *Transfer*.

G

Garnishment Legal process subjecting to the plaintiff's claim the defendant's property that is in the hands of a third person, or "garnishee." This term sometimes applies to both a provisional remedy and a type of execution. See *Attachment.*

General Appearance An appearance by defendant in an action that has the effect of waiving any threshold defenses of lack of territorial authority to adjudicate or lack of notice. See *Limited Appearance; Special Appearance.*

I

Immunity Governmentally granted protection from effective service of process, or from liability.

Impleader A procedural device that allows a defending party to assert a claim against a nonparty who is or may contingently be liable to that party for all or part of a claim already made against that party. Federal Rule 14. See *Interpleader.*

Indispensable Party A necessary party who cannot be joined because of the restrictions of jurisdiction and venue, and whose nonjoinder forces the court in equity and good conscience to dismiss the action. Federal Rule 19(b). See *Necessary Party; Proper Party.*

Interest Analysis A choice-of-law technique that entails comparing the interests of the involved sovereigns in having their own law applied to the issue in question.

Interlocutory Decision Any decision prior to a final decision. See *Final Decision.*

Interpleader A procedural device that allows a person to avoid the risk of multiple liability by requiring two or more persons with actual or prospective claims against him to assert their respective adverse claims in a single action. Federal Rule 22. See *Impleader.*

Interrogatories A discovery device governed by Federal Rule 33, or the written questions used thereunder. Also, the former name of the written questions that may be submitted to the jury under Rule 49(b).

Involuntary Dismissal A dismissal under Federal Rule 41(b) or some state equivalent. See *Voluntary Dismissal.*

Involuntary Plaintiff A person who is involuntarily joined as a plaintiff in order to circumvent the requirement of service of process on him. However, this procedural tactic is very narrowly available. Federal Rule 19(a)(2).

Issue Pleading A procedural system under which the pleadings are intended to yield the contested issues of law or fact. This was the common-law approach. See *Fact Pleading; Notice Pleading.*

J

Judgment An appealable decision. Federal Rule 54(a); Wright's Hornbook § 98.

Judgment as a Matter of Law A judgment entered upon the order of the trial judge, who thereby takes the case out of the jury's hands because a reasonable jury could not decide the case in any other way. Federal Rule 50.

Judgment n.o.v. A judgment non obstante veredicto, or notwithstanding the verdict. Federal Rule 50(b), which now calls this a judgment as a matter of law.

Judgment on Partial Findings A judgment entered upon the order of the trial judge, who thereby short-circuits the nonjury trial because a party has been fully heard on a dispositive issue and the court finds against the party on that issue. Federal Rule 52(c).

Jurisdiction Any of a wide variety of power-related concepts, but most notably referring to either subject-matter jurisdiction or territorial jurisdiction.

Jurisdiction to Determine Jurisdiction A special branch of res judicata that, upon an attack on a judgment in subsequent litigation, may foreclose relitigation of a prior determination of the existence of subject-matter jurisdiction, territorial jurisdiction, or adequate notice. Also, an entirely different doctrine that authorizes punishment by criminal contempt for the violation of a court order that is judicially determined to have been improper (even for lack of subject-matter jurisdiction), although this doctrine authorizes such punishment only if the violator was personally bound and had an opportunity to pursue full review of the order without incurring destruction of a significant right in question. Wright's Hornbook § 16. Finally, still another doctrine that authorizes a court to issue binding orders necessary to determine its own jurisdiction.

K

Klaxon Rule A rule that derives its name from *Klaxon Co. v. Stentor Elec. Mfg. Co.*, 313 U.S. 487, 61 S.Ct. 1020 (1941), which held that for matters governed by state law under *Erie*, the forum state's conflicts law determines which state's law governs.

L

Last-in-Time Rule The judge-made rule providing that if by failure to invoke or apply res judicata two inconsistent judgments are rendered, then the judgment later rendered has the controlling preclusive effects.

Limited Appearance The procedural technique by which defendant restricts her appearance to defending a nonpersonal action on the merits, without submitting to personal jurisdiction. See *General Appearance; Special Appearance.*

Local Action Any of a rather arbitrary group of actions that must be brought in the place where the subject matter of the action is located. See *Transitory Action.*

Long-Arm Statute A state statute enacted to extend the state's personal jurisdiction beyond common-law limits toward modern constitutional limits. Kevin M. Clermont, Civil Procedure: Territorial Jurisdiction and Venue 69–72 (1999).

M

Magistrate Judge A lower-level federal judicial officer, with a jurisdiction defined in 28 U.S.C.A. § 636.

Mandamus "We command." A writ issued by a court to a governmental officer or a lower court ordering the performance of some specified act. Mandamus is used as an irregular and extraordinary means of review of the district courts by the federal courts of appeals. 28 U.S.C.A. § 1651(a).

Master A parajudicial officer specially appointed to help the federal district judge handle litigation. Federal Rule 53.

Motion An application to the court for an order. A motion is not a pleading. Federal Rule 7.

Motion to Dismiss An application to the court to have a claim dismissed, usually in the form of an attack on the complaint before trial, as under Federal Rule 12(b).

Motion to Quash Service An application by defendant to the court to void service of process, thus not dismissing the case but instead requiring plaintiff to serve process again, in a proper manner. This form of relief is available under Federal Rule 12(b)(4) or (5) as a less drastic alternative to dismissal, and it is granted in the court's discretion when there is a reasonable prospect that plaintiff ultimately can serve defendant properly. 5B Wright & Miller § 1354.

Motion to Strike An application to the court to have material eliminated, usually from a pleading, as under Federal Rule 12(f).

N

Necessary Party A proper party who is so closely connected to an action that she must be joined, unless joinder is not feasible under the requirements of jurisdiction and venue. Federal Rule 19(a). See *Indispensable Party; Proper Party*.

Nonpersonal Action A case that proceeds within a category of territorial jurisdiction other than in personam, i.e., jurisdiction in rem or quasi in rem.

Notice Pleading A procedural system under which the primary purpose of pleadings is to give the court and the adversary fair notice of the pleader's contentions. This has been the Federal Rules' approach. See *Fact Pleading; Issue Pleading*.

O

Objection An act that calls the court's attention to an alleged impropriety, or the reason for so objecting. Also, a motion for a more definite statement or a motion to strike any redundant, immaterial, impertinent, or scandalous matter in a pleading—these responses being distinguished from defenses.

One-Motion Rule The rule generally requiring consolidation of objections and defenses into a single pre-answer motion. Federal Rule 12(g).

Other Action Pending An affirmative defense that will result in dismissal without prejudice if another action on the same claim between the same parties was pending in the same state, or in the same federal district, when the present action was commenced and if that other action is still pending. 1 C.J.S. Abatement and Revival §§ 19–86 (2005).

P

Permanent Injunction A final remedy ordering defendant to do or not to do something. See *Preliminary Injunction; Temporary Restraining Order*.

Personal Delivery Service of process in a personal action by handing defendant a copy of the process. See *Personal Service; Substituted Service*.

Personal Service Service of process in an action in personam. However, some courts and commentators use this term as a synonym for "personal delivery." See *Personal Delivery; Substituted Service*.

Preliminary Injunction A provisional injunctive remedy granted after a hearing. See *Permanent Injunction; Temporary Restraining Order.*

Preponderance of the Evidence A degree of persuasion, usually applicable in civil actions and meaning more-probable-than-not.

Prior Pending Action See *Other Action Pending.*

Privy A person legally related in interest to another. In particular, this label is used to describe a person who was a nonparty to an action but who is nevertheless subjected to generally the same rules of res judicata as are the former parties, the basis for this treatment being some sort of representational relationship between former party and nonparty.

Procedure The societal process for submitting and resolving factual and legal disputes over the rights and duties recognized by substantive law. See *Substantive Law.*

Process The judicial mode of operation in general. Also, the summons or any other writ. The summons is sometimes termed "original" process to distinguish it from "mesne" and "final" process. See *Service of Process.*

Proper Party Any person that a pleader may join when pleading his claim, in compliance with the rules of permissive joinder, real party in interest, and capacity. See *Indispensable Party; Necessary Party.*

Protective Order A court order designed to protect a party or person from annoyance, embarrassment, oppression, or undue burden or expense. Federal Rule 26(c) governs orders designed to

protect from discovery abuse.

Provisional Remedy Temporary relief given the claimant to protect him from loss or injury while his action is pending—this kind of relief being distinguished from a final remedy.

Public Law Litigation Modern complex lawsuits, such as desegregation and some antitrust cases, wherein there is lessened adversariness and a greatly more active role for the judge. Abram Chayes, The Role of the Judge in Public Law Litigation, 89 Harv.L.Rev. 1281 (1976).

R

Realignment The process by which the court, for determining diversity jurisdiction, realigns the parties as plaintiffs and defendants according to the ultimate interest of each.

Real Party in Interest A person entitled under applicable substantive law to enforce the right sued upon. Federal Rule 17(a).

Reification In a nonpersonal action, the process of identifying the thing in dispute and of attributing an in-state situs to it. This term is most commonly used when an intangible is treated as the in-state target of the action.

Remittitur A procedure whereby a judge can grant, on the ground of excessive damages, a new trial that plaintiff can avoid by agreeing to give up the excessive damages. See *Additur.*

Res Judicata A former-adjudication doctrine that encompasses both claim preclusion (merger and bar) and issue preclusion (direct and collateral estoppel). Robert C. Casad & Kevin M. Clermont,

Res Judicata: A Handbook on Its Theory, Doctrine, and Practice 9–12 (2001).

Reviewable Issue An issue that the appellate court will consider on appeal from a trial-court decision. See *Appealable Decision*.

Rules Enabling Act of 1934 A federal statute that delegated comprehensive procedural rulemaking power to the Supreme Court and resulted in the Federal Rules of Civil Procedure. The statute is now, with some changes, 28 U.S.C.A. §§ 2072–2074.

Rules of Decision Act of 1789 A federal statute that declared the obligation of the federal courts to apply state law on certain issues. The statute is now, with slight changes, 28 U.S.C.A. § 1652.

S

Service of Process Delivery of the summons or any other writ. Usually, "service of process" refers to that step in instituting an action by which the persons whose interests are to be affected receive official notice that plaintiff has brought an action and by which power over the target of the action is formally asserted. Federal Rule 4. See *Process*.

Speaking Motion A motion that requires consideration of materials outside the pleadings.

Special Appearance The procedural technique by which defendant can raise any threshold defenses of lack of territorial authority to adjudicate or lack of notice. See *General Appearance; Limited Appearance*.

Special Verdict A verdict "in the form of a special written finding on each issue of fact." Federal Rule 49(a).

Stakeholder A person who invokes interpleader to avoid the risk of multiple liability.

Stay A suspension of all or part of the proceedings in a case. For example, enforcement of a judgment may be stayed by court order pending appeal.

Substantive Law The body of enforceable rights and duties that concern primary conduct in the private and public life transpiring essentially outside the courthouse or other forum. See *Procedure*.

Substituted Service Service of process in a personal action other than by personal delivery. However, some courts and commentators define this term more narrowly. See *Personal Delivery; Personal Service*.

Summary Judgment A judgment given without trial to a movant "entitled to judgment as a matter of law" if "there is no genuine issue as to any material fact." Federal Rule 56.

Supplemental Pleading A pleading setting forth transactions, occurrences, or events that have happened since the date of the pleading sought to be supplemented—this kind of pleading being distinguished from an amended pleading. Federal Rule 15(d).

Supplementary Proceedings Procedures other than execution for enforcing a judgment for the payment of money. See *Execution*.

T

Temporary Restraining Order A stopgap, provisional injunctive remedy granted without a hearing; also termed a "t.r.o." See *Permanent Injunction; Preliminary Injunction*.

Third-Party Practice Impleader.

Transaction A broad term linked to a general episode or natural congeries of facts, and broader than occurrence. A transactional test is frequently encountered in modern procedure, being relevant in such areas as amendment of pleadings, supplemental jurisdiction, joinder of claims and parties, and claim preclusion. In these different contexts, the word "transaction" proves to be a malleable one, being flexibly and varyingly defined in a functional way.

Transfer Moving, without dismissing, a case from one venue or court to another in the same court system. 28 U.S.C.A. §§ 1404(a), 1406(a), 1407, 1631. See *Forum Non Conveniens*.

Transitory Action Any action other than a local action. See *Local Action*.

Two-Dismissal Rule The rule providing that a notice of dismissal operates with prejudice when filed by a claimant who has in any federal or state court previously dismissed the same claim by notice of dismissal. Federal Rule 41(a)(1)(B).

V

Variance A discrepancy between pleading and proof, which was often fatal to a party's case under traditional systems of procedure.

Verification Sworn or equivalent confirmation of truth. For example, a verified complaint typically has an attached affidavit of plaintiff to the effect that the complaint is true.

Voluntary Dismissal A dismissal under Federal Rule 41(a) or some state equivalent. See *Involuntary Dismissal*.

Vouching In An old procedural device that allows a defending party to bind by judgment someone obliged to cover that party's liability on a claim already made against that party. To bind the vouchee, the party must give simple notice of the action and offer control of the defense. See *Impleader*.

W

Work Product Litigation-related materials and thought processes given special protection from discovery by *Hickman v. Taylor*, 329 U.S. 495, 67 S.Ct. 385 (1947), and Federal Rule 26(b)(3). Wright's Hornbook § 82.

Writ A written judicial order to perform a specified act, as in a writ of mandamus or certiorari, or as in an "original writ" for instituting an action at common law.

Writ System The common-law procedural system, under which plaintiffs commenced most actions by obtaining the appropriate kind of original writ. This pigeonholed approach shaped both procedural and substantive law. See *Form of Action*.

APPENDIX D

Text Correlation Chart

Civil Procedure: Black Letter Series	B. Babcock, T. Massaro & N. Spaulding, Civil Procedure: Cases and Problems (3d ed. 2006)	R. Brousseau, Civil Procedure: A Functional Approach (1982)	R. Casad, H. Fink & P. Simon, Civil Procedure: Cases and Materials (2d ed. 1989)	J. Cross, L. Abramson & E. Deason, Civil Procedure: Cases, Problems and Exercises (2d ed. 2008)	D. Crump, W. Dorsaneo, R. Perschbacher & D. Bassett, Cases and Materials on Civil Procedure (5th ed. 2008)
PART ONE: GENERAL CONSIDERATIONS					
I. Civil Procedure Analyzed	xxvii–xxviii	v–vi	vii	v–vii	v–vii
II. Civil Procedure Synthesized	48–96, 262–81, 757–87	1–1 to –3, 2–1 to –21	1–4, 399–430	1–9, 533–50	1, 279–95, 895–978
PART TWO: LITIGATING STEP–BY–STEP					
III. Preliminary Considerations	261–62	1–6 to –19	4	—	1–49
IV. Pretrial	281–593, 912–40	8–1 to 10–64	430–527, 673–819	265–393, 464–532, 550–83, 656–703	296–381, 459–625
V. Trial	593–756	11–1 to 13–2	821–94	584–655, 704–25	627–768
VI. Judgment	—	2–21 to –40	895–900	739–40	847–94
VII. Appeal	—	13–7 to –28	915–51	807–43	773–803

Civil Procedure: Black Letter Series	B. Babcock, T. Massaro & N. Spaulding, Civil Procedure: Cases and Problems (3d ed. 2006)	R. Brousseau, Civil Procedure: A Functional Approach (1982)	R. Casad, H. Fink & P. Simon, Civil Procedure: Cases and Materials (2d ed. 1989)	J. Cross, L. Abramson & E. Deason, Civil Procedure: Cases, Problems and Exercises (2d ed. 2008)	D. Crump, W. Dorsaneo, R. Perschbacher & D. Bassett, Cases and Materials on Civil Procedure (5th ed. 2008)
PART THREE: AUTHORITY TO ADJUDICATE					
VIII. Subject–Matter Jurisdiction	204–58, 826–65	1–3 to –6, 4–1 to –69	222–94	52–119, 844–57	173–233
IX. Territorial Authority to Adjudicate	96–203, 258–60, 865–78	3–1 to –128, 5–1 to –25	5–159, 211–13, 294–327	123–219, 241–62	51–117, 134–71
X. Notice	1–48	7–1 to –39, 2–40 to –50	159–211, 214–22	219–41	119–34, 833–47
XI. Procedural Incidents of Forum–Authority Doctrines	138–39	3–128 to –143, 4–69 to –80	327–41	119–22, 262–64, 795–98	117–19
PART FOUR: COMPLEX LITIGATION					
XII. Preliminary Considerations	—	15–1 to –2	4	10–11	383–89, 401–02, 431–32
XIII. Multiclaim Litigation	—	15–2 to –18	529–41	21–31, 39–44	389–95
XIV. Multiparty Litigation	879–912, 940–1054	15–18 to –79	541–671	11–20, 31–39, 394–463	396–458
PART FIVE: GOVERNING LAW					
XV. Choice of Law	172–73	6–1 to –5	319	318–26	263–66
XVI. Choice Between State and Federal Law	789–826	6–5 to –50	343–98	326–40, 857–904	235–77
PART SIX: FORMER ADJUDICATION					
XVII. Preliminary Considerations	1055–73, 1128–29	14–1 to –2, 13–1 to –6	953–57, 900–13	44–51, 725–38, 740–42, 799–806	768–72, 832
XVIII. Claim Preclusion	1073–104	14–3 to –12	958–90	742–53	805–12
XIX. Issue Preclusion	1104–13, 1129	14–12 to –15	990–1004	754–72	812–19
XX. Nonordinary Judgments	1129	14–12 to –15	996–97	—	815–19
XXI. Nonparty Effects	1113–29	14–16 to –23	1004–26	772–86	812, 819–27
XXII. Nondomestic Judgments	1129–72	14–23	977–89, 1021–22	786–99	828–31, 894

Civil Procedure: Black Letter Series	R. Field, B. Kaplan & K. Clermont, Materials for a Basic Course in Civil Procedure (9th ed. 2007)	R. Freer & W. Perdue, Civil Procedure: Cases, Materials, and Questions (5th ed. 2008)	J. Friedenthal, A. Miller, J. Sexton & H. Hershkoff, Civil Procedure: Cases and Materials (rev. 9th ed. 2008)	J. Friedman, J. Landers & M. Collins, The Law of Civil Procedure: Cases and Materials (2d ed. 2006)	G. Hazard, C. Tait, W. Fletcher & S. Bundy, Cases and Materials on Pleading and Procedure: State and Federal (9th ed. 2005)
PART ONE: GENERAL CONSIDERATIONS					
I. Civil Procedure Analyzed	iii–v	vii–viii, 14–19	v	v, 1	iii–ix
II. Civil Procedure Synthesized	2–31, 244–329, 1008–121	1–3, 7–14, 795–824	1–4, 465–512, 1239–68	369–74, 875–902	19–35, 47–64, 95–144
PART TWO: LITIGATING STEP–BY–STEP					
III. Preliminary Considerations	32–33	3–7	4–62	1–47	1–19
IV. Pretrial	33–58, 64–136, 1124–306	283–434, 482–507	513–605, 764–924, 1069–81	325–41, 367–555	546–647, 821–989
V. Trial	136–84, 1308–508	435–82, 508–32	925–1066	673–765	990–1150
VI. Judgment	184–98, 823–35	—	1067–69, 1081–91	303–66	35–46, 1151–53
VII. Appeal	198–205, 222–23, 1510–73	767–93	1092–145	767–96	1257–302
PART THREE: AUTHORITY TO ADJUDICATE					
VIII. Subject–Matter Jurisdiction	205–23, 408–74	177–238	246–338	157–230	346–412
IX. Territorial Authority to Adjudicate	223–28, 475–645	21–142, 239–71	63–179, 215–21, 345–75	49–140, 231–58	145–281, 303–16, 412–48
X. Notice	225–27, 646–72	143–76	183–215, 221–45, 1070–71	141–56, 325–33	64–95, 281–303
XI. Procedural Incidents of Forum–Authority Doctrines	408–12, 497–99, 511–14, 816–23	273–82	179–82, 338–44	807–14	317–27, 410–12
PART FOUR: COMPLEX LITIGATION					
XII. Preliminary Considerations	228–31, 242–43	641–42	606	557–59	648–53
XIII. Multiclaim Litigation	58–64, 238	645–54, 666–78	606–27	559–74	651–69
XIV. Multiparty Litigation	231–42, 838–1005	642–45, 654–66, 678–766	627–763	574–672	669–820
PART FIVE: GOVERNING LAW					
XV. Choice of Law	343–44	62–63	376–77	259	327–46
XVI. Choice Between State and Federal Law	332–406	533–88	377–464	259–302	449–545
PART SIX: FORMER ADJUDICATION					
XVII. Preliminary Considerations	674–79, 685, 715–16, 810–16	589–91, 602–03	1060–66, 1146–47, 1184–91	796–806, 815–22	1153–59, 1198, 1251–56
XVIII. Claim Preclusion	680–716	591–608	1147–67	823–43	1159–83
XIX. Issue Preclusion	717–42	609–37	1167–84	843–59	1183–98
XX. Nonordinary Judgments	678, 770–71, 789–92	635–36	1191–95, 1236–38	858–59	1196, 1227–28
XXI. Nonparty Effects	743–86	599–602, 618–34	1195–217	860–73	1175–76, 1198–228
XXII. Nondomestic Judgments	499–502, 787–810	637–40	1217–36	836–43	1229–51

Civil Procedure: Black Letter Series	A. Ides & C. May, Civil Procedure: Cases and Problems (2d ed. 2006)	D. Karlen, R. Meisenholder, G. Stevens & A. Vestal, Civil Procedure: Cases and Materials (1975)	A. Levin, P. Shuchman & C. Yablon, Cases and Materials on Civil Procedure (2d ed. 2000)	M. Lipson & R. Catz, Materials on the Process of Federal Civil Litigation (1988)	J. McCoid, Civil Procedure: Cases and Materials (1974)
PART ONE: GENERAL CONSIDERATIONS					
I. Civil Procedure Analyzed	xxxi–xxxii	xi–xiii	vii	vii–x	xiii–xiv
II. Civil Procedure Synthesized	24–47, 391–92, 531–54, 654–59	1–63	516–603, 634–51	xxxv–xxxvi	1, 24–25
PART TWO: LITIGATING STEP–BY–STEP					
III. Preliminary Considerations	1–24	190, 209–17	1–11	xxxi–xxxv	1–28
IV. Pretrial	529–652, 867–935, 938–41	218–344, 359–528	234–515, 604–33, 652–703	37–81, 6–21, 105–12, 294–303, 312–578	229–413
V. Trial	937–38, 941–1013	692–784, 786–841	813–86	578–655, 303–10	28–215, 779–815
VI. Judgment	1016	785	10	629–30, 1–35, 837–906	—
VII. Appeal	1015–95	842–47	953–85	773–835	215–28
PART THREE: AUTHORITY TO AD-JUDICATE					
VIII. Subject–Matter Jurisdiction	279–391	64–94	2–4, 166–89, 925–29	162–283	492–98
IX. Territorial Authority to Ad-judicate	49–215, 254–64, 393–439	94–189, 202–09	76–154, 189–233	113–62, 283–94	498–620
X. Notice	217–54, 264–78	169–77, 165, 190–202	12–60, 68–76	61–80, 82–103	522–30, 594–95, 555, 569
XI. Procedural Incidents of Forum–Authority Doctrines	208–14, 384–89	89–94, 152–59, 877–81	154–66	311–12	550
PART FOUR: COMPLEX LITIGATION					
XII. Preliminary Considerations	653–59	541–42, 556–59	704–05	56–57	660
XIII. Multiclaim Litigation	659–82	344–59, 586–93	709–12	358–65	660–82
XIV. Multiparty Litigation	682–866	529–691	705–09, 712–812	298–303, 365–72, 715–72	683–778
PART FIVE: GOVERNING LAW					
XV. Choice of Law	—	—	—	452	—
XVI. Choice Between State and Federal Law	441–527	80–88, 191–98	61–68	452–63	414–91
PART SIX: FORMER ADJUDICATION					
XVII. Preliminary Considerations	1097–98, 1120–26, 1183–84	848–61	887–903	655–72, 712–14	621, 624–25
XVIII. Claim Preclusion	1099–128	898–916	903–06	672–85	622–34
XIX. Issue Preclusion	1140–67	861–64	906–25, 929	697–712	634–46
XX. Nonordinary Judgments	1098	882–86	924–25	695–97	—
XXI. Nonparty Effects	1128–40, 1167–83	864–77, 882–98	906–23, 949–52	698–703	646–59
XXII. Nondomestic Judgments	1117–20, 1177–78	881–82	929–49	685–97	—

Civil Procedure: Black Letter Series	R. Marcus, M. Redish & E. Sherman, Civil Procedure: A Modern Approach (rev. 4th ed. 2008)	J. Parness, Civil Procedure for Federal and State Courts (2001)	M. Rosenberg, H. Smit & R. Dreyfuss, Elements of Civil Procedure: Cases and Materials (5th ed. 1990)	T. Rowe, S. Sherry & J. Tidmarsh, Civil Procedure (2d ed. 2008)	A. Scott & R. Kent, Cases and Other Materials on Civil Procedure (1967)
PART ONE: GENERAL CONSIDERATIONS					
I. Civil Procedure Analyzed	v–viii	61	xix–xx	1–2	vii
II. Civil Procedure Synthesized	1–25, 84–86, 108–31	1–60, 229–91	1–31, 1111–35, 46–78	2–18, 24–28, 203–26	1–4, 26–251
PART TWO: LITIGATING STEP–BY–STEP					
III. Preliminary Considerations	25–26	—	31–45	18–24	5–25, 1061–105, 313–15
IV. Pretrial	131–227, 332–520, 1205–24	219–27, 343–76, 391–434, 521–676	543–748, 781–827, 119–52	29–202, 207–15	458–581, 599–677, 433–34, 983–41, 872–73
V. Trial	521–689	677–724	828–929, 749–80	227–304	678–872
VI. Judgment	67–108	725–34	930–31, 78–118, 943–54	315	928–31, 941–50, 990–1019
VII. Appeal	1017–91	749–86	1031–110	305–14	1020–60, 931–33
PART THREE: AUTHORITY TO ADJUDICATE					
VIII. Subject–Matter Jurisdiction	860–918, 1224–43	63–109	153–222	519–86	252–65, 311–13
IX. Territorial Authority to Adjudicate	690–829, 840–59	111–87, 201–17	222–329, 1136–43, 335–50	407–97, 506–18	316–457
X. Notice	27–67, 835–40	187–200, 377–89	330–35, 121–45	497–506	354–55, 380, 315
XI. Procedural Incidents of Forum–Authority Doctrines	829–35	—	230–32, 325	489–90	312–13, 366–77, 450–57
PART FOUR: COMPLEX LITIGATION					
XII. Preliminary Considerations	228	435–38	399, 434	353–60	874
XIII. Multiclaim Litigation	207–12, 234, 265–67	439–52	412–26, 435–37	360–70	874–80, 581–96
XIV. Multiparty Litigation	228–331	452–519	400–12, 426–34, 437–542	371–406, 640–707	880–927
PART FIVE: GOVERNING LAW					
XV. Choice of Law	806–09	293–307, 339–42	351–52	587	—
XVI. Choice Between State and Federal Law	919–1016	309–38	352–98	587–639	265–310
PART SIX: FORMER ADJUDICATION					
XVII. Preliminary Considerations	1092–95	735–48, 787–94, 827–29	955–58, 1002–03, 931–42	296–304, 315–22, 350–52	950–51, 968–71
XVIII. Claim Preclusion	1095–125	795–809	958–78, 1003	323–31	951–62, 236–45, 544–48, 714–17, 747–48, 596–99
XIX. Issue Preclusion	1142–64	817–18	978–86, 1001–08	331–35, 343–44	957–71
XX. Nonordinary Judgments	1186	809–16, 829–31	1020	—	987–88
XXI. Nonparty Effects	1164–203	818–26	964–74, 986–1001, 1008–21	335–47	971–89
XXII. Nondomestic Judgments	1125–42	797–802	953–54, 1021–30	347–50	344–47

Civil Procedure: Black Letter Series	L. Silberman, A. Stein & T. Wolff, Civil Procedure: Theory and Practice (2d ed. 2006)	A. Spencer, Civil Procedure: A Contemporary Approach (2d ed. 2008)	S. Subrin, M. Minow, M. Brodin & T. Main, Civil Procedure: Doctrine, Practice, and Context (3d ed. 2008)	L. Teply, R. Whitten & D. McLaughlin, Cases, Text, and Problems on Civil Procedure (2d ed. 2002)	S. Yeazell, Civil Procedure (7th ed. 2008)
PART ONE: GENERAL CONSIDERATIONS					
I. Civil Procedure Analyzed	xxv–xxvi	1–8	xxvii–xxx	iii–iv	xxv–xxvi
II. Civil Procedure Synthesized	1–2, 576–81, 1135–75	18–20, 734–45	1–10, 68–92, 264–83, 418–24, 553–607	1–20, 65–74, 935–43	1–2, 261–68, 481–526
PART TWO: LITIGATING STEP–BY–STEP					
III. Preliminary Considerations	2–61	9–18	10–19, 183–92	21–65	2–56, 257–59
IV. Pretrial	575–76, 581–698	403–30, 441–505, 589–734, 745–69, 867–81	94–113, 192–264, 283–98, 332–418, 463–503, 550–52	545–656, 793–935	316–21, 333–481, 526–49
V. Trial	699–743	771–865	425–63, 504–47	944–1022, 1024–31	551–623
VI. Judgment	745–86, 801–04	882–84	93, 113–81	98–99, 1022–23	268–316
VII. Appeal	1069–134	884–96	547–50	1031–71	625–65
PART THREE: AUTHORITY TO ADJUDICATE					
VIII. Subject–Matter Jurisdiction	317–457	187–280	763–815	75–196	175–220
IX. Territorial Authority to Adjudicate	63–227, 279–315	21–165, 281–331	609–742, 750–61	197–321, 337–423	56–139, 154–73
X. Notice	203–05, 258–79, 786–801	165–86, 430–41	19–68, 742–50	321–36, 638–56	140–54, 321–31
XI. Procedural Incidents of Forum–Authority Doctrines	454–56	164–65	—	202–04, 218–21, 1151–55	72–74, 722–29
PART FOUR: COMPLEX LITIGATION					
XII. Preliminary Considerations	933, 1064–65	507	298–307	657, 687	735–36
XIII. Multiclaim Litigation	934–49	507–20	307–11	657–86	737–49
XIV. Multiparty Litigation	933–34, 949–1068	521–87	311–32, 927–98	687–792	749–846
PART FIVE: GOVERNING LAW					
XV. Choice of Law	227–58	—	817–18	23–24	59–60
XVI. Choice Between State and Federal Law	459–573	333–402	818–64	424–544	221–55
PART SIX: FORMER ADJUDICATION					
XVII. Preliminary Considerations	805–06, 885–88	861–64, 897, 948–50	865–67, 923–25	1071–93	667–68, 688, 729–33
XVIII. Claim Preclusion	806–41	897–908, 916–27	867–90, 908–16	1093–111	688–93, 715–17
XIX. Issue Preclusion	841–60	927–35	890–97	1111–38	694–702, 717
XX. Nonordinary Judgments	894–904	—	896–97	—	717–22
XXI. Nonparty Effects	861–85, 888–91	909–16, 935–48	897–908, 916–22	1138–51	702–15
XXII. Nondomestic Judgments	891–932	927	922–23	1155–79	722–23

APPENDIX E

Table of Cases

*

APPENDIX F

Table of Statutes and Court Rules

*

APPENDIX G

Index

†